Sustainable Architecture

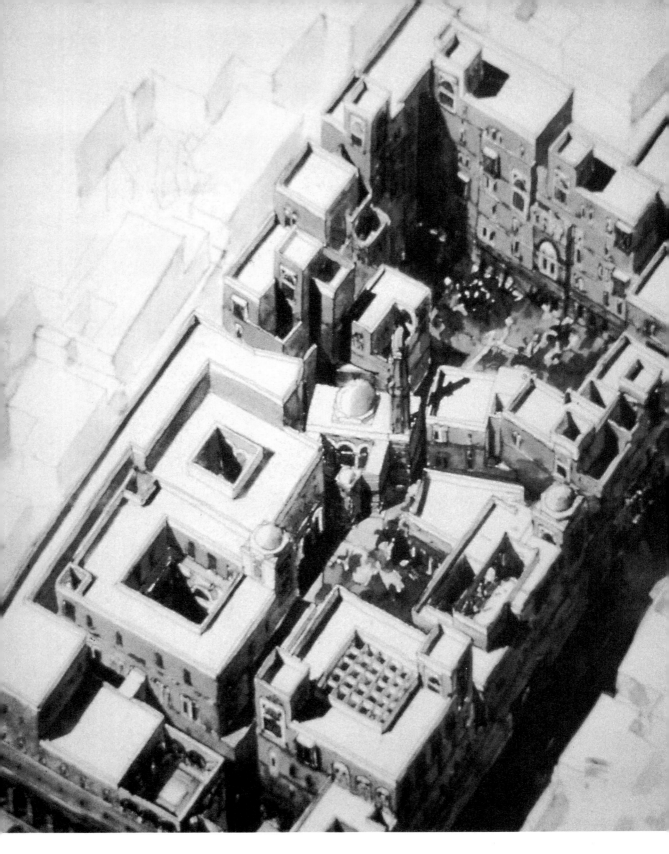

Sustainable Architecture

Principles, Paradigms, and Case Studies

James Steele

McGraw-Hill

New York   San Francisco   Washington, D.C.   Auckland   Bogotá
Caracas   Lisbon   London   Madrid   Mexico City   Milan
Montreal   New Delhi   San Juan   Singapore
Sydney   Tokyo   Toronto

Library of Congress Cataloging-in-Publication Data

Steele, James.
    Sustainable architecture / James Steele.
        p.   cm.
    Includes bibliographical references and index.
    ISBN 0-07-060949-7 (acid-free paper)
    1. Architecture—Environmental aspects.   2. Architecture—Environmental
aspects—Case studies.   3. Architecture, Modern—20th century.   I. Title.
NA2542.35.S82   1997
720'.47—dc21
                        96-45681
                             CIP

McGraw-Hill

A Division of The McGraw·Hill Companies

   2 3 4 5 6 7 8 9 0   DOC/DOC   9 0 2 1 0 9 8 7

ISBN 0-07-060949-7

The sponsoring editor for this book was Wendy Lochner, the editing supervisor
was Patricia V. Amoroso, and the production supervisor was Suzanne W. B. Rapcavage.
It was designed and set by Silvers Design.

This book is printed on acid-free paper.

McGraw-Hill books are available at special quantity discounts to use as premiums and
sales promotions, or for use in corporate training programs. For more information,
please write to the Director of Special Sales, McGraw-Hill, 11 West 19th Street, New
York, NY 10011. Or contact your local bookstore.

For Ian McHarg

CONTENTS

INTRODUCTION

THE NAME OF THE FUTURE

It is hard to find definitive terms that are not encumbered by value judgment and subjectivity. The recent proliferation of "buzz words" within architecture exemplifies this, but when these are combined with terms borrowed from the fields of economics and ecology, the picture becomes muddier still. *Sustainable architecture* is a provocative title and begs questions that must be addressed.

The term *sustainable* has its own evolution, but some of its immediate nuances are colored by the political, economic, social, and psychological climate of the here and now and make it particularly prone to dating. *Sustainability* is, I suggest, evocative of optimistic and protective ideas, recalling *sustenance* and, therefore, a nurturing, or at least good common sense. Linked as it has been to *development*, which implies its own set of desirable goals and growth, *sustainability's* connotations are those of building a solid future and achieving prolonged, lasting, worthwhile progress. No wonder, then, that in the present climate of urgency to find solutions to the now unavoidably obvious repercussions of years of long-term abuse of the environment, *sustainability* has become not only an attractive and fashionable phrase, but also a "comfort word" that is prone to being viewed with suspicion.

Panaceas also abound in the area of development, but, increasingly, the abuse of the Third World, like the damage to the environment, is an unavoidable truth. Every new publication in the field of development brings a new set of comparisons that bring into sharp focus the ironies and iniquities that abound, making our goals seem nothing short of absurd—as water from a single spring in France is bottled and shipped to prosperous countries, nearly 2 billion people drink and bathe in water contaminated with deadly parasites and poison; the cost of keeping a cat in the West is more than the average annual income of the 1 billion people who live in the world's poorest nations, and the list goes on. Moreover, the "First World" is beginning to realize that its silent, usually tacit involvement represents a vested interest in keeping the Third World poor, that the implications of land clearance for export crops such as coffee and tea are marginalization of subsistence food crops, and that promoting the free market economy is another way of crippling the Third World. It is no longer possible to see development as a nonpolitical issue or as a neocolonial process of "giving aid" to the poor (although as imaginative national media campaigns have shown, this undoubtedly is an impulse with mass public appeal and potentially dramatic results). The question that arises, and is faced by agencies every day, is what sort of aid and to whom and how this aid can be used for truly constructive purposes of empowerment rather than as part of the cycle that keeps the Third World dependent on the First. In aid terms, technology has been replaced by "appropriate technology," which is in many cases less appealing and less attractive, bringing us face to face with the real priorities of life in a poor country rather than the priorities of our own societies: Raising money to donate symbols of our technological advancement such as scanners inevitably has a broader public appeal than raising money to fund exchange of skills or the construction of equally or sometimes more valuable low-technology pit latrines.

In architecture, the parallels are just as powerful. In the West, we think of *architecture* as a building that somehow has connotations of something elevated or ennobled; architecture becomes, in this new context, *building* or, more precisely, *building to meet essential needs,* and is often shelter. Vast strides have been made in First World consciousness about this issue; what were once thought of as "primitive" mud buildings are beginning to be valued more highly for their appropriateness and simple beauty. Our concept of *sophistication* is changing from something that is based on high technology and materialism to accommodate the concept of suitability or *appropriateness.* Among the many complex reasons for this is, simply, a greater visual awareness of what exists in cultures and countries so different from the West. Anyone looking at the towering mud "high-rise" buildings of Yemen—pictures of which can now be found not only in obscure and enlightened books by well-travelled enthusiasts and companies brave enough to publish them but also in travel brochures—is challenged to think beyond our concepts of modern high-rise housing. The nagging suspicion that we don't have all the answers—or that the goal of progress has negated even asking the right questions—is enforced further by the unremitting failures of sophisticated buildings of the West to cater for our psychological needs or even to improve our built environment in a purely visual way. An awareness of the built environment as part of the wider environment, and the negative impact of high technology and construction itself, in maintaining the environment, has made this broader understanding still more imperative.

Once we have become self-effacing enough to accept that technology, or technology as we know it, does not have all the answers, once we can go beyond the guilt and well-intentioned but hollow cliches of "nobility" of the "primitive" that still separate us from a real and constructive understanding of other cultures, and once we take on sustainability as part of the agenda for progress and true development, the question is what we can learn and how we can use it back in the world of the freeway and the skyscraper and profitability and client demands? The tempting conclusion in the overwhelming light of evidence that the two worlds are too incompatible and that the political and social goals of our cultures are too different denies instances of real progress that can be made and negates the possibilities of adjustment and change that can begin to make a difference.

Returning to the ever-present issue of meaning for anyone writing and working in the field of development, the use of terminology is unavoidable. The term *Third World* has obvious negative connotations but, as one development worker recently commented, carries with it an unspoken acknowledgment of its own shortfall and somehow continues to be considered acceptable. It has been supplanted to some extent by the more benign *developing world*, a term which is particularly problematic in a climate that is calling into question the whole notion of this value judgment and which implies the disquietingly complacent corollary *developed world*, for industrialized countries. Attempts to define and ascribe this terminology also run into problems. It is difficult to be satisfied with the rather messy categorization that of the 4.8 billion-plus people on the earth, 1.2 billion live in less developed nations, the "more" or "less" developed status being awarded almost solely on the basis of economic indicators. The terms *North* to describe the rich, industrialized countries and *South* to describe other nations, while spotlessly clean, can be misleading shorthand, given that the position of these countries on the map is of abstract relevance to the meaning of these terms. I use all three descriptions, in the understanding that all are flawed and in the hope that as more true progress is made in this field, and consequently in the collective consciousness, they will be supplanted by more adequate and appropriate changes in the vocabulary.

ACKNOWLEDGMENTS

The author would like to recognize the invaluable contribution of Jo Newson in the initial stage of this project, especially in advising on the introduction, helping to determine which case studies to use and procuring information on them, and generally serving as a second conscience on many of the controversial issues involved. This book has benefited greatly from her help.

I would also like particularly to thank the people at McGraw-Hill for their patience and understanding during the extended preparation of this book. Their tolerance with delays has allowed many ideas in a fast-breaking field of study to be included that might otherwise have been missed.

I would also like to recognize the assistance given to me by Dr. Ismail Serageldin, Vice President of Environmentally Sustainable Development and John O'Connor at the World Bank on sustainability and the specific role of environmental economics, respectively. Thanks also to Douglas Gardner and Maguire Thomas Partners, James O'Connor and Moore Ruble Yudell, Stefanos Polyzoides and Elizabeth Moule, Michael Hopkins and Claire Endicott, Alan Short and Brian Ford, Norman Foster Associates and Katy Harris, Richard Rogers and Fiona Charlesworth,

Rasem Badran, Eric Dudley, Jaime Hartzell, Ralph Knowles, Benedict Dousset and Pierre Flament, Victor Regnier, and Edward Blakely for helping to make it possible to realize this work. Finally, Deeba Haider and Ngan Wan Lau helped greatly with their thorough research and have my gratitude.

James Steele

THE SOURCE OF SUSTAINABILITY

Earth Day in June 1970 was a dramatic event, the first consensus to arise out of the growing concerns that began to be voiced in the socially conscious 1960s with ecology as a rallying cry. That consensus seemed especially prescient when supplies of fossil fuel from the Middle East were curtailed and prices drastically increased 3 years later, with public anger at long lines at the pump finally prompting minimal conservation efforts. A report entitled *Limits to Growth,* published by the Club of Rome in 1972, focused on the idea of progress and, most particularly, on the fact that global industrial activity was increasing exponentially, predicting drastic consequences if such growth were not altered. This report, later considered naive in several of its assumptions, succeeded in popularizing the axiom of "zero growth" which has been a subject of debate among environmentalists ever since.

The basic environmental issues raised on that first Earth Day—of resource degradation, population growth and agricultural limits leading to global famine, pollution of air and water, the disastrous potential climatic effect of the concentration of greenhouse and ozone-depleting gases in the atmosphere, and their corollaries—have all been examined in exhaustive detail, and incontrovertible evidence of the irreparable damage being inflicted on the planet mounts daily. The subtle but significant philosophical shift that has taken place since that first Earth Day has been an emphasis on the concept of sustainability rather than ecology, making it important to understand where this term has come from and its implications for the future, particularly for those in the design professions.

The first use of the word *sustainability* in connection with the environment was in 1980 in a publication produced by the International Union for the Conservation of Nature (UCN) in Gland, Switzerland, entitled *World Conservation Strategy,* in which sustainability was inextricably linked to development. This was intended to defuse the progrowth-antigrowth debate that had raged throughout the 1970s, between those who argued that economic progress was necessary to finance environmental protection on the one hand and those who were against such growth because its inevitable result was resource degradation and waste on the other. However, *World Conservation Strategy* had a limited impact on governmental policy. A more effective initiative was the Brandt Commission, named after Willy Brandt, then also chair of the Social Democratic Party of the Federal Republic of Germany. In a speech delivered in Boston in January 1977, then president of the World Bank Robert S. McNamara proposed the formation of a Commission on International Development, also to be chaired by Willy Brandt, and repeated the call during his address at the annual meeting of the International Monetary Fund and the World Bank in Washington later that same year. As a result, the Commission, which was independent, with members serving in a private capacity rather than being under governmental restriction, held its first meeting in Gymnick, Germany, on 9 December 1978. The membership of the 20-person committee reflected McNamara's intent that it not be dominated by representatives from industrialized countries. After ten meetings, the committee unanimously endorsed a report of their findings entitled *North-South: A Program for Survival,* published in 1980. Among many other issues, the report contained recommendations for changes in the operational procedures and policies of the International Monetary Fund and the World Bank, indicating a close connection to those institutions. Following this publication, the Commission visited several countries at the invitation of their governments to assess its results. They met in The Hague, Berlin, Kuwait City, Brussels, and Ottawa between the spring of 1980 and December 1982. This, in turn, led to an addendum published in 1983.

THE BRANDT COMMISSION

The proposals put forward by the Commission happened at a time when the global economic pendulum had taken a turn in favor of the industrialized countries following an attempt at autonomy by OPEC a decade earlier and revolved primarily around the issue of trade and self-sufficiency. The proposals were related to the negotiating process between North and South, and, although their description inadequately defined the tragic situation of dependency by the developing world, it did succeed in drawing attention to the debilitating spiral of exports produced to offset debt. For the developing countries, the connections between trade and finance make economic management peculiarly difficult. Without adequate finance, imports cannot be paid for; without essential imports, production and exports decline; and without adequate exports, countries are not sufficiently creditworthy to borrow to service their debts. The combined grip of inadequate trade and finance on developing economies has become devastating.

The "decline" the report recorded became even more manifest shortly after the Commission ceased the global assessment of its findings, in 1982. Mexico sent out danger signals that it could no longer maintain payments, followed by Brazil, Argentina, and other heavily leveraged borrowers in the developing world. This sent shock waves through the banking community, with economic repercussions that made the inequities between North and South discussed in the report clearly visible. Further collapse of commodity prices has shown the extent to which the report was prophetic.

The link between the Brandt Commission and high-level financial institutions, regardless of the independent nature of its composition, now make it appear to some to be little more than a thinly veiled promotional device to encourage developing world borrowers to seek more loans, continuing the destructive spiral of dependence. The Brandt Commission's focus on the oil-producing countries and somewhat abstract attitude toward the extremity of the adverse aspects of trade inequities—the poverty, famine, and death so graphically described at the same time by writers like Susan George—make it difficult to view the contributions of the Commission objectively. And yet it did initiate awareness of the need for global consensus and coordination on environmental policy, through tactics such as "global negotiations," to be carried out at the United Nations. Through emphasis on trade, finance, and the essentials of development in the Third World, the Commission opened the door for the increasing focus on the search for a rapprochement between economics and ecology that was to follow.

THE BRUNDTLAND COMMISSION

The gap between isolated internal conservationist debate and a higher international possibility of sustainable development was finally bridged by the World Commission on Environment and Development, which was established by the United Nations as a strategic means of compromise between the growth and no-growth factions. The proceedings of the Commission, entitled *Our Common Future,* were published in 1987. The document is also known as the *Brundtland Report,* after the president of the panel, the Norwegian Prime Minister Gro Harlem Brundtland.

Central to the Brundtland Commission's findings was the concept of sustainability, which the Commission defined as the principle that economic growth can and should be managed so that natural resources be used in such a way that the "quality of life" of future generations is ensured. Sustainable development involved "those paths of social economic and political progress that meet the needs of the present without compromising the ability of future generations to meet their own needs."

The use of such a qualitative, subjective phrase as *quality of life* left the concept open to critical interpretation, since the exact component and extent of that heritage could not be specified, leading to speculations as to whether it related to manufactured or natural assets. This means, as some have suggested, that either per capita utility or well-being is increasing over time with free exchange or substitution between natural and human-made capital or that capita utility or well-being is increasing over time subject to nondeclining wealth. In spite of a vagueness on this central issue, the *Report,* by holding out the prospect of the perpetual satisfaction of human needs within a satisfactory natural framework, provided a compelling vision of the middle ground that could be attained.

The outcome of the publication of *Our Common Future* was that it offered a potential area of rapprochement between agencies, raising official awareness that a realistic compromise might be feasible. By holding out the promise that environment and economic development are potentially compatible or complementary objectives, sustainable development offered a welcome relief from the paradigm of conflict that had characterized the debate on limits of growth during the 1970s. Having been placed at the forefront of the political debate about the feasibility of development, the concept of sustainability offered decisionmakers a means with which to reconcile what had previously proved to be an intractable division.

The concept of sustainability, then, has been inextricably linked to development and by extension to economics. From the outset, the focus of the commission was to arrive at a determination of the general perception of the impact of development, by holding community hearings in key industrialized countries to gauge public opinion. Rather than being made up of environmentalists, the UN Commission members were primarily political figures, with a different agenda—to combine rather than separate environmental and development issues to attempt a worldwide view of how this might be achieved and to bring environmental policy into the political arena. Also adopted as articles of faith were the efficacy of extending production with more efficient technology and conservation, the need to reduce the growth of worldwide population, and, perhaps more important, definition of a mechanism to allow the redistribution of resources from profligate countries predominantly in the northern hemisphere to the poor, predominantly in the South.

The search for such a mechanism was based on a recognition that, since the beginning of the twentieth century, the industrially rich countries have thrived at the expense of the poorer ones and have caused a great deal of the environmental damage now evident. Also highlighted is the hypocrisy of the expectation that the poor, who are now industrializing, suspend development as a result of this damage. Bringing attention to the dichotomy of both standards of living and values is one of the Brundtland Commission's greatest contributions to the current ecological debate. The years since the report have seen important distinctions arise between development and sustainability: One of these has been the observation that, "Sustainable development requires a broader view of both economics and ecology than most practitioners in either discipline are prepared to admit, together with a political commitment to ensure that development is 'sustainable'.... Is it possible to undertake environmental planning and management

Sustainable Architecture

in a way that does minimum damage to ecological processes without putting a brake on human aspirations for economic and social improvement?"[1] The qualifier in this crucial question is obviously the aspirations of those people at the bottom of the economic ladder in the developed countries involved, as well as those which have been rapidly ascribed by the acronyms of *RDC* (rapidly developing country), *LDC* (less developed country), and NIC (newly industrialized country).

THE EARTH SUMMIT—AGENDA 21

The more recent impetus for the concept of sustainability has been the Earth Summit held at Serrado Mar, near Rio de Janiero, Brazil, in late spring 1992. As an extension of the work of the *Brundtland Report,* this conference, also sponsored by the UN Commission on Environment and Development, was organized by Maurice Strong, who unequivocally stated, when he was appointed head of the Earth Summit in 1989, that his intention was to use it as a vehicle to further explore the idea of sustainable development and "to move the environment into the center of economic policy."[2]

Strong's background as a self-made businessman is relevant to the shaping of the outcome of the Rio Summit. Starting as an executive with the Western Canadian Oil Company, Dome Exploration (where he became vice-president at the age of 25), he became vice-president of Power Corporation of Canada in 1962, head of Canada's foreign aid program under Prime Minister Lester Pearson in 1966, which he reformed into the Canadian Development Agency (CIDA), and head of Petro Canada. Petro Canada had been formed by Prime Minister Pierre Trudeau in 1976, on Strong's advice, to negotiate directly with the OPEC cartel following the price rises that took place earlier in the decade. Strong's experience in helping to organize the UN World

Conference on the Human Environment, held in Stockholm in 1972, which resulted in consensus by 112 nations on a global environmental plan, and his background as head of the UN famine relief effort in 1985 made him the proper choice to tackle the daunting task of organizing the heads of state from 175 member countries to forge what Strong described as "an environmental bill of rights." As a first step in achieving a fusion between economics and the environment, Strong expressed his belief in typically businesslike terms that it is necessary to "put a price tag on the elements of nature" and that "depreciation of natural resources has to be taken into account, literally, by nations all over the world. The loss of a country's natural resources must be subtracted from the GNP. When businesses have to pay for the loss of things, they have a powerful incentive not to pollute or over-consume."[3]

The 1992 Rio Earth Summit, in which more than 100 world leaders participated, with the notable exception of the President of the United States, who claimed that research into environmental damage was inconclusive and untrustworthy, did not produce Strong's much desired "Earth Charter." However, the publication of its proceedings, *Agenda 21,* named after the century in which it is to be implemented, has provided a much more comprehensive outline of the possible scope of sustainable development, as conceptualized by its most powerful proponents. Based on the fundamental premise that the First World must subsidize development in the Third World in order to redress past inequities and reverse the destructive cycle of resource depletion, *Agenda 21* is a complex document with 40 separate sections addressing different areas of concern. It also has 120 program outlines, and 1000 proposals, grouped under a general directive best expressed in the first paragraph of introduction to the document:

> Humanity stands at a defining moment in history. We are confronted with a perpetuation of disparities between and

Figure 1.1
Pollution spews into the air in Estonia, an unwelcome surprise at the end of the Cold War. Courtesy World Bank Archive.

within nations, a worsening of poverty, hunger, ill health, and illiteracy and the continuing deterioration of the ecosystems on which we depend for our well-being. However, integration of environment and development concerns and greater attention to them will lead to the fulfillment of basic needs, improved living standards for all, better protected and managed ecosystems and a safer, more prosperous future. No nation can achieve this on its own, but together we can in global partnership for sustainable development.[4] (Fig. 1.1)

The daunting complexity of the multivolume document can best be summarized by conceptualizing it in six subject areas, corresponding to the terminology used by the report. These areas are: (1) the quality of life on earth, (2) efficient use of the earth's materials, (3) the protection of our global commons, (4) the management of human settlements, (5) chemicals and the management of waste, and (6) sustainable economic growth.[5] Quality of life on earth, which is conceptually as indebted to the *Brundtland Report* as the idea of sustainable development itself, relates primarily to the disparity between rich nations of the world, now characterized by conspicuous, wasteful consumption, and poor nations, characterized by poverty, starvation, preventable disease, and nonexistent or inadequate health care and education. This part of *Agenda 21* focuses on strategies to alleviate poverty, changing patterns of consumption, and improving standards of health, all within the framework of reducing population growth. The document advocates programs which will assist the "most vulnerable" social groups, which it identifies as "women, children, indigenous people, minority communities, landless households, refugees, and migrants."[6] The report proposes to achieve this by structural changes in the systems of land ownership in poor countries to allow more equitable access to resources and the free exchange of "environmentally sound technologies" from the developed to the developing world, provided that these are adaptable to particular circumstances.

Agenda 21, elaborating on the dilemma of population growth, examines the difficulties involved in social change, especially given the pervasive influence of mobility, which makes a lifestyle revolving around high levels of consumption seem so appealing to those in the developing world, and the intrinsic connection in the industrialized world between economic growth and resource depletion.

Agenda 21 divides the second main theme, the efficient use of the earth's natural resources, into renewable and nonrenewable resources, such as land, water, energy, biological, and genetic resources, and here it becomes clear that a single philosophical framework guided recommendations for programs and activities in each of the six subject areas. This section consists of largely decentralized policies and advocates putting control into the hands of local rather than national authorities, encouraging public participation in decision making, identifying ecosystems as units to be managed uniformly, developing new technologies to halt and combat degradation and depletion and increase productivity and efficiency, and implementing extensive research in each area of development.

Translated into policy recommendations, these principles, when applied to the seminal resources of land and water, result in a plea for an awareness of the finite capacity of each and the systematic characteristics that produce complex interaction. This complexity, the report reiterates, argues for an integrated approach in relation to land. This integration has two components, the need for a comprehensive assessment of the negative impact of any proposed human intervention into the environment or use of natural resources and the careful balance that must be maintained when economic and environmental factors are weighted against each other, with social welfare as a primary criterion. Specific recommendations relating to land are surprisingly inspired for a document of this scope. One proposal calls for a study of traditional approaches to land use as exemplified in terraced agriculture practiced in Yemen and Indonesia, the Hema reserves used in Islamic societies, and "pastoralism" (seasonal patterns of pasture use practiced by nomadic societies) as possible solutions for appropriately scaled areas. (Fig. 1.2) Another series of proposals which restate the emphasis on analysis, recommend establishment of detailed land inventories to determine local capacities and ecosystems, to be collected by individual communities and pilot projects for curricular changes at the vocational, technical, and university level to expand education about land use and other avenues of public participation. The subject of water, which is given extensive coverage in *Agenda 21*, includes emphasis on its importance for the environment, its manifestations within the ecological network, and its geopolitical implications.

The third main thrust of *Agenda 21*, related to what has been referred to as a "global commons," views the atmosphere and the oceans as belonging to everyone, whereas it characterizes resources as falling into geopolitical jurisdictions. The proceedings refer to industrial development and transportation, as well as the energy used in each and land use, in terms of their negative impact

Figure 1.2
Terracing as a traditional
farming technique in
Yemen. Courtesy World
Bank.

on air and water and looks at "marine living resources" in a view toward encouraging increased international cooperation in their use.

Of all sections of the report, the fourth area of concern, management of human settlements, is of most interest to architects and urban planners, referring in detail to the need for adequate environmental infrastructure and changes in the construction industry. This section advocates international environmental conferences to address directly issues of the built environment, examines the present structure of the construction industry, and notes its destructive capacity, which it identifies as "a major source of environmental damage through the degradation of fragile ecological zones, damage to natural resources, chemical pollution, and the use of building materials, which are harmful to human health."[7]

Specifically, as a corrective the report recommends:

1. The use of local materials and indigenous building sources (Figs. 1.3, 1.4)
2. Incentives to promote the continuation of traditional techniques, with regional resources and self-help strategies
3. Recognition of the toll that natural disasters take on developing countries, due to unregulated construction and use of inadequate materials and the need for improvements both in use and manufacture of materials and in construction techniques, as well as training programs
4. Regulation of energy-efficient design principles
5. Standards that would discourage construction in ecologically inappropriate areas
6. The use of labor-intensive rather than energy-intensive construction techniques
7. The restructuring of credit institutions to allow the poor to buy building materials and services[8]
8. International information exchange on all aspects of con-

Figure 1.3 (right)
Windcatch in Bahrain.
James Steele Photo.

Figure 1.4 (opposite)
Adaptation of traditional
windcatch into new
building in Saudi Arabia.
Courtesy Rasem Badran.

Sustainable Architecture

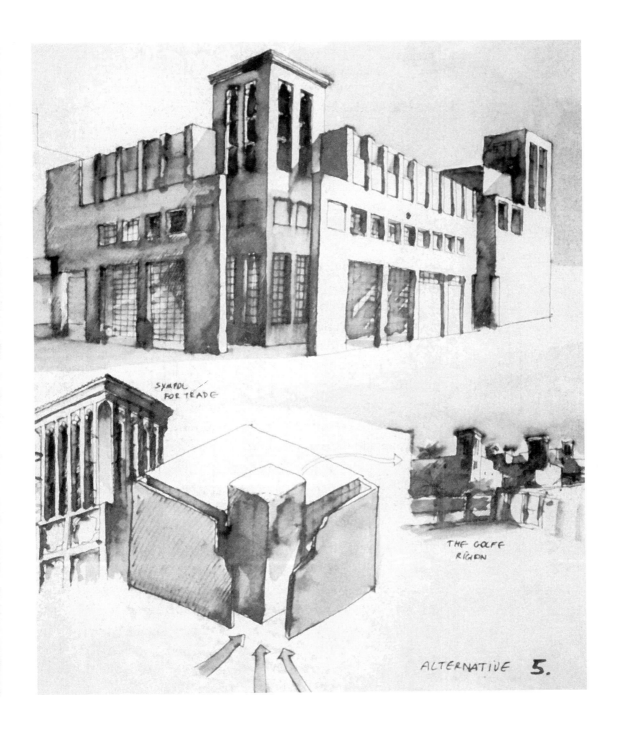

SYMBOL FOR TRADE

THE GOLFF RIGION

ALTERNATIVE **5.**

The Source of Sustainability

struction related to the environment, among architects and contractors, particularly about nonrenewable resources

9. Exploration of methods to encourage and facilitate the recycling and reuse of building materials, especially those requiring intensive energy consumption in their manufacture

10. Financial penalties to discourage the use of materials that damage the environment

11. Decentralization of the construction industry, through the encouragement of smaller firms

12. The use of "clean technologies"

Following the release of these recommendations, several members of the American Institute of Architects, together with others representing the International Union of Architects, issued an addendum to this section of *Agenda 21*, published as part of the *AIA Environmental Resource Guide*. Stating that the built environment represents on average 50 percent of global energy consumption related directly to the construction industry, this groups proposes to expand the *Agenda 21* proposals, which the group criticizes in emphasis rather than omission. The group suggested the following additions, revealing specific professional viewpoints:

1. An extension of the view of the built environment beyond shelter, to include "energy harvesting, waste management and reuse, food production and distribution, water harvesting and handling, as well as facilities for recreation, health, education, commerce, etc."

2. Reduction of construction processes that damage the environment in favor of those that restore it

3. The strict implementation of reuse and recycling of building materials

4. Encouraging the creation of self-reliant communities to reduce transportation, energy, and material use

Sustainable Architecture

5. A return to well-established methods of design that conserve energy and natural resources
6. A further examination and exploration of the potential of self-help in the "making, remaking, and use" of sustainable settlements
7. The encouragement of community participation in the design and construction process, an idea that was first popularized in the early 1970s in the United States by Charles Moore
8. Urban energy and harvesting, forestry, food production and hydrology, and wildlife management supported by the involvement of UN agencies[9]

Although these recommendations reveal little that is at exception with *Agenda 21* proposals, the reiteration of the need for reduced environmental degradation and resource depletion by the building industry, of which architects are a part, and for self-help and sustainable settlements, underscores the importance accorded them by the official voice of the profession. What is significant in the second list is a claim for a wider scope for architects in the future and the need to go beyond physical constructs into planning processes. In this respect, the emphasis on "harvesting" of energy, especially in urban areas, along with related concepts of the city as an environmental asset, rather than liability, is indicative of a current vision in the profession.

In its fifth and sixth sections on chemicals and the management of waste and sustainable economic growth, *Agenda 21* returns to topics of more general concern, presented, as all others, in terms of the cost required to correct existing problems and to implement new programs. In these two sections, discussion of international trade policies in connection with environmental damage, technology transfer, and the economic policies necessary to support sustainable development, are again of interest to architects and planners because they heighten awareness of the implications of design choices in a comprehensive way.

Agenda 21 was an ambitious undertaking, accurately reflecting many of the values of the organizers. Regardless of recognized shortcomings, the report has managed to establish firmly the term *sustainability* in relationship to ecology in the public consciousness, adding to the impact of the Brundtland Commission. By continuously using this term in connection with such a wide range of factors related to the environment, *Agenda 21* has helped to make it seem to be an indispensable means of solving current environmental problems.

The question, for those concerned about trying to implement the ideas embodied in the idea, is what does sustainability mean? And, more specifically, for those trying to find pragmatic ways to integrate its lofty ideals into the structure of the built environment, there is the question of the possibility of achieving a truly sustainable architecture, since its boundaries seem so ephemeral. To begin to circumscribe those boundaries more tightly, it is necessary to identify several of the terms that have caused confusion and to attempt to clarify them.

A C O N T R A D I C T I O N   I N   T E R M S

In its final evolution from the Brandt and Brundtland reports through the Rio Summit and the proceedings published in *Agenda 21,* the concept of sustainability has gained wide acceptance at both the institutional and popular levels, but several ambiguities in the description of sustainable development as "paths of social, economic and political progress that meets the needs of the present without compromising the ability of future generations to meet their own needs" continue to elude definitive explanation. Other aspects of the concept, which are implicit in the definition, have also not been properly addressed.

The aspects that seem to have caused the most controversy and confusion in this definition and the unspoken subtext related to it are as follows (in no particular order of priority):

1. The belief that it is possible to place quantifiable values on each of the myriad parts of the complex ecological web that make up the environment and to "manage" natural resources. This belief has spawned the new speciality of environmental economics described in detail in Chap. 5. (Fig. 2.1)

Figure 2.1
Rainforest in Brazil.
Courtesy World Bank.

2. The meaning of the word *development*. The term has historic connotations related to the destruction of the natural, as well as the human-made, environment, as in the widespread destruction wrought by "urban development" in the 1960s and 1970s. Because of its implicit connection with a belief in progress, which has become so questionable in view of the undeniable legacy of destruction left at the end of the twentieth century, the term *development* is now viewed with considerable suspicion by many concerned with stopping further ecological degradation. As used in this new definition, however, the term ostensibly embodies enlightened improvement of global inequities and is necessary to guarantee that present and future "needs" are met. The question remains, development, how, of what, and for whom?

3. The word *needs* is also vague. Used in conjunction with development, it implies material enrichment, rather than emotional and spiritual well-being, unless one assumes that in a pure, consumer-oriented society, these relate to the same thing. Needs obviously vary a great deal according to social and economic differences. The needs of a Saiidi family in Aswan are not the same as a family in the Bronx.

4. At the level of subtext congruent with an implied reaffirmation of the notion of progress is the tacit suggestion that technology will once again intervene to save the day. Just as in a seemingly interminable list of recent Hollywood thrillers, where expensive gadgets spell the difference between salvation and doom, technological transfer and scientific invention continue to be looked upon as solutions to the environmental crisis, an important component in the unstated weaponry of sustainable ideology.

5. In addition to the subtext of technology, there is the unspoken, but keenly understood political agenda related to this initiative, stemming out of the highly charged polarization that characterized the beginnings of the ecological movement in the 1960s. That agenda may not be quite as clear as the only partly humorous analogy offered by a high-ranking official in a major lending institution that advocates of sustainability today are either kiwis or watermelons, since kiwis are green on the inside and green on the outside, while watermelons are red on the inside and green on the outside. There is no doubt, however, that sustainability has been taken up as a rallying cry by two completely different factions and has entirely opposite meanings for each.

For the kiwis, whose green interior may be shaded by financial as well as ecological concerns, that meaning relates to a businesslike and undeniably capitalistic view of the earth, as a repository of resources needing management to optimize profit. Any architectural expression related to their theory, in their view, should make use of finite resources and industrial materials and such optimization should be proved to be a corollary of their use. For the watermelons, however, the stress is one focused on people, land reform, indigenous architecture, natural materials, self-help, and nongovernmental organizations. Visionaries, wishing to proselytize for sustainability, have attempted to give it wide public appeal by attempting to incorporate and reconcile both viewpoints, but evidence continues to point to the fact that, like the compounds of oil and water which may be said to symbolize them, they will never mix.

To understand the ramifications of each of the dichotomies inherent in the definition and their possible impact on architecture in the future, it may be helpful to discuss several of them in more detail. Among them, the idea of management is the most contentious.

GLOBAL MANAGEMENT AND CHANGING ALLEGIANCES

A strong criticism leveled against the notion of sustainability is that it is "capitalism with a green face" providing a politically correct screen behind which business may be carried out as usual. This stems from the stress its proponents place on the necessity of resource management. To ensure that future needs be met without sacrificing those of the present, these proponents argue that we must systematize the environment, break it down into its component parts, and measure the commensurate gains and losses in each. In this quantitative, rather than qualitative approach, which treats ecology as a business, susceptible to cost-benefit analysis, terms such as *stock constraints, environmental indicators,* and *efficiency analysis* abound, which are all notoriously inimical to many architects. In this evolving discipline, the earth is viewed as the repository of both renewable and nonrenewable resources, calculated at a potential rate of "throughput." This view is in direct contravention to the idea of Gaia, first put forward by James Lovelock in the early 1960s in a hypothesis that soon became an article of faith among many environmentalists.[1] In Lovelock's view, which echos that of ecologists, the matter the earth is made of, the resources now being added up by economists, are part of an ongoing process, the evolution of the species and the evolution of that matter are compiled in a single, indivisible living process beyond price. To come to terms with the idea of sustainability, however, one must accept a more compartmentalized view of the biosphere, comprised of air, water, soil, minerals, flora and fauna, as a stock of resources available for human use, or "environmental services." Michael Jacobs has summed up the essence of the movement by saying that "The important point about defining sustainability in this way is that each of these components of environmental capacity—soil volume and productivity, the size of aquatic stocks and the quantity and quality of water supplies—is measurable. Moreover, it is quite feasible, through proper management, to maintain them over time."[2]

Once this emphasis on management is understood, the theoretical position of an extensive and burgeoning body of literature becomes clear. One of its most consistent themes relates to patterns of consumption long known to be inequitable in which industrialized nations are consistently portrayed as being roughly three time more profligate with energy resources than developing countries. Total energy consumption, including liquid gas, solid and electrical energy in 1989, for example, expressed in petajoules, totaled 82,133 in North America, 49,304 in western Europe, 15,160 in central Europe, 7875 in Latin America, and 4486 in Africa. Or, put more graphically, as it has been by Denis Hayes, "The typical American uses 11.5 kilowatts of energy per day. That is to say that if you take all of the energy that is used in the United States by industry and commerce, residential, transportation, and all other purposes, divided by the population equals 11.5 kilowatts. In Japan, it is 5 kilowatts and in the third world it is less than one."[3] A similar case is made for the production of carbon dioxide; the United States produces 23.8 percent of carbon dioxide in the world. The output from all of western Europe and Japan is 23 percent. The former Soviet Union and eastern Europe, vastly inefficient economies, produce about 25.8 percent. Production from the rest of the world is: Latin America, 4.4 percent; the Middle East, 2.5 percent; Korea and Taiwan, 1.5 percent; China, 11.4 percent; the rest of Asia, dominated by India, 4.9 percent; Africa, 2.7 percent—about one-tenth that consumed by the United States.[4] All this in a country which represents only 5 percent of the world's population and in a group of nations, once the industrialized north, that now share post-industrial status that comprises 24 percent of it. The North uses 80 percent of the world's iron and steel reserves, to the South's 20 percent and, in many specific, critically limited resources, relies heavily on reserves located almost entirely in less developed countries. The statistics of such shocking inequities are typically quoted to support the position that management of the earth, as if it were a corporation, expanding on proven budgetary techniques, would introduce efficiency.

The degree of exchange of such resources indicates the extent to which the countries of the developing world are integrated into the international economy through trade and investment. One economic theory holds that this integration is symbiotic, since it provides important commodities needed by the North, while providing the financial means necessary for the development of the South, but a dissenting view sees such links as a barrier to development and a means of perpetuating underdevelopment. The proponents of this dependency theory point to what has been referred to as "Iron law" of commodity prices, a vicious and intentionally perpetuated trend related to the continually devalued terms of trade on Third World commodity exports and the historical deterioration of their prices in terms of the reciprocal capacity of such Third World countries to then purchase the manufactured imports, particularly those deriving from the raw materials supplied by the First World. In the mid-1970s, as the awareness of the diminishing stock of rare resources, particularly those related to energy and building materials, began to rise, there was a sense of increased optimism in their countries of origin that the higher prices that could be demanded would finally break this cycle, and cartels were formed to expedite the process.

The moral imperative that the poor of the world must be allowed to raise their standard of living by having recourse to the same global resources as the developed countries once used to achieve industrialized status is as undeniable as the fact that the vicious cycle of international trade has prevented them from doing so. The rationale that the developed sector must continue to grow so that, by purchasing more commodities from the underdeveloped world, it will help lift it out of poverty is one of the less convincing justifications for this cycle and is now largely discredited. A more tenable position is that the stabilization of consumption and curtailing of runaway consumerism would allow the measured redistribution of these resources in a way that will more directly assist the underdeveloped nations and allow more time for conservation and protection practices to be implemented. The debate about "lifting the bottom without lowering the top" versus "lowering, or at least transforming the top" so that the bottom can rise is still heavily enjoined as a more sophisticated variant of the growth versus no-growth argument that raged among environmentalists in the 1960s and 1970s. The harsh reality of Third World dependency, however, is beyond debate.

One of the most blatant examples of this dependency, as an aside from the tragic instances of famine that now occur so frequently that public sensitivities have been numbed by their repetition, occurred in the spring of 1994, when U.S. troops left Somalia. In a front-page story entitled, "Chaos Grips Somalia as Peace Keepers Leave," the *Los Angeles Times* reported how a profitable black market had developed in the sale of U.S. garbage in Mogadishu, which, with troop withdrawal, threatened to cut off supplies that supported an estimated 200,000 Somalis. All this from garbage trucks that hauled trash for 20,000 U.S. troops.[5]

Such graphic examples of the extent of differences between national expectations, lifestyles, and thresholds of survival are legion and seem to lose their ability to shock, through continuous exposure in the media. Looked at carefully, however, they reveal the distance that must be traveled for global equity to occur.

Sustainable Architecture

THE DILEMMA OF DEVELOPMENT:
A QUESTION OF MEANING

What has now become apparent in progressive research along the paths pointed out by *Our Common Future* and *Agenda 21,* is that development, as the second precept of sustainability, is a relative and culturally loaded term and that a greater percentage of income growth worldwide exacerbates, rather than diminishes, the tremendous disparities that now exist between the developed and the developing world. Increases in growth, in fact, take place in much more random ways, especially with the advent of trading blocs and favored nations. This issue of *global inequality* institutionalized by treaty is another frustrating barrier to parity, raising further doubts about the possibility of achieving equitable and homogenous benefits from development for entire societies. The environmental consequences of inappropriate development are now painfully clear.

The role of governments and lending institutions in promoting such values in the past has also proved critically generative, as evidence of the negative consequences of inflicting alien values on other countries continues to mount.

THE ASWAN DAM: A CASE STUDY OF THE WRONG KIND OF DEVELOPMENT

As a classic example of what development has often constituted in the recent past, the Aswan Dam in Egypt illustrates many of the problems involved and, as such, deserves extensive review here as a case study of the disastrous consequences that often accompany national "progress" following the Western model. Dedicated by Gamal Abdul Nassar on 14 May 1964, and completed 6 years later, the dam was not the first attempt to contain the Nile. In his aim to convert Egypt into a modern state, the Khedive

Mohammed Ali, who ruled from 1805 to 1849, was the first to introduce cotton and sugar cane into the economy of the country as cash crops. By doing so, he ensured that farmland would be more intensively used, with grain being grown during the winter and cotton and sugar occupying the same field during the spring and early summer. This agricultural recycling, which has eventually been extended into three cycles, led to the construction of a barrage in the delta region. Although it had no real storage capacity, the barrage did slow the flow of the river until it was high enough to reach the inlets of the irrigation canals located above normal water level.

As the demand for water caused by this new system of perennial irrigation began to increase in the years following the reign of Mohammed Ali, leading to what has been considered an agrarian revolution between 1820 and 1890, a more pragmatic solution to the use of the Nile's water became more pressing. British engineers proposed the construction of a dam near Aswan that would store, rather than impede, the flow of the river to allow its release months after the flood had passed. There were three main factors which characterized this first Aswan Dam that refined its emphasis on water storage: First, sluice ways, which were evenly spaced across the face of the barrier, allowed the early rush of the flood, as well as the silt that was carried with it, to pass more freely. Second, in addition to these sluice gates, which were eventually designed to operate smoothly, navigation locks were also located on the western side of the dam to allow for the free passage of ships from one level of the river to the other. Third, a barrage was built across the Nile near Assiut, almost half-way between Aswan and Cairo. This barrage was intended to divert any water released from storage into a system of canals so that it might be more efficiently used for irrigation.

When completed in its first phase in 1902, the Aswan Reservoir was over 1 mi long, 106 m above sea level, and capable of storing 1 billion cubic meters of water in a lake that stretched

225 km to the south behind it. To increase water storage capacity and irrigation further, this first dam was raised to 113 m in 1912 and to 121 m once again, in 1934. An additional heightening was even discussed as late at 1945, but it was never implemented. Although not widely acknowledged as one of the sociological ramifications of the first Aswan Dam, much disruption was caused to the Nubian district of Dekka, which was then located between those of Kurta and Kashtumna. After the first heightening in 1912, this lake extended as far as Wadi el Sebou, 150 km south of Aswan. This flooding increased with the second heightening in 1934 to finally reach the Sudanese border itself, nearly 290 km away.

Soon after the successful takeover of the government on 23 July 1952, one of the first long-range goals for Egypt announced was to achieve "century storage" of the Nile. This aim marked a significant change in the national attitude toward annual reliance on this important natural resource, indicating a long-range view toward self-sufficiency. First conceived by an engineer, Adrian Danitos, as early as 1948, the idea of storing the water of the river for generations, rather than 1 year, closely paralleled Gamal Abdul Nasser's vision of future propriety for his country, and the president accepted it within 2 months of coming to power.

The best location for the new dam deemed necessary to achieve this goal was determined to be over 6 km south of the old Aswan Reservoir, at a point on the river where a natural basin had already existed to hold the water required. At this point, the banks on either side of the river rise up sharply to create a natural foundation for a dam. Several obvious comparisons between the old and new dams at Aswan indicate the dramatic change in viewpoint that separated them. At over 5 km in length, the High Dam is more than twice as long as the older reservoir and 1 km thicker at its base.

In 1952, the German engineering firm of Hochtief Dortmund designed a structure that would comfortably hold back the 164 billion cubic meters of water. This was the amount deemed necessary to achieve enough storage capacity for annual agricultural needs, as well as to hold sufficient water in reserve for emergencies and as protection against flood surges. The designers responded to this challenge with a human-made mountain of coarse sand and rock built upon a concrete plug drilled into the riverbed. On the eastern side of this mountain, called "Saad el Aali" in Arabic, the Nile is diverted into an intake tunnel nearly 2000 m long which is drilled into the steep granite cliff on this side. Six spillway tunnels, lined with reinforced concrete, branch out from this intake to serve the hydroelectric power station located on the down river side of the dam. A spillway on the western side of the barrier, which is controlled by a regulator, acts as a safety valve in times of high flood and provides a means of diverting the river away from the dam during construction. The hydroelectric component of the structure is enormous; its generating capacity is 2,100,000 V, with an electric power of 8 billion kwh per annum. In 1976, Egypt also completed an impressive rural electrification program that became feasible only after construction of the dam.

Construction of the Aswan High Dam was actually delayed until 1960 because, after making positive gestures of support for the project, the United States finally withdrew from the project in 1956, causing a major international incident. Because of this impasse, the dam was finally backed by the Soviet Union and built with the help of USSR advisors. With a final cost of over $994 million, the dam now has enough water capacity to irrigate 2 million acres in Egypt.

There is no question that Saad al Aali, which was completed in 1970, has significantly expanded the agrarian potential of Egypt; as a direct result of this project agriculture has managed to retain a large share of the economy. According to a report by the World Bank in 1980, that share occupied 44 percent of Egypt's workforce, 30 percent of its total exports, and 29 percent of the gross national product. This large market share for agriculture also means that any factors that adversely affect it also negatively impact the rest of the economy. The Aswan High Dam has made possible the reclamation of a great deal of land near the desert fringe, which, because of increased irrigation, have been added to the 5.6 million feddans of arable land that was previously in use.

The dam has made an equally impressive contribution to the energy needs of Egypt, which has had a direct impact upon industrial output and the national standard of living. Since 1970, the Aswan hydroelectric plant has been a primary source for a complex network of hydro and thermal generating stations throughout the country, operated under the authority of the Ministry of Electricity and Energy. A 500-kV, double-circuit transmission line nearly 838 km long connects the delta with Aswan and is the main lifeline of this system. (Fig. 2.2)

Along with these rather remarkable benefits, however, an equally remarkable number of ecological, sociological, and economic problems have arisen that are directly attributable to the High Dam. These, in no order of priority, are as follows:

1. Several million tons of fertile silt, which has nourished the fields of Egypt for thousands of years, have been blocked because no means have been provided for their passage. This means that the existing topsoil must serve without any natural regeneration, into the future.
2. The greater speed and constant volume of the Nile is now causing an alarming amount of erosion of the river bank, as well as of the coastal dunes near the Mediterranean Sea. Water speed has also scaled the riverbed, blocking natural drainage from the surrounding fields.
3. Lack of adequate provision for drainage of the increased amount of water used for irrigation has resulted in waterlogging of the soil and a drop in crop production.

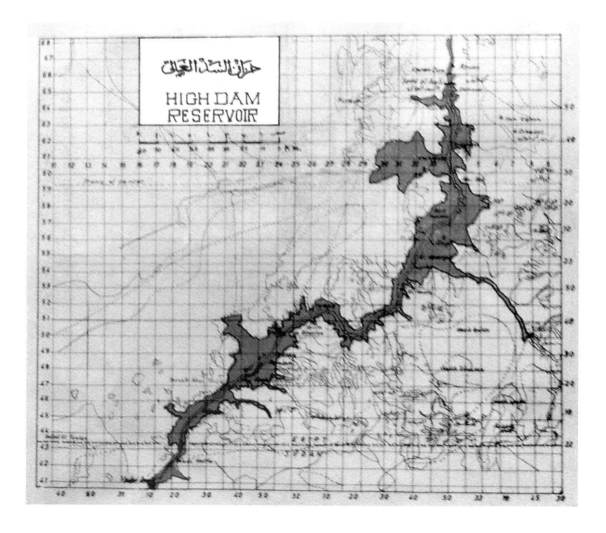

Figure 2.2
Aswan High Dam. Photo
of plan by James Steele.

4. Salinity has begun to penetrate into the river delta from the Mediterranean and continues to move further into the river.

5. Excessive water loss, due to evaporation and seepage, has been recorded in Lake Nasser.

6. The incidence of malaria and bilharzia has increased because more breeding areas for mosquitoes and schistosomes have been provided by the dam.

Sustainable Architecture

7. The choice of the dam has meant that irreplaceable archae-
   ological monuments were put in danger of flooding from
   Lake Nasser. Only intervention of international organizations, like UNESCO, which have spent millions of dollars
   to rescue these monuments, has been able to save these
   monuments. In the case of the Abu Simbel, for example,
   the entire complex had to be lifted above water level.
8. Finally, and perhaps most tragically, more than 90,000
   Egyptian and Sudanese Nubians were ousted from their
   traditional homeland because it was flooded by Lake
   Nasser.

While each of these problems is important, three of them
in particular require further elaboration, because they have direct
bearing on later changes in village life in Upper Egypt and, hence,
demonstrate the real long-term impact of this particular development.

The first of these is the loss of the rich sediments that are
brought down the Blue Nile from the Ethiopian highlands. Unlike
the first Aswan Reservoir, which allowed the primary flood state of
the river and the silt it carried to pass through sluice gates, the
High Dam was not designed to allow silt to pass through it.
Although supporters of the High Dam claim that this loss is negligible since the nutritive value of the sediment had been depleted
before construction began and that the use of artificial fertilizers
has not increased significantly since 1970, such claims are not convincing. Far more output is now being demanded of the Nile
Valley topsoil than at any time in the past, and the soil cannot be
regenerated naturally. Increased use of chemical fertilizers and the
leaching of these chemicals from the soil into the Nile has already
done considerable environmental damage to water quality and
marine life in the river, which is already suffering from indiscrimi-
nate dumping of industrial waste. Ironically, the Kima fertilizer

plant near Aswan, which is one of the major industrial beneficiaries of this blockage of silt, is also one of the biggest customers of the electricity produced by the High Dam. Usage is so high, in fact, that the company is currently subsidized by the Egyptian government to offset the cost of this service.

For the Saidi of Upper Egypt, who have historically used mud brick for house construction because it is the one building material they can afford, the inability to continue to do so represents an economic hardship. An official government ban against the stripping of the now irreplaceable top soil for use in making mud brick was enforced soon after the High Dam was completed. A factory to use silt deposits from behind the dam to produce mud bricks was inaugurated by President Sadat in early 1980, but it is unclear to what extent production there offsets the absence of this traditional building material.

The second factor from the long list of complications presented by the dam is the intensified use of agricultural land which is made possible by increased irrigation and the lack of adequate drainage provided for that land. Whereas increased irrigation seemed to allow for more production and subsequently to provide more income for farmers, this increased irrigation capacity has actually caused production to drop. As one observer explained:

> An important share of the agricultural investment went into the Aswan High Dam, which brought perennial irrigation to an additional .7 million feddans of the old lands. The planners estimated that the dam could bring another 1.2 million feddans under cultivation and by 1970 about 805,000 feddans of new land (desert, swamp, and saline soils) had been treated. With the quantum increase in the capacity of the irrigation system and with no means to control usage, however, the outmoded drainage system was unable to handle the amount of water farmers put on

their land. Another adverse consequence is that the high cost of the dam fixed the pattern of public investment and closed major development options. Choices of strategy were, and to a considerable extent still are, limited by the need to reap the full benefits of the original investment in the High Dam and to invest heavily in drainage works. This need explains much of the pattern of public investment in the sector and the shortage of funds for other agricultural purposes. Moreover, much of the reclaimed land is of poor quality [and] 76 percent of the new land is shallow to rock; other parts are covered with windblown sand, having a high water table in an unirrigated state; some are coarse textured, gravely and loamy sands that will not use irrigation water efficiently. These soils are not good and cannot be expected to give returns on inputs comparable to those from old lands.[6]

With this drop in soil production and the growth of the rural population throughout Egypt, revenues and wages in agriculture have fallen far below the national average in other sectors of the economy. This drop in income has also been aggravated by the small plot sizes made available to many farmers, which further inhibits productivity. As a result of the land reforms enacted by the Nasser government in September 1952, land holdings were abolished and a limit on ownership of 50 feddans per person was set. Strict inheritance laws, which progressively divide property from one generation to the next, also tended to reduce plot sizes to between 2 and 4 feddans each, continuing a cycle of rural poverty that had been commonplace in Egypt in the past.

The third and most widespread sociological effect of the Aswan High Dam was the flooding of the ancient Nubian homeland which had stretched from Aswan in Egypt southward to the fifth cataract near the joining of the Blue Nile and the Atbara River in northern Sudan. The Nubians, who are known to have lived and prospered in this region in a symbiotic relationship with pharaonic Egypt since the Archaic period, when they capitalized on their neighbor's need for ivory, gold, and slaves, still retain a distinct cultural character and language. Although there is some disagreement on the exact number of groups that constitute Nubia, there is agreement that it consists of four tribes: the Maha, Danaqla, Fadaykiyya, and Kenuzi. The Fadaykiyya and Kenuzi, who are named after the Banu Kanuz Arabs and are the only one of the four groups to speak Arabic, made up the majority of the Nubians inside the Egyptian border north of Aswan. In the early part of 1964, 50,000 Nubians on the Egyptian side of the border were relocated from the area between the first cataract at Aswan and the second at Wadi Halfa. An equal number of Sudanese Nubians, mostly from the Danaqla group, were relocated southward to Khasm el-Girba, nearly 500 km away from their traditional villages. The resettlement plans organized by each government were initially intended to replicate existing village life as much as possible. Proposals for designs of the resettlement camps at Kom Ombo, for example, which is 50 km north of Aswan, were requested from such notable architects as Hassan Fathy, who was a great admirer of Nubian culture and architecture and was very sympathetic to their plight. Unfortunately, restraints of schedule and budget prevented these original intentions from being carried out in the Nuba El-Gedida, or New Nubia at Kom Ombo, and over 40 villages there are almost uniformly characterized by extremely regimented and unimaginative planning.

In the majority of these new villages, small, rectilinear dwellings, made up of between one and four rooms, are tightly organized within a grid pattern, with hardly any space between them for ventilation or privacy or any courtyards of the type that had characterized Nubian homes in the past. In addition to these crowded conditions, and the use of stone, concrete block, and reinforced concrete for house construction, which raised ambient

Sustainable Architecture

temperature levels to dangerous and sometimes fatal levels, the designers of Nuba El-Gedida also greatly underestimated the need for flexibility for the future in their plans. As Hassan Fathy explains, planners overlooked the significant numbers of people who were pouring into the area. "The demographic, social and health consequences of the relatively overcrowded villages and living quarters, aggravated by the inadequate services and insufficient economic opportunities, will definitely increase the flow of people out of the new community."[7]

In comparison to these minuscule barracks, the traditional houses of the Nubian villages were generously proportioned and ingeniously proportioned so as to accommodate both the formal rituals of hospitality and the privacy necessary for the family. As can be seen today in remnants such as Aboul-Riche near Aswan, the Nubians have been forced to abandon an architectural tradition which they have practiced for thousands of years, which resulted in noble, environmentally harmonious and sensitive structures, wedded closely to the land.

The Aswan Dam is only one of many environmental disasters, originally cloaked in the guise of progress and actually proposed to developing countries by the lending institutions to which they are so heavily in debt, which have had equally damaging effects on the people they were meant to serve. David Nicholson Lord extends this particular example to the broader sphere, "Dams have had a bad press recently, with good reason. Dams line the pockets of politicians, supply electricity to urban elites by drowning the homes of peasants, look good on lists of prestigious aid projects but bad everywhere else."[8]

DEVELOPMENT WITH A FRIENDLY FACE: INTERMEDIATE TECHNOLOGY

In stark contrast to such intrusive approaches to development as the Aswan High Dam, which characterized many national initia-

Figure 2.3
Ataturk Dam in Turkey,
which will control the
flow of the Euphrates.
Courtesy Turkish Tourist
Board.

Sustainable Architecture

tives in the 1950s and 1960s and may still be found in the Tarbela, Terri, and Euphrates projects today, advocates of sustainable development now point to a dramatic change in direction. Now, development includes efforts to help reduce air and water pollution, manage forest resources, strengthen national environmental institutions, structure solid waste management systems, fund urban transport projects, and derive environmental strategies for cities. (Fig. 2.3)

It is significant, however, that many of these institutions are still predicated on imported technologies of the type described by Susan George in her classic study, *How the Other Half Dies,* within the late 1970s. Not surprisingly, George's work is anathema to those promoting sustainable development, a Cassandra to whom they turn a deaf ear, but her descriptions of the way that commodity prices continue to be controlled to perpetuate dependency make compelling reading. George focuses on the potentially destructive power of imported technologies, as related to monopolies on credit in general and on fertilizers, pesticides, and research, in particular, in the agricultural sector, but her study goes much further as a thoroughly documented, scathing indictment of how advanced technologies transferred to the Third World actually exacerbate rather than alleviate underdevelopment, while continuing to profit suppliers. The iniquitous conditions she portrays of plenty and waste on one hand and deprivation and hunger on the other have deteriorated rather than improved in the nearly two decades since her book was released, underscoring the disastrous effects of such policies even more. When George's book was released, an approach stressing appropriate technology had an equal chance of gaining the kind of public recognition and institutional backing that sustainable development now enjoys.

Maurice Strong, the organizer for the Rio Conference and primary force behind *Agenda 21* coined the term *ecodevelopment,* which was first used at the Stockholm Conference in 1972. This concept differs from that of sustainability in its emphasis on regional, rather than imported, resources and paradigms and the encouragement of local expertise. Ecodevelopment focuses, instead, on the question of development for whom? Unlike the econometric model finalized in Rio, ecodevelopment implies an affinity with Gandhian principles, in which the concept of productivity itself is questioned and replaced by the notion of a social system based on the bartering of services.

Like Gandhi's approach, ecodevelopment has been criticized for being romantic and retrograde and has been partially subsumed in the repeated call in *Agenda 21* for a return to reliance on regional initiatives. Some, however, see the idea as a potentially viable less developmentally focused alternative to sustainability, if its inherent relationship to particular contexts can be expanded. Ecodevelopment rejects the "trickle-down" economics tacitly implied in *Agenda 21,* favoring the creation of "trickle-up" activities as an alternative. Resource allocation in this alternative view looks less at cost-benefit analysis and investment in the status quo of the industrialized North and more toward the ecological definition of regional ecosystems. Using Maurice Strong's definition, "Ecodevelopment emphasizes the capacity of people themselves to invent and generate new resources and techniques to increase their capacity to absorb them and to put them to socially beneficial use, to take a measure of command over the economy and to generate their own way of life."[9]

Two examples suffice to highlight the critical difference between the two viewpoints of sustainable versus ecodevelopment. The first is the project at Rajastan, a direct contrast to the intrusive approach taken at Aswan, illustrating the dramatic difference between development as it has been understood in the past and appropriate or intermediate technology. Using traditional techniques, villagers in the Aravalli hills east of Jaipur have erected earthworks called *johads* to preserve rainwater to see them through times of drought and, more important, to raise the water table, retain well pressure, and prevent erosion. This new initiative to reinstate an old idea began in 1985 when an ashram called Tarun Bharat Sangh was set up by a group of young university graduates interested in implementing Mahatma Gandhi's ideas of indigenous technology carried out through village organization. In spite of a dramatic increase in crop production, water well dependability, and soil fertility, the *johads* were initially declared illegal by the government, who claimed they were in competition with the state-built dam nearby.[10] The real issue has proved to be the proliferation of this technique of water control throughout many other villages, whose inhabitants have been impressed by its effectiveness and by the establishment of *gram sashas,* or self-governing committees. The possibility of resistance by these communities, as well as the reduction in soft revenue that an indigenous alternative to state-run water control projects represents, is the basis of the "competition" than the *johads* have been characterized as presenting.

A second, equally instructive example of the ecodevelopment approach is offered by a fascinating experiment carried out in Kenya. David Hopcraft has recorded how desertification has occurred in the Sahel and has proposed a natural alternative to alleviate it. Hopcraft was convinced that the human substitution of domestic cattle for indigenous animals, prompted by the advice of foreign agricultural experts and the need for more trade exchange, had prompted a destructive process which now results in the loss of at least 14 million acres a year to desert as grasslands deteriorate and loosened vegetation is eroded by wind and rain, leaving nothing to eat. He devised a controlled comparison to test his theory by fencing off a 300-acre plot of land in Kenya, dividing it down the middle and stocking it with equal number of cattle on one side and gazelle on the other, to compare the ecological effects on the range, the yield of meat, and the financial return. The difference between the two control groups and the range they inhabited when measured over a 3-year period, was astonishing. Hopcraft's suspicions that cattle were adversely affecting the semiarid range land were confirmed. Since cattle depend so heavily on water, they crush the grass and other vegetation on their daily trek to water, destroying the root systems. They have specific food preferences, wiping out selected grass species instead of grazing on all the vegetation evenly, as indigenous animals do. As Hopcraft noted, in his final study, "A series of changes in species composition and a loss of vegetational cover result, reducing the productive quality of the whole. Each year the situation becomes worse where cattle are used, and in many African countries this same deleterious progression has led, and is continuing to lead to the point of land disaster, followed by starvation and death of the stock and the owners."[11]

In the other categories of his study, in which the yield of lean meat per acre per year was measured, Hopcraft found that the gazelle, in addition to doing far less damage to the range, since they had adapted to their environment, could exist on virtually no water, yielded a 20 percent heavier usable carcass with far less fat, and, because of lower overhead related to dipping, inoculation, water supplies, and shelter, cost only 20 percent of income as opposed to 60 percent for cattle, providing a much higher financial yield. His conclusion as a result of this study is that nature's technology, when given the chance, is far superior to misguided interference. As he says, "The western world, through its major institutions, banks, and foundations, continues to pour money, expertise, time and energy into the livestock industry in Africa. Any amount of money is available for livestock development. All of the scientific institutions and universities in 40 or more African countries are studying cattle, sheep and goats, but not indigenous animals."[12]

His recommendations for systems that conform to evolved patterns and are multicultural and diverse, just as nature is, rather than monocultural, are reminiscent of the principles recommended by many other proponents of appropriate and intermediate technologies which do not rely on large quantities of imported energy to succeed.

A HIDDEN AGENDA

A hidden agenda of sustainability is related to political divisions and has been an unexplored topic. An unspoken premise is that if sustainability is achieved, it will be so within the framework of a new social structure, variously referred to as "green" or "ecopolitics." This construct, it is assumed, will be born out of the necessity for survival under extreme conditions, which require that historical political disparities be put aside for global benefit and the common good of humankind, the tacit understanding being that ecology must be free of temporal intersticine labels. An objective overview of the voluminous body of literature now available on various aspects of human degradation of the environment, however, indicates that longstanding divisions are still present, and it is naive to assume they will magically disappear in deference to some as yet undefined utopian vision.

Sustainability, which is being put forward by its enthusiasts as the theoretical apologia for this new brand of utopian ecological politics, appears through its lineage and implementation to be nothing more than capitalism striving for political correctness. Many issues reiterated in *Agenda 21*, such as land reform, decentralization, reparations, and changes in value systems are fraught with political overtones involving nothing less than revolutionary change in many existing government systems, and yet these implications have yet to be addressed by any of the most influential proponents of sustainability.

Decentralization is also implicit in governmental reform, and decentralization implies self-contained communities as well as the end of detached object buildings and houses because they consume so much more energy and materials than a plan using party walls. For many advocates, sustainable development means improving cities and communities and building new ones, reducing or eliminating the need for the automobile, now necessary for the commute from home to work. Detached houses are estimated to use five times as much energy as a condominium or apartment, because more wall surface is exposed to the elements.

Concentrated development patterns, already provided in many existing cities, abandoned in the rush to the suburbs in the four decades after World War II, are now being studied more carefully, and the energy implications of a multitude of configurations has become a specialty of its own. The vision of a new *eco-city*, in which an existing urban area is transformed from a hard concrete and asphalt wasteland with a center nearly deserted after dark into an amenable and efficient natural and social organism, now seems closer to being realized as local initiatives gather force. These have been augmented by simultaneous, if not parallel, efforts by sociologists and law enforcement experts in cities such as Los Angeles, where a repeated incidence of civil violence has led to studies on the relationship between crime and recreational areas. Although still in their infancy, and far from conclusive, these studies suggest a direct correlation between urban violence and the amount of public land available. After Watts in 1965 and the South Central riots in 1992, pollsters were able to determine a connection between the two. This has resulted in the formation of The Trust for Public Lands, which has now initiated a $2.5 billion campaign to make 12 U.S. cities greener.[13]

Rather than large expanses of the Hyde Park or Central Park variety, these areas will be carved from vacant lots and derelict properties bought through private donations and public bond bills, creating a network of interconnected greenery throughout each city. Others advocate the use of these areas as agricultural commons, planted with species that will replace carbon monoxide with vitally needed carbon dioxide. This effort works in conjunction with an understanding that planning decisions, material, and construction choices all affect fossil fuel emissions and that, taken together, the decisions can convert an inhuman environment into one that is environmentally harmonious. Along with this broader campaign, there are detailed proposals on both sides of the Atlantic to increase urban biodiversity by altering present methods of building design to allow "colonization" by plants, birds, and animals. This is not a new idea, but new legislation, such as Directive 92/43 EEC on the Conservation of Natural Habitats and of Flora and Fauna, indicates a decided change in attitude on such ideas relative to a general social conversion from the idea of protecting the environment to that of actively working to improve degradation.[14] (Figs. 2.4 to 2.7)

THE CONTINUING LURE OF TECHNOLOGY

Sophisticated techniques for measuring the effectiveness of various land use configurations, particularly in urban areas, have now been developed. Bénédicte Dousset, for example, has been using surface temperature statistics taken from satellite images of the Los Angeles basin compared with urban land cover classified from a multispectral SPOT (*Satellite pour l`Observation de la Terre*) image to correlate the effect of industrial and fully built-up areas as well as vegetation on urban microclimates. (Fig. 2.8)

Fascinated by the capacity of urban areas to induce an infinite number of microclimates, linked to the composition of the surfaces and the relationships of their structures, Dousset has measured how changes in the surface properties (albedo, heat capacity, and moisture content), changes in the air flow due to streets and tall buildings, and heat released by human activities contribute to the modification of the thermal balance of the atmospheric boundary layer and generate the "urban heat-island" effect.

By the year 2000, she notes, 47 percent of the world population will be urbanized, and 24 cities will exceed 10 million inhabitants. The impact of such cities upon the atmosphere and

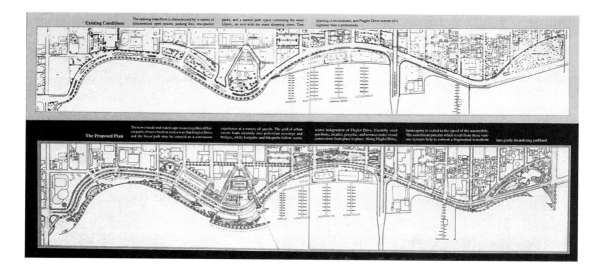

Existing Conditions The existing waterfront is characterized by a variety of disconnected open spaces, parking lots, vest-pocket parks, and a central park space containing the main library, on axis with the main shopping street. Tree planting is inconsistent, and Flagler Drive is more of a highway than a promenade.

The Proposed Plan The new islands and waterscape weave together different paths of movement in such a way that Flagler Drive and the linear park may be enjoyed as a continuous experience at a variety of speeds. The grid of urban streets leads naturally into pedestrian crossings and bridges, while footpaths and bikepaths follow scenic routes independent of Flagler Drive. Carefully sited pavilions, arcades, pergolas, and terraces make visual connections from place to place. Along Flagler Drive, landscaping is scaled to the speed of the automobile. The curvilinear patterns which result from these various systems help to convert a fragmented waterfront into gently meandering parkland.

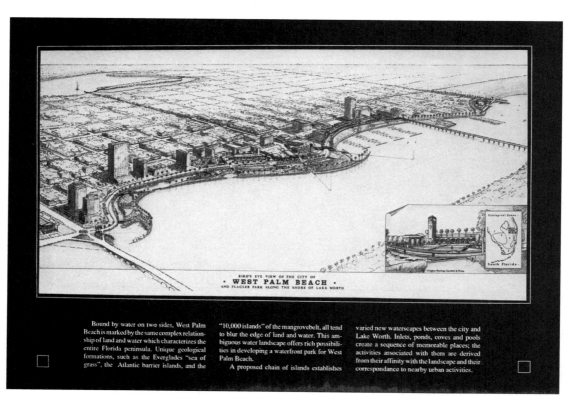

BIRD'S EYE VIEW OF THE CITY OF
· WEST PALM BEACH ·
AND FLAGLER PARK ALONG THE SHORE OF LAKE WORTH

Bound by water on two sides, West Palm Beach is marked by the same complex relationship of land and water which characterizes the entire Florida peninsula. Unique geological formations, such as the Everglades "sea of grass", the Atlantic barrier islands, and the "10,000 islands" of the mangrovebelt, all tend to blur the edge of land and water. This ambiguous water landscape offers rich possibilities in developing a waterfront park for West Palm Beach.

A proposed chain of islands establishes varied new waterscapes between the city and Lake Worth. Inlets, ponds, coves and pools create a sequence of memorable places; the activities associated with them are derived from their affinity with the landscape and their correspondance to nearby urban activities.

46   Sustainable Architecture

Figure 2.4 (top left)
James O'Conner,
Douglas Suisman West
Palm Beach Park. An
example of urban
initiatives to add more
greenspace.

Figure 2.5 (bottom left)
West Palm Beach Park.

Figure 2.6 (top right)
West Palm Beach Park.

Figure 2.7
(bottom right)
West Palm Beach Park.

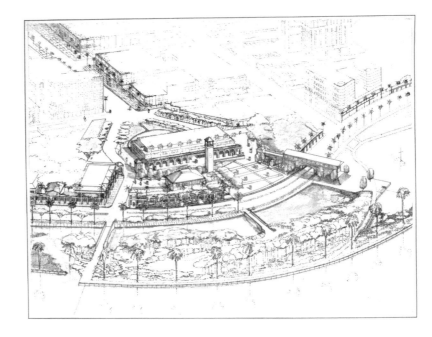

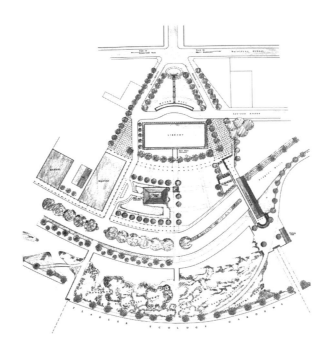

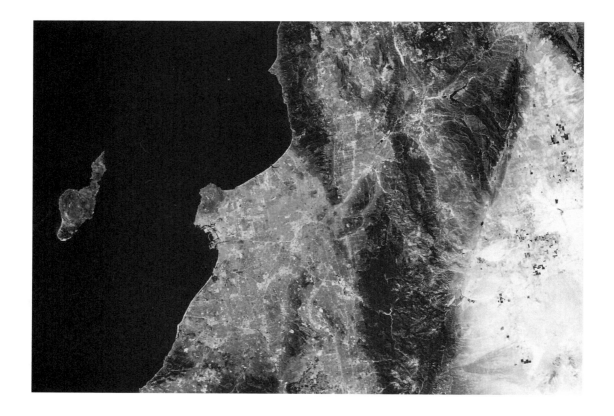

Figure 2.8 Landsat image of Los Angeles. The gray area is the city. Courtesy Jet Propulsion Laboratory.

regional ecosystem is becoming a critical issue for urban planners and designers. Dousset believes the development of sustainable cities requires accurate microclimate databases and a better understanding of the energy exchange at the urban surface in order to

- Optimize energy-efficient designs at the urban and building scale
- Mitigate the urban heat-island effect by selecting the distribution of vegetation, the layout of city blocks, building size and clustering, and the properties of surface materials
- Predict the climatic responses of alternative urban planning and designs

Sustainable Architecture

- Coordinate strategies that ensure a healthy environment for the inhabitants and prevent alterations of the regional ecosystem

Realizing that the sparse network of weather stations located in parks and suburban airports, currently used to monitor urban climates, does not represent the urban environment and lacks spatial resolution, Dousset noted that parameters such as diurnal temperature amplitude and mean insolation can have large spatial gradients impossible to detect using this recording system. Among the climatic parameters recorded from space, radiant surface temperature and cloudiness are collected by infrared scanners on polar orbiting satellites. They provide data over the entire globe twice daily at a resolution of 1 km. The frequency and global extent of satellite coverage creates new capabilities for the analysis of the urban environment. Additional data from high-resolution multispectrum-visible and microwave sensors enable the interpretation of urban microclimates as a function of land classification, vegetation index, and surface properties such as reflectivity or moisture capacity. Optical sensors are unable to penetrate cloud cover. This often prevents the collection of surface temperature statistics in tropical countries but nevertheless allows the mapping of cloud-cover variability.

Remote sensing within the visible to near-infrared range of the electromagnetic spectrum is extensively used to classify static or dynamic phenomena such as city size, road patterns, and population statistics. However, urban climatology using the infrared advanced very high resolution radiometers (AVHRR) on meteorological satellites of the National Oceanic and Atmospheric Administration (NOAA) is a relatively new field.

In her Ph.D. dissertation, Dousset analyzed a series of infrared images from the NOAA-AVHRR over the Los Angeles basin to demonstrate that satellite-derived temperature and cloudiness statistics can yield useful information on urban microclimates.

Composite images of cloud frequency and average surface temperatures were constructed for each set of images at the times of satellite passage. The diurnal frequency of the cloud cover displayed large temporal and spatial variations. The afternoon thermal-composite image indicated a 90°C heat-island between downtown and rural areas. The temperatures were interpreted as a function of the urban land cover classified from a multispectral high resolution SPOT image. Maximum and minimum temperatures were well correlated with the distribution of industrial, densely built areas and parks and golf courses, respectively. A significant negative correlation was found in the afternoon between the vegetation index derived from the multispectral image and the mean intensity of temperature. (Figs. 2.9 to 2.11)

RESEARCH OBJECTIVES AND METHOD

The radiant temperature sensed by the AVHRR represents the amount of electromagnetic radiation reflected and/or emitted by the surface as a function of its emissivity and of the absorption by water vapor in the atmosphere. For most cities, a correction for atmospheric absorption would be necessary. The multichannel temperature correction, developed by McClain in 1985 and commonly used over the ocean, does not work over urban areas, because, unlike the ocean, the emissivity of land surfaces may vary significantly with wavelength. For the first time, the along track scanning radiometer (ATSR) on board the Earth Resource Satellite (ERS), through its dual viewing angle, offers the capability to correct for water vapor using a single wavelength independent of emissivity variations. This capability allows the study of urban microclimates without being restricted to dry regions.

Dousset's research aims to answer the following questions:

- How do urban temperature statistics vary as a function of location?

Figure 2.9
First-stage screen to measure albedo over Los Angeles. Benedicte Dousset.

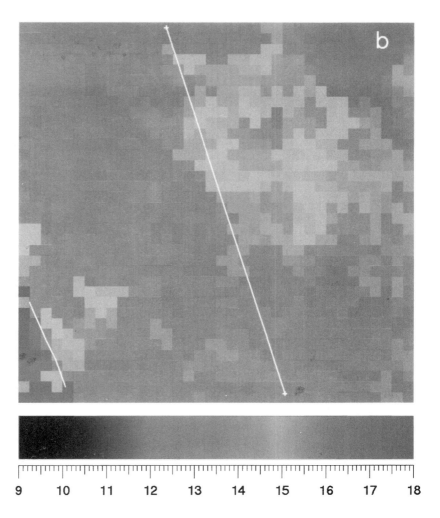

- Is there a correlation between temperature increase and surface ozone concentration?
- Are temperature and cloudiness patterns correlated with land uses such as industrial or residential areas and urban parks?
- Does the magnitude of the heat-island differ for old and new developments, and if so why?
- How do urban heat-island effects differ with season?

Figure 2.10
Second-stage screen.

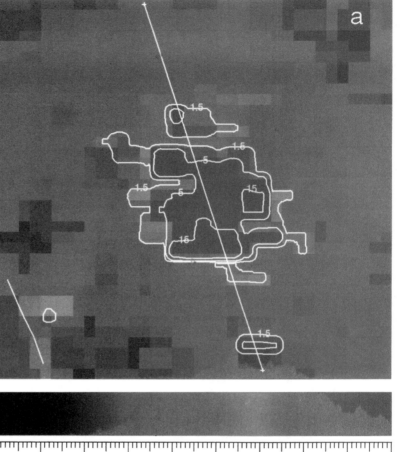

8 9 10 11 12 13 14 15 16 17

- How does urban design influence the microclimates?
- What are the thermal effects of different materials such as asphalt or cement?
- Is the cooling effect of vegetation very different in urban parks within densely built areas as compared to residential areas, garden cities, and suburban areas?
- Is there any common pattern in the thermal behavior of the observed cities?

Figure 2.11
Third-stage screen
showing albedo levels
caused by built-up areas
over Los Angeles.

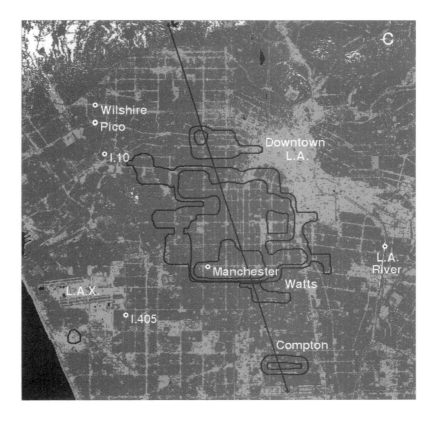

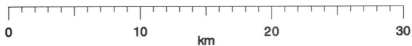

Dousset's research has many applications, from the interpretation of the thermal impact of given urban planning and land
uses to the database needed to design energy-efficient buildings.
This research will allow us to mitigate the urban heat-island effect,
to predict the climatic responses of alternative urban developments, and to coordinate strategies that ensure a healthy environment for the inhabitants and prevent alterations of the regional
ecosystem. Furthermore, systematic analysis of different cities
could explain some of the relationships between microclimates,

energy demand, and urban designs. Although the analysis of series of images will focus on two cities because of limited resources, the method is general and could be applied to any city viewed by the polar orbiting satellites, including those in developing countries for which little conventional data are available.[15]

Regardless of the refinement of such technological methods of prediction and modeling, architects and planners are also becoming aware that many of the techniques they are now discussing to increase urban vitality, environmental harmony, and biodiversity were common practice in cities throughout the developing world until they were radically altered by the influence of the industrialized north. It is ironic that as industrial production has been transferred from the developed to the developing sector, the former must cope with readjustment to an information economy. Many large architectural firms now find that a majority of their work is in the developing world. This has forced many architects to closely examine cultures previously unknown to them and to reevaluate their assumptions of technological superiority.

Mixed use, for example, and the high densities it made possible, were, and still are, common in the developing world, and yet the hierarchical mixture of open and enclosed space does not make these seem oppressive. A recent trend toward mixed-use housing in Santa Monica, in which commercial space is located at street level with living quarters above to reduce commuting, is being hailed as revolutionary, and yet this was the prevalent model in medieval Cairo 700 years ago. The problems now endemic to this city, of overcrowding due to rural urban migration and a resulting failure of existing infrastructure, poor sanitary facilities, and polluted water causing serious health problems, traffic congestion, and lack of services are common throughout the Third World, and yet the lessons Cairo has to teach are there to be found beneath the detritus that has resulted from a change in allegiance to "modern planning" trends by Mohammed Ali at the end of the nineteenth century. (Fig. 2.12)

Figure 2.12 Plan of the
medieval quarter of
Cairo.

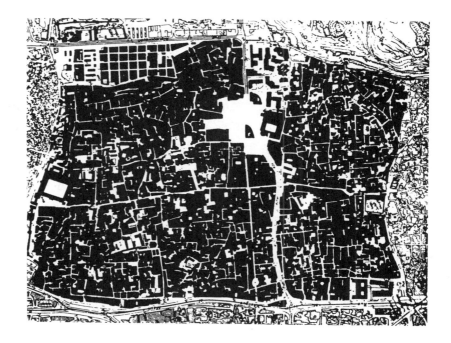

Although somewhat less desirable in the sustainable ethos,
because they require the use of energy, materials, and land to
build, and regardless of the efficiency of their design, self-contained communities are also seen as an attractive and logical alternative to detached suburban houses in the postindustrial age. First
brought to public attention by Peter Calthorpe and Sim van der
Ryn in *Sustainable Communities,* as well as by Andreas Duany and
Elizabeth Plater-Zyberk in town plans such as Seaside, Florida, in
the 1980s, this third alternative to city or suburbs is gathering sur-
prising strength. Calthorpe, who argues that cities are an idea
whose time has gone because permanent changes in household
composition and workplace location have eliminated the necessity
for them, advocates "pedestrian pockets" in their place.

The difference between Calthorpe's perception of the
direction that home ownership and working and commuting patterns are taking in the postindustrial nations is reflected in the
community he proposes. Calthorpe describes the change as "the

Figure 2.13 (Opposite)
Dogan Village, Mali.
World Bank Photo
Archive.

signal of a deep shift in the structure of our culture. The computer and the service industry have led to the decentralization of the workplace, causing new traffic patterns and 'suburban gridlock.' Where downtown employment once dominated, suburb to suburb traffic patterns now produce greater commute distances and driving time. Over 40 percent of all commute trips are now from suburb to suburb."[16]

The pedestrian pocket, by comparison, is intended to align with a light rail system, with cluster housing, retail space, and offices all within a quarter-mile radius or within easy walking distance of it. Calthorpe is pragmatic enough to realize that the model he proposes does not preclude urban improvement or continued suburban growth.

IMPLICATIONS FOR ARCHITECTS

At the close of the twentieth century, as the global network becomes smaller and the interrelationship between nations becomes more delicate, architects who tend, in spite of their preferred image as leaders of teams of experts, to be isolationists, can no longer console themselves that, by making token gestures toward energy conservation, they are doing their bit for environmental protection. A burgeoning body of literature not strictly confined to construction has a direct impact on the architect's world, and architects must become familiar with this literature to maintain professional responsibility to a wider global constituency that is increasingly demanding consideration.

One of the first and most shocking realizations is that the very traditional societies of the kind displaced by the Aswan Dam have been the most effective in managing environmental resources over time, of true sustainable development. What distinguishes the 250 million indigenous peoples that remain in more than 70 countries in which they have managed to survive is their approach

toward the land. As Julian Burger has said, "For most indigenous peoples, land is not viewed as a 'commodity' which can be bought or sold in impersonal markets, but rather a substance endowed with sacred meanings which defines their existence and identity. Similarly, the trees, plants, animals, and fish, which inhabit the land are not 'natural resources,' but highly personal beings which form part of their social and spiritual universe."[17] There are difficulties in squaring this realization with the views of the land management advocates and the proponents of environmental economics, and it is significant, if confusing, to note that in its search for the parameters of sustainability, the Brundtland Commission has also recognized that such indigenous groups are repositories of vast accumulations of traditional knowledge and that when they are destroyed this knowledge will be irretrievably lost. As *Our Common Future* indicates, "Their disappearance is a loss for the larger society, which could learn a great deal from their traditional skills in sustainably managing very complex ecological systems. It is a terrible irony that as formal development reaches more deeply into rain forests, deserts, and other isolated environments, it tends to destroy the only cultures that have proved able to thrive in the environments."[18] (Fig. 2.13)

The case studies that follow in Chapter 3 were chosen largely because the architects involved have realized that, to a greater or lesser degree, providing models for others to follow in a future that is riddled with difficulty is a necessary part of helping to change social patterns. Sustainability as a concept may now be on the verge of becoming a fashionable buzzword because of its increasing alliance with economic and institutional interests. It would also be unfortunate if it became associated with an architectural style with all the inherent dangers that becoming a contemporary trend now implies. The following examples indicate that there is a strong probability that this will not happen.

CASE STUDIES

DE MONTFORT UNIVERSITY ENGINEERING BUILDING
Short and Ford Architects

De Montfort Engineering Building is historically significant because of its scale, institutional use, and success. Leicester was the United Kingdom's Environment City in 1992, and the focus on sustainable design during that time encouraged university administrators, in cooperation with the local council, to attempt this radical departure from standard design policies. The vice chancellor of the university had actually commissioned the design in 1988, which was finalized, following government review, in mid-1989, but official consensus could not be reached at that time. An impressive list of advisors were recruited to assist in the design process, including the Department of Architectural Research at Cambridge, the Environmental Computer Aided Design and Performance Group at De Montfort, Thomas Lawson, from Bristol University, and Max Fordham Associates, who provided direction on everything from general ventilation and air flow physics to advice on building services. (Figs. 3.1 to 3.19)

Figure 3.1
Axonometric of
DeMontfort University,
Short and Ford
Architects.

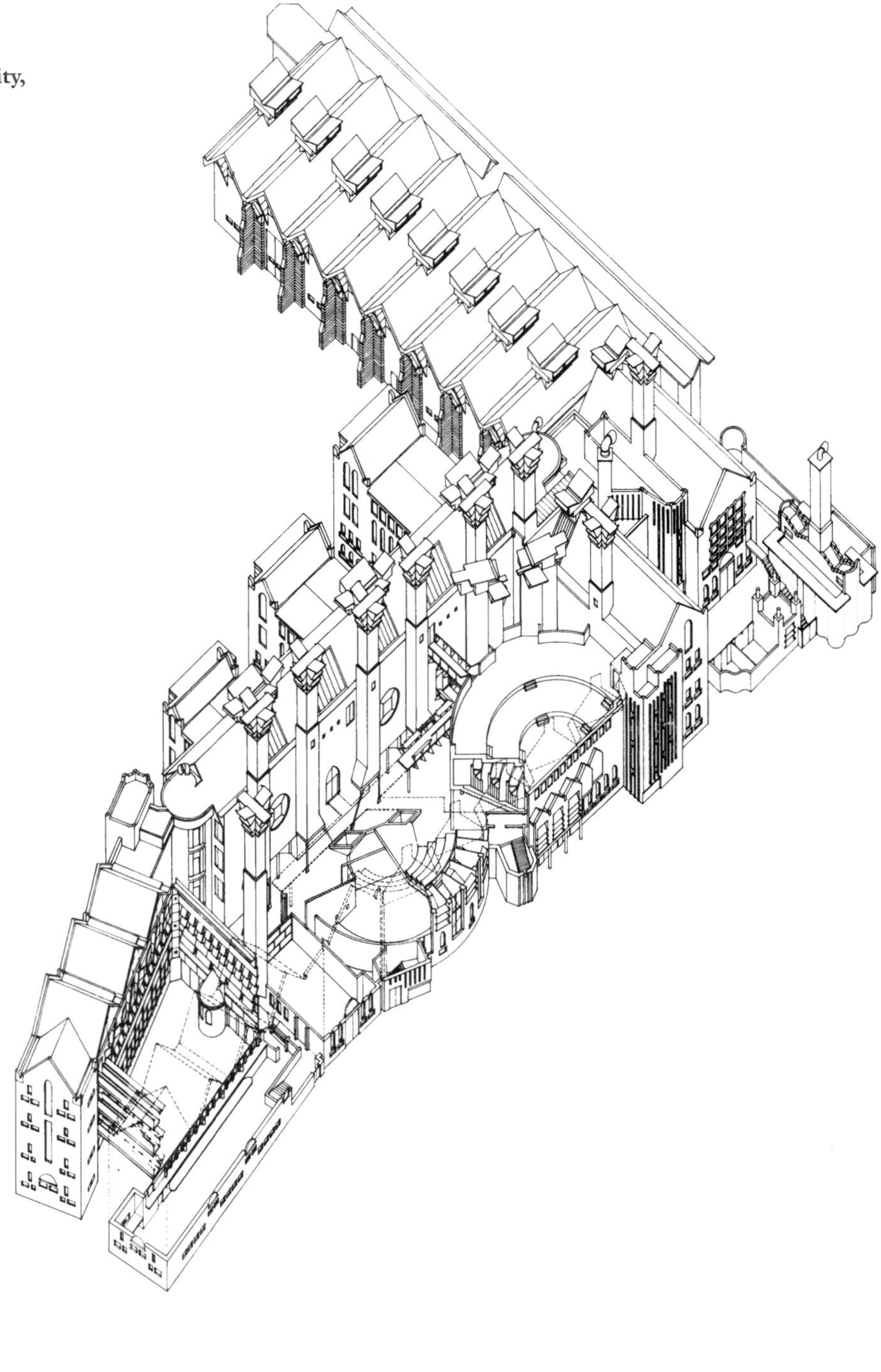

Figure 3.2
Labeled version of
Fig. 3.1.

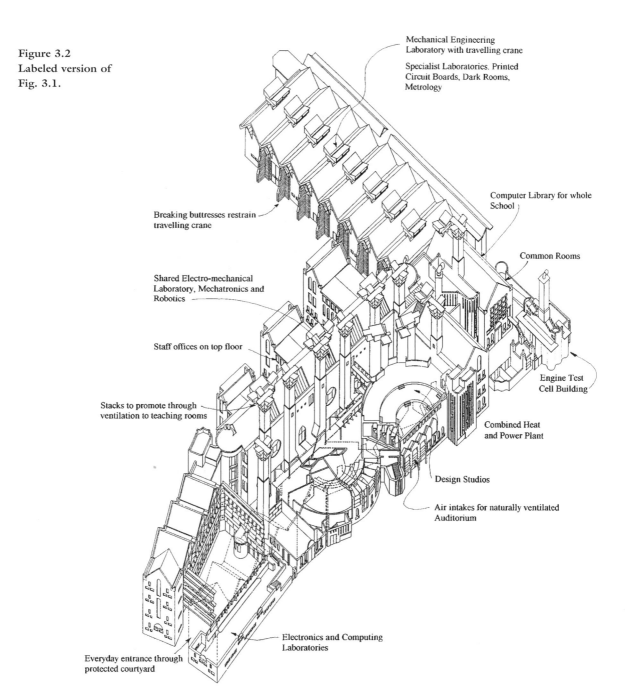

Mechanical Engineering
Laboratory with travelling crane

Specialist Laboratories. Printed
Circuit Boards, Dark Rooms,
Metrology

Computer Library for whole
School

Common Rooms

Breaking buttresses restrain
travelling crane

Shared Electro-mechanical
Laboratory, Mechatronics and
Robotics

Staff offices on top floor

Engine Test
Cell Building

Stacks to promote through
ventilation to teaching rooms

Combined Heat
and Power Plant

Design Studios

Air intakes for naturally ventilated
Auditorium

Electronics and Computing
Laboratories

Everyday entrance through
protected courtyard

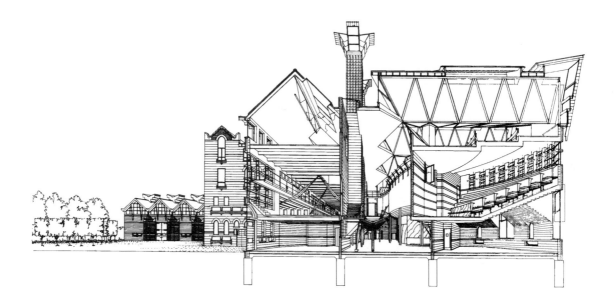

In spite of all this attention the initial parti proposed by the architects remained relatively unchanged throughout; a north-east-southeast orientation dictated by prevailing winds and a thin profile to encourage cross ventilation. Functional adjacencies however, requiring that two separate auditoria be located centrally, amidst the various laboratories strung out along them, caused complications which Short and Ford solved with a central linear "concourse" that allows air to escape through the deepest midline of the plan. This is where the majority of the distinctive ventilation chimneys are located, since stack effect rather than straightforward air currents had to be the main cooling strategy in this part of the complex. The comfort levels required in the auditoria, where large groups remain for extended periods, made this section even trickier. Computer simulations indicated that the most important factor was the size and position of the chimney openings or "extracts."

Sustainable Architecture

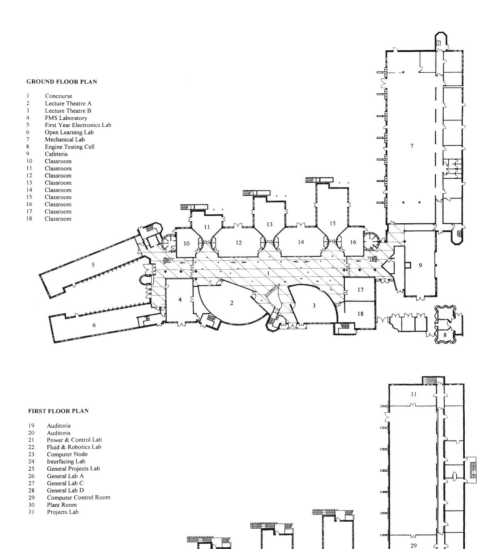

Figure 3.4
Ground floor
plan,
DeMontfort
University.

Figure 3.5
First-floor
plan,
DeMontfort
University.

GROUND FLOOR PLAN

1   Concourse
2   Lecture Theatre A
3   Lecture Theatre B
4   FMS Laboratory
5   First Year Electronics Lab
6   Open Learning Lab
7   Mechanical Lab
8   Engine Testing Cell
9   Cafeteria
10 Classroom
11 Classroom
12 Classroom
13 Classroom
14 Classroom
15 Classroom
16 Classroom
17 Classroom
18 Classroom

FIRST FLOOR PLAN

19 Auditoria
20 Auditoria
21 Power & Control Lab
22 Fluid & Robotics Lab
23 Computer Node
24 Interfacing Lab
25 General Projects Lab
26 General Lab A
27 General Lab C
28 General Lab D
29 Computer Control Room
30 Plant Room
31 Projects Lab

Figure 3.6
Second-floor
plan,
DeMontfort
University.

Figure 3.7
Third-floor
plan,
DeMontfort
University.

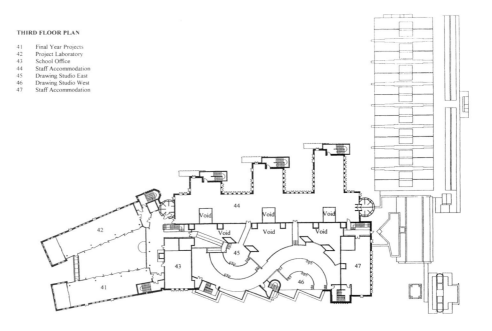

SECOND FLOOR PLAN

32	Auditorium 1
33	Auditorium 2
34	Staff Accomodation
35	Heads of Schools and Departments
36	Heads of Schools and Departments
37	Network and Communications Lab
38	Electronic Computer Aided Design
39	Staff Accomodation
40	Computer Node Mezzanine

THIRD FLOOR PLAN

41	Final Year Projects
42	Project Laboratory
43	School Office
44	Staff Accommodation
45	Drawing Studio East
46	Drawing Studio West
47	Staff Accommodation

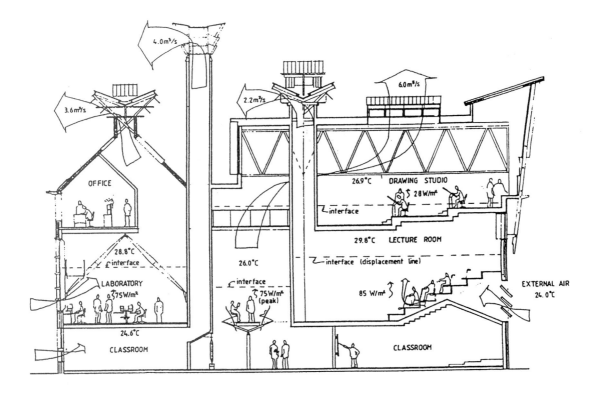

Displacement Ventilation & Temperature Stratification Predicted by Saline Bath Simulation.

Figure 3.8
Diagramatic section showing path of natural ventilation, DeMontfort University.

Central Building The compacted plan of the central building precludes cross-ventilation. The various laboratory and general teaching spaces are independently conditioned via low-level openings, stacks and rooftop vents. Each activity is separated to cope with acoustic and fire prevention needs. Daylight penetrates deep into the laboratory and concourse area via rooflights and glazed gables over the drawing studios. Acoustic attenuation is achieved within the air supply and exhaust routes to the auditoria, which have the highest noise reduction needs.

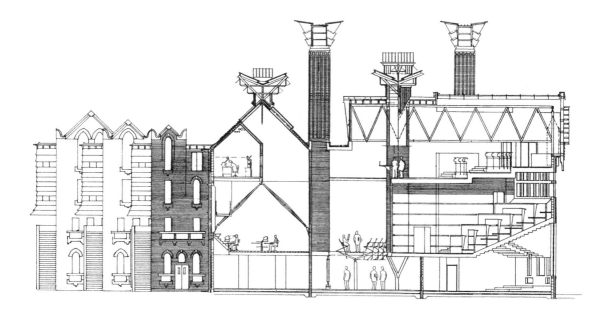

Figure 3.9
Section, DeMontfort
University.

Technically, this analysis indicated, as the architects have described, that

the opening had to be sized so that the boundary of the 1 meter thick layer of hot polluted air was below the top lip of the extract opening, but above head height on the top row of seats. The system comprises a fresh air plenum serving grilles under the raked seats, the vitiated air being exhausted through a 13 meter high stack. In winter, finned tubes located behind the inlet grilles heat the fresh air. A carbon dioxide detector controlling automatic dampers in the stack is intended to prevent excess ventilation in winter. Temperature sensors will control the heating and override the CO_2 detector to open the dampers as space temperature rises.

Other concerns, such as unexpected, opposing eddy currents and backflow caused by external cooling of the chimney sur-

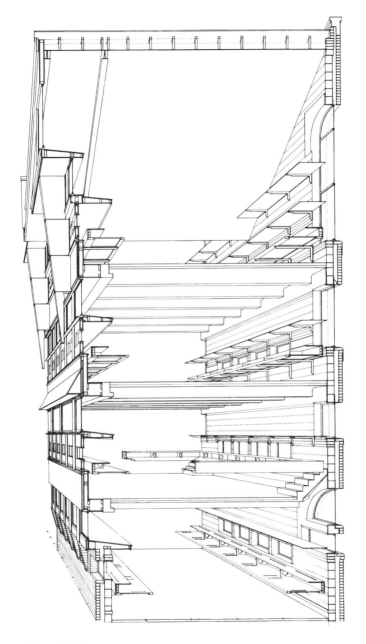

Figure 3.10
Section detail, DeMontfort University.

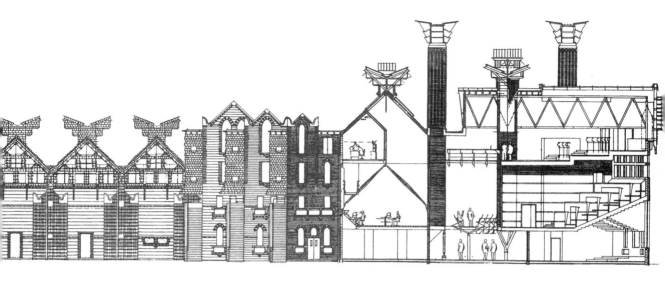

Figure 3.11
Diagramatic section,
DeMontfort University.

face, also had to be accounted for, with sizing and insulation used
to reduce this possibility to a minimum. The general design goal
through the complex was to maintain an internal mean temperature of 19°C, a minimum of 13°, and a maximum of 25°, and this
has been maintained, with only rare extreme cases of 28° temperatures in summer, when school use is low.

As the largest naturally ventilated building in Europe,
using only minimal mechanical equipment for dampers, fans to
induce stack effect, and heating by a two-pipe weather-compensat-
ed system, the De Montfort University School of Engineering has
set a significant precedent. This is especially true considering that
it has been realized in one of the most highly regulated areas in
the European Economic Community (EEC) with a strong tradition in conservative high technology. Several observers have noted
the irony in the fact that Leicester is also well known as the location of James Stirling's iconic Engineering Building of 1963,
which gave new impetus to the Brutalist phase of the Modern
movement. Although the notion that there may be any similarity

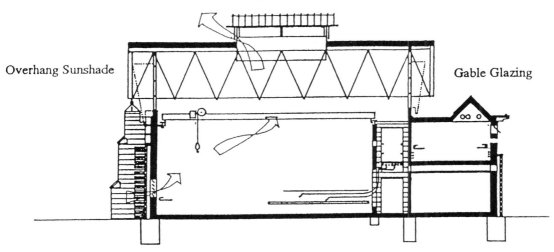

Rooflight / Ventilator

Overhang Sunshade

Gable Glazing

Diagramatic Section through Mechanical Laboratory.

Figure 3.12
Diagramatic section,
DeMontfort University.

Mechanical Laboratory The main hall of the mechanical laboratory suffers periodic high internal heat gains from large machines. Ventilation air is introduced at low level via 'perforated' brick buttresses which incorporate acoustic quilt to reduce noise transfer and brace the travelling gantry. High light levels are achieved by glazed gables and rooflights, which also act as ridge ventilators. Roof overhangs and deep reveals prevent penetration of direct sunlight onto the laboratory floor.

between the two buildings will undoubtedly seem unlikely to De Montfort enthusiasts, as well as its architects, there are obvious parallels related to the honest use of materials and clear expression of form. The difference is one of intent. Stirling's listed Modernist monument, which has proved to be an environmental disaster, formalized function rather than its relationship to climate and the

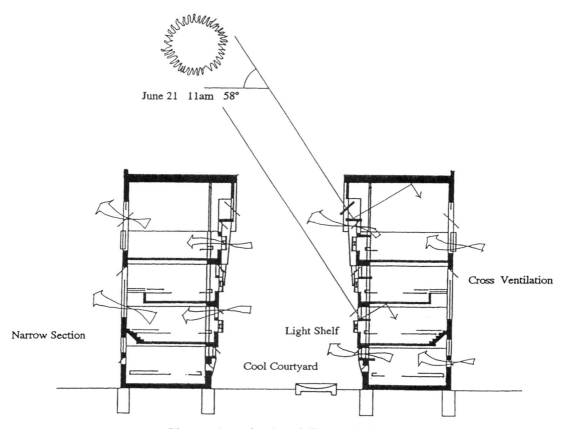

June 21   11am   58°

Cross Ventilation

Narrow Section

Light Shelf

Cool Courtyard

Diagramatic Section through Electrical Laboratories.

**Figure 3.13
Diagramatic section,
DeMontfort University.**

Electrical Laboratories The shallow
section of the two 'wings' promotes cross
ventilation. Low- and high-level openings
(some electronically operated) provide
sufficient air changes to remove high
internal heat gains from computers and
other small machines. Daylight is controlled partly by 'light shelves' which protect occupants from direct sunlight and
reflect light onto the ceiling, providing an
even distribution across the laboratory.

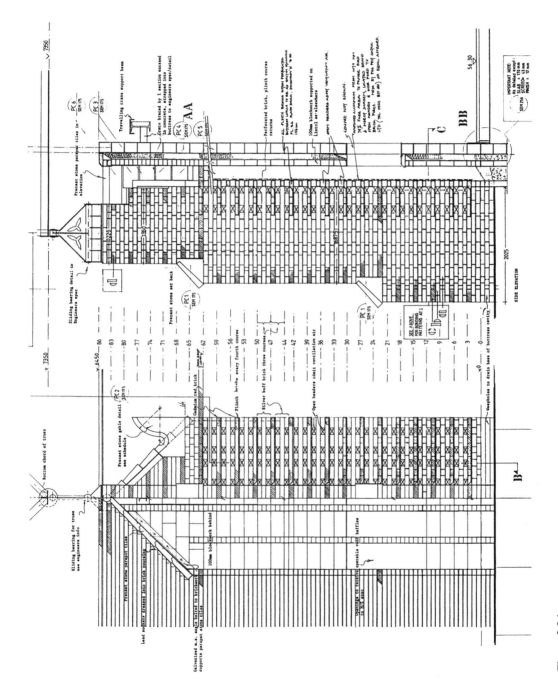

Figure 3.14
Elevation of ventilation stack, DeMontfort University.

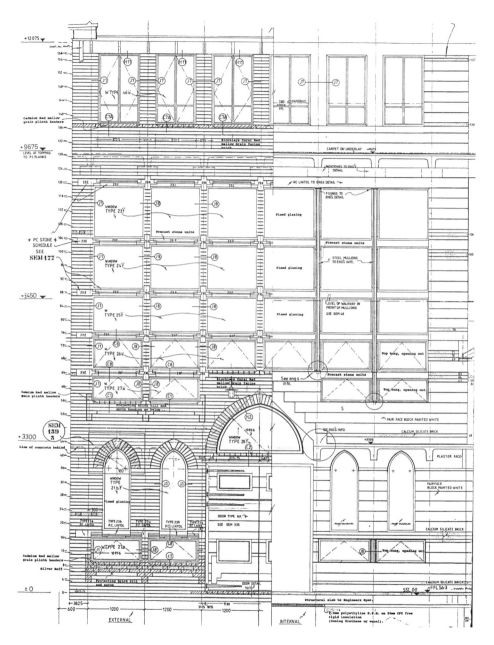

Figure 3.15
Detail of elevation, DeMontfort University.

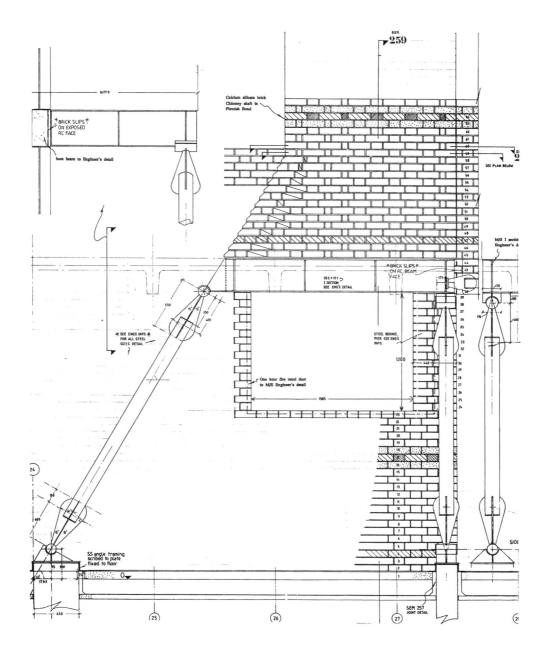

Figure 3.16
Detail of elevation, DeMontfort University.

Figure 3.17 (left)
Queen's building,
DeMontfort University.
Photo Courtesy
DeMontfort University.

Figure 3.18 (top)
Detail of vent stack,
DeMontfort University.
Credit Peter Cook.

internal processes necessary to harmonize with it. The materials chosen, primarily glass over the central reading room, forced dependence on a mechanical air handling system that was then purposefully expressed as part of the technological image that Stirling wanted. Alan Short and Brian Ford, however, have allowed air dynamics to shape their building; a secondary agenda being to get as much natural light into the interior as possible, with brick chosen as cladding to assist thermal mass rather than to act as a visual foil. This difference of intent speaks volumes about the

Figure 3.19
Detail of vent stack,
DeMontfort University.

significant transformation that has taken place in basic architectural principles in the three decades that separate these two historically important structures; De Montfort would previously have been unthinkable in the public sector.

Beyond serving as a symbol of change, this building will also provide much needed statistical data through an extensive and sophisticated monitoring system propitiously included by its originators. A Building Environment System (BES) has been installed with over 900 control points, to allow finetuning as time goes on. The building will also provide the students using it with a firsthand example of an efficient natural cooling system, proselytizing through performance.

THE VILLAGE OF NEW BARIZ, EGYPT

Hassan Fathy

Hassan Fathy first achieved international recognition with the publication of *Architecture for the Poor* in 1977, which followed soon after the OPEC price rise, and a surge in interest in conservation measures. The book details the ill-fated history of the project of New Gourna, a compelling narrative that captures all the depressing nuances of dealing with Egyptian bureaucracy as well as the prejudice against indigenous materials and traditional methods of construction in that country. Because of the success of the book, Fathy has since become identified with New Gourna in the public consciousness, and primarily with its failure, to the exclusion of other, equally significant work. A comprehensive redress of this media-induced myopia that was abetted by a quirk of current events is long overdue.

Upon his return to Egypt after a self-imposed 5-year exile in Greece from 1957 to 1962, following the debacle at New Gourna, Fathy was asked by Dr. Salah Hidayat, the head of the Ministry of Scientific Research, to undertake the design and supervision of a new settlement near the village of Bariz in central Egypt. *Bariz*—the Arabic pronunciation of Paris, a holdover from the Ptolemaic period—is an oasis in the western desert, 60 km to the south of the town of Kharga, the capital of the region. In 1962, it was discovered that the artesian wells that feed the oasis are more extensive than originally believed. Millions of cubic meters of fresh underground water were found beneath the desert floor, flowing from the equatorial African plateau toward the Mediterranean. This water is calculated to be sufficient to irrigate 2 million acres of desert, and a governmental directive was issued to construct a well to tap this resource and to build an agricultural center near it, to serve a region 40 km in diameter to include 1000 cultivated acres and six smaller villages. (Figs. 3.20 and 3.21)

Figure 3.20 (top)
Site plan of New Baris.
Hassan Fathy.

Figure 3.21 (bottom)
Plan of New Baris.
Hassan Fathy.

Sustainable Architecture

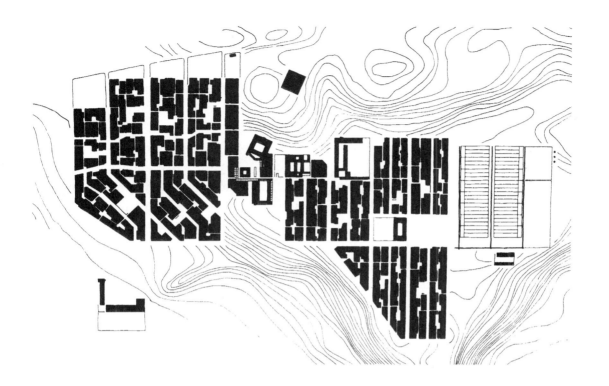

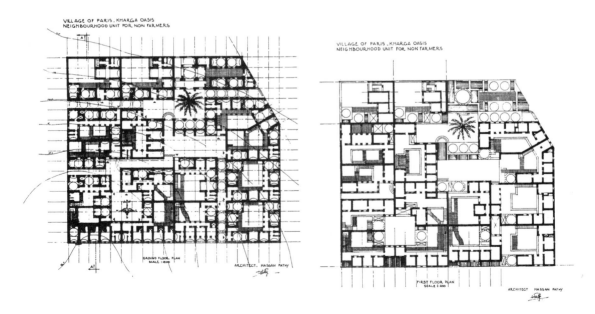

VILLAGE OF PARIS, KHARGA OASIS
NEIGHBOURHOOD UNIT FOR NON FARMERS

GROUND FLOOR PLAN
SCALE 1:200

ARCHITECT. HASSAN FATHY

VILLAGE OF PARIS, KHARGA OASIS
NEIGHBOURHOOD UNIT FOR NON FARMERS

FIRST FLOOR PLAN
SCALE 1:200

ARCHITECT HASSAN FATHY

Case Studies

79

As at New Gourna, Fathy saw this opportunity, for the design of the agricultural center of New Bariz, as an ideal chance to provide a prototype, not only for the additional six villages that would follow but also for housing for the rural poor, using traditional techniques and materials. He began by visiting towns in the area, noting that many of their narrow streets were partially covered, and that the houses were introverted, primarily opening onto inner courtyards, to combat temperatures that frequently exceed 48°C in July and August. Based on these examples and his own research on the *Takhtaboosh,* or opening between one paved and one planted courtyard, arranged to induce convective cooling, Fathy decided to employ a system of internal courtyards as a primary means of climate control in his design of the village of New Bariz, along with shading. In his initial presentation, he stressed that thermal comfort in the housing design he proposed depended on the natural control of air temperature, air movement, relative humidity, and radiation. Air movement was to be generated by creating a pressure differential and by convection, utilizing the basic physical principle that hot air rises and is replaced by cooler air to best advantage. To bring air into the series of internal courtyards planned for each house, he proposed wind towers, or *Badgirs,* to catch the higher cooler breeze above the desert, and bring it into each house. His refinement, also used in the market, where cool temperatures were essential to preserve agricultural perishables awaiting shipment to larger markets, consisted of two shafts. One of these has an opening facing the windward side, and the other faces the leeward side with a metal-bladed funnel pointed downward, which ensures suction by Venturi effect. This second stack and funnel have been painted black to draw air from below as they are heated by the sun. To add to their cooling capacity the windward towers had straw mats hanging inside them which were dampened by a hand pump at regular intervals during the day. (Fig. 3.22)

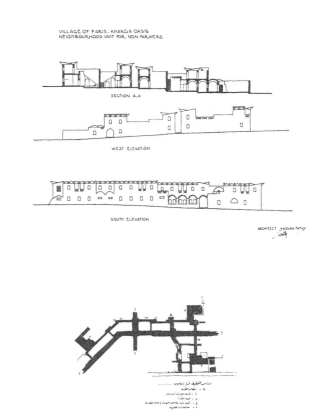

VILLAGE OF PARIS - KHARGA OASIS
NEIGHBOURHOOD UNIT FOR NON FARMERS

SECTION A.A

WEST ELEVATION

SOUTH ELEVATION

ARCHITECT . HASSAN FATHY

VILLAGE OF PARIS - KHARGA OASIS
NEIGHBOURHOOD UNIT FOR NON FARMERS

ROOF PLAN
SCALE 1:7200

ARCHITECT . HASSAN FATHY

Figure 3.22
Plan sections and
elevations of New Baris.
Hassan Fathy.

In addition to these cooling strategies, a shortage of viable building materials indicated a repetition of the same vault and dome system in mud brick, used at New Gourna, with paraffin and bitumen emulsions used as stabilizers, since the soil at Kharga Oasis is of poorer quality than that near the Nile. Fathy specifically recommended a social mix in the community of 150 families occupied in agriculture and 100 families in other occupations, broken down with neighborhoods of 20 families each to promote cooperative building. This was based on Fathy's studies of traditional societies which showed that this was a critical size; the possibility

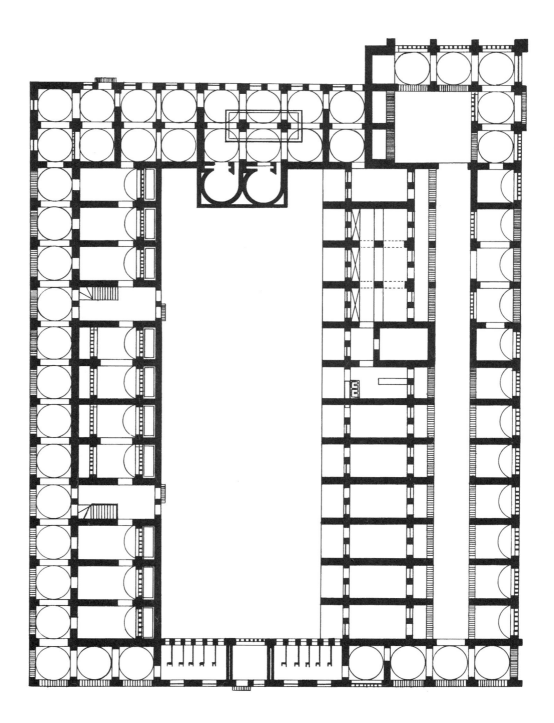

Figure 3.23
Plan of Market, New
Baris. Drawing by James
Steele.

of cooperation declined thereafter. He estimated that a team of two masons and four laborers could build a house in 45 days, and that 20 families, which would provide 4 such teams, could build their own neighborhood in 8 months. Realizing that many of the residents coming to New Bariz would have had no prior experience in building, Fathy proposed an in-service training program which he also initiated at New Gourna as well as at Faris where a school, built using a self-help system, has been in constant use since 1956. (Fig. 3.23)

Unfortunately, hostilities in the region, in 1967, derailed plans for New Bariz, leaving the market as the only part of the village to be completed. It performs just as Fathy said it would, its basement constantly cold enough to serve as a refrigerated locker for produce. Its stark verticality and clean contemporary lines give the lie to those critics who have characterized the architect as a hopelessly retrograde romantic. As the majority of initiatives being labeled as sustainable architecture now show, Fathy's sensibilities were remarkably prophetic, and New Bariz, rather than New Gourna, represents them best.

The housing, had it been built, would undoubtedly have functioned equally well, but we only have his working drawings to show us what it would have looked like. Rather than the domes that predominate in New Gourna, he relied mostly on a Barasti truss system; a lighter reed and wire frame roof that was easily built and helped to promote better convection. The repetitive, triangular forms of the Barasti roof, topping off the linear, two-story housing blocks, would have been as visually distinctive as the Badgirs of the market. (Fig. 3.24)

Describing his approach at New Bariz, Fathy said: "Over many centuries, the people in each part of the earth have learned, by trial and error, how to deal with their environment; their solutions to the problems of housing grew out of countless experi-

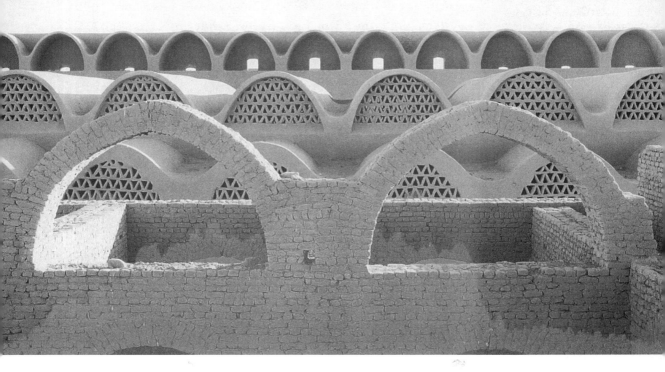

Figure 3.24
Roofscape of market at
New Baris. Photo by
Tina Wik.

ments and accidents, out of the experience of generations of builders who kept what worked and rejected what did not, and these solutions were passed on as tradition."

It has taken the architectural profession half a century to finally begin to appreciate the importance of Fathy's realization.

Sustainable Architecture

UNIVERSITY OF ARIZONA CAMPUS PLAN

Moule and Polyzoides

While involved in general master planning for the University of Arizona, architects and urbanists Elizabeth Moule and Stefanos Polyzoides were asked to develop a more detailed scheme for one specific part of the campus. This 100,000-ft^2 district includes mixed residential use for more than 500 students and faculty as well as classrooms, computer rooms, a dining hall, and a parking garage.

In response, Moule and Polyzoides have proposed a series of buildings lined up against Highland Street, which is a main circulation artery in their general scheme, broken down into units grouped around interior courtyards. These courtyards, which serve as entryways into the buildings, are narrow, to provide adequate shade from the hot desert sun, in configurations based on a variety of American, Mexican, and Middle Eastern examples. The most local typologies were Spanish missions, and the pueblos at Taos, Tumcacori, and East Vahan. To replicate the thermal mass that is a consistent feature of each of these in more institutionally acceptable materials, concrete block and brick were used throughout. Brick screens have also been incorporated into these exceptionally thick walls to allow light and air to penetrate into the buildings. (Figs. 3.25 to 3.41)

Eleven courtyards of various sizes are placed throughout the complex, and the largest two of these anchor it at its northern and southern ends. The strategies used in the design of each of the outdoor rooms, which occupy as much space in plan as the buildings themselves, vary according to location and purpose. These outdoor rooms range from spaces that are partially surrounded by building walls to those that are completely enclosed with only a

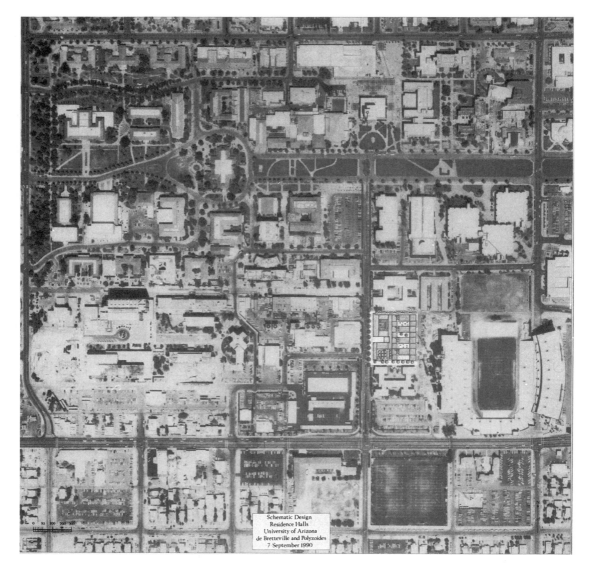

Schematic Design
Residence Halls
University of Arizona
de Bretteville and Polyzoides
7 September 1990

Figure 3.25
Aerial view of the
University of Arizona
showing location of the
new residence hall by
Moule and Polyzoides.

Sustainable Architecture

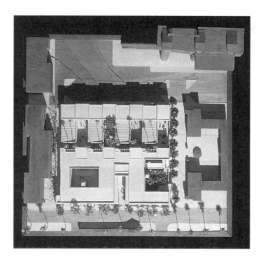

Figure 3.26
Elevation of courtyard of
University of Arizona
residence hall.

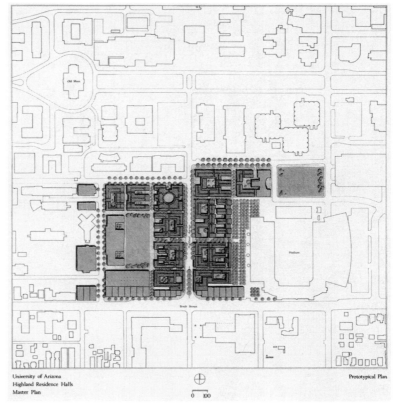

Figure 3.27
Preliminary layout of the
University of Arizona
residence hall.

University of Arizona
Highland Residence Halls
Master Plan

Prototypical Plan

0   100

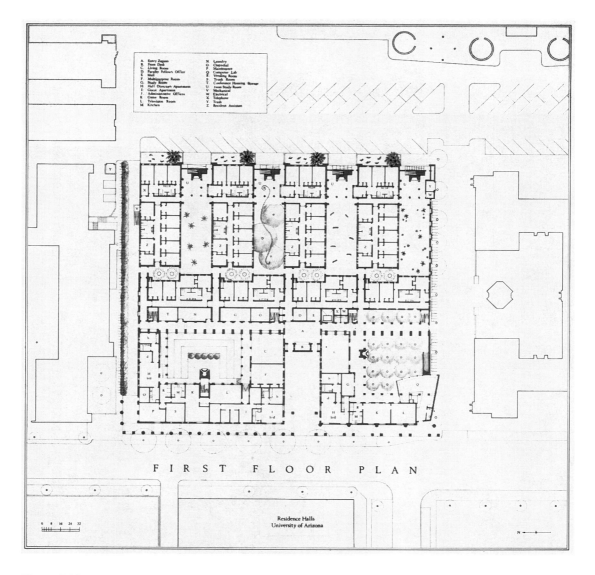

F I R S T   F L O O R   P L A N

Residence Halls
University of Arizona

Figure 3.28
Plan of residence hall,
ground floor.

Sustainable Architecture

Figure 3.29
Aerial perspective of
residence hall.

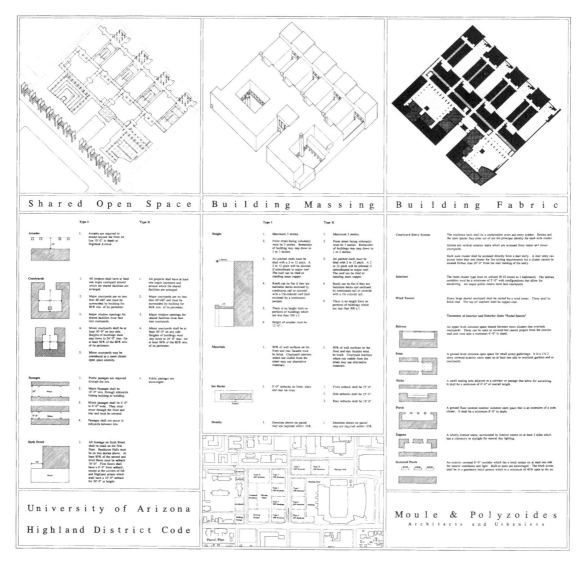

Figure 3.30
New district code
proposed by Moule and
Polyzoides.

Figure 3.31 West elevation.

Figure 3.32 North elevation.

Figure 3.33 East elevation.

Figure 3.34 South elevation.

Figure 3.35 (right)
Axonometric of Iwan
and court.

Figure 3.36 (bottom)
Axonometric of front
entry court.

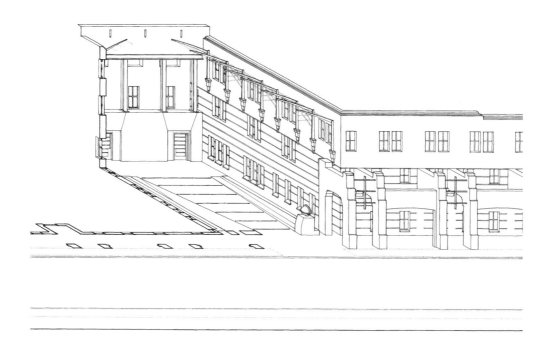

Figure 3.37
Axonometric of south
court.

Figure 3.38
Axonometric of north
court.

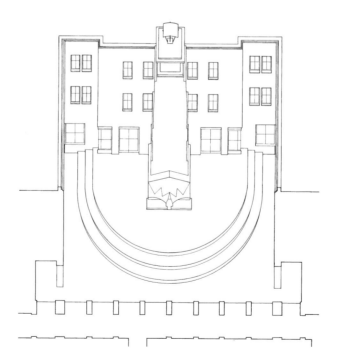

Figure 3.39
(pages 94–96)
Working drawing of
details of University of
Arizona residence hall.
The wind catchers, which
are a prominent
architectural feature, are
sculptural forms in the
courtyards.

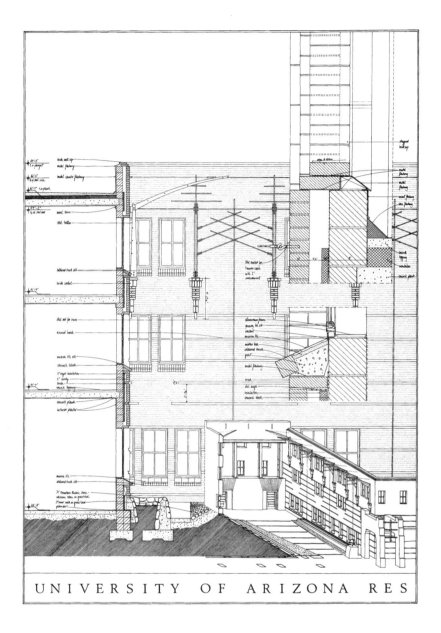

UNIVERSITY OF ARIZONA RES

Sustainable Architecture

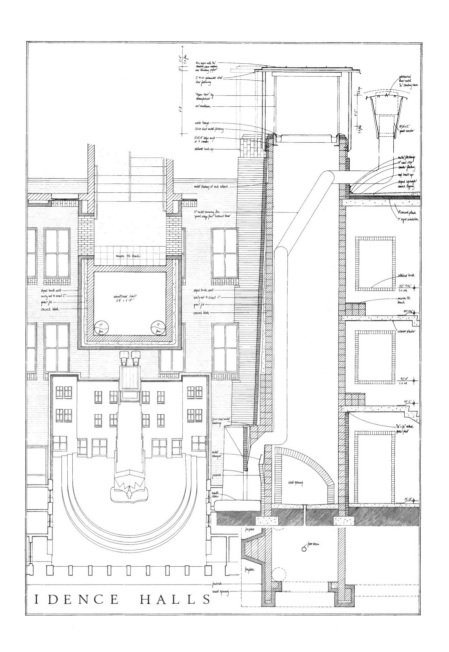

I D E N C E   H A L L S

Figure 3.40
Windcatch, University
of Arizona residence
hall. Courtesy Moule
and Polyzoides.

Figure 3.41
Arcade in residence hall.

relatively small opening at the top, and all are recessed below grade, to take advantage of cooler air at ground level.

Water has also been used in conjunction with these various courtyards to help in cooling them, with wide liquid bands lining the edges of all entrances. Each of the courts is also graded downward from a crown in the center, to direct the scant rainfall that does occur in Arizona toward cisterns at the sides, from which the rain is then directed toward gardens on the southern edge of the complex. This filtration system has also been adopted throughout the rest of the campus, since it is more efficient than that previously in use.

Wind towers located in the largest north and south courtyards are 65 ft tall and 12 ft square at the base, to allow an adequate amount of air to circulate in summer and to provide heat in winter. The central shaft of the towers is divided into two flues, to allow one to act as a chimney for a fireplace. In the summer, metal mesh at the top of the second flue is kept constantly wet with misted spray, so that as the air runs through it, it is cooled, and accelerated downward as it becomes heavier. The University of Arizona is well known for its contributions to research on wind towers, and their implementation here has dual significance, symbolic and functional.

HOUSING IN YEMEN

Rasem Badran

Although much attention is now being given to discovering regional typologies, Jordanian architect Rasem Badran has been successfully adapting elements from his own local context for decades, before it became fashionable to do so. His field of study has primarily been the historical fabric of the most significant cities in the Islamic world. He has concentrated primarily on constants between them as well as the reasons for differences, when they occur, continually questioning how best to reinterpret the architectural morphology of the past, given the multiplicity of forms represented. He has arrived at what he has termed "a dialectic methodology" of investigation in determining the basic architectural characteristics of a specific place, which he unravels through a heuristic, graphic process of topological study. (Fig. 3.42)

A recent project, for housing in Sana'a, Yemen, demonstrates Badran's approach, reflecting the architect's belief that "Architectural expression is bound up in a set of interconnected factors, including socio-cultural, environmental, ecological and technical issues. I see my role in activating these factors, in giving value to human needs by emphasizing the character of a place as well as its architectural and morphological patterns."

Badran's studies of Sana'a began with an analysis of the process of urbanization in Yemen relative to defensive requirements and tribal divisions. Badran compared urban growth in Yemen with that in other nearby cities, such as Cairo and Baghdad, to find points of similarity and difference. By so doing, he found that a recognizable center, along with a large mosque, or Masjid Al-Jami'i, and related commercial and residential functions are constant in all of them, but housing in Yemeni cities differs. Rather than spreading out horizontally, with individual courtyards in each

**Figure 3.42
Traditional tower houses
in Yemen. Courtesy
World Bank Photo
Archive.**

house, as elsewhere, urban residential groups in Yemen are stacked
vertically, and clustered around a common garden, or *Bustan*.
Badran and others have traced this vertical residential cell to earlier
houses created by a nomadic agricultural society to adapt to the
hilly topography of Yemen, where terracing is used and tower
houses help to save valuable land, as well as to visually protect it.
(Figs. 3.43 to 3.46)

As they evolved, the tower houses were increasingly
designed to relate to sun and natural ventilation, with the highest
room, the *Mafraj*, articulated with openings to create a direct visual relationship with the outside. The ornamentation used on these

Case Studies

openings, in addition to being a means of controlling glare, also became an indication of socioeconomic status, much as the richness of decor in the internal courtyards of houses throughout other cities in the Middle East has been used to indicate familial wealth, but the outsides remain plain.

The tower house, moving down from the *Mafraj,* became less ceremonial, with family quarters and bedrooms located in the middle, and the ground floor used for reception, cooking, and storage. Because of the importance accorded to view and orientation, Badran found that south-facing elevations were more highly

Figure 3.43
Survey sketch of Yemeni village. Rasem Badran.

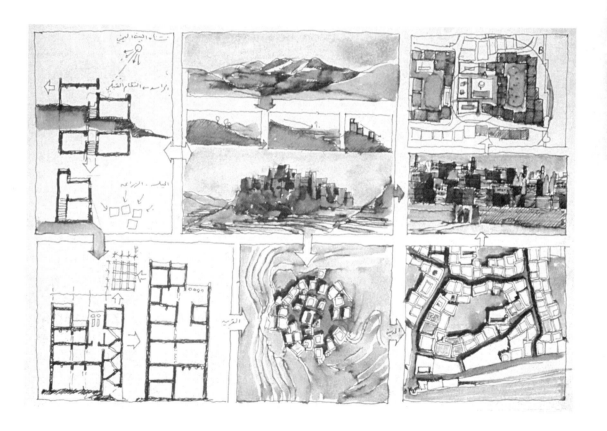

Sustainable Architecture

Figure 3.44
Survey of Yemeni
window types. Rasem
Badran.

prized than others, and that houses with this aspect were called
"complete."

Tracing the house to the urban setting, Badran then identified other typological elements historically associated with it.
These, in addition to the *Bustan* and mosque already mentioned,
were found to be a commercial district or *suq*, a specialized commercial center or *Samsara*, a water well or *Abiyar*, and defensive
walls and gates. In this system, Badran identified that residential
units usually occupy about 30 to 40 percent of the land available,
in linear organization, and he attempted the same configuration in

Case Studies

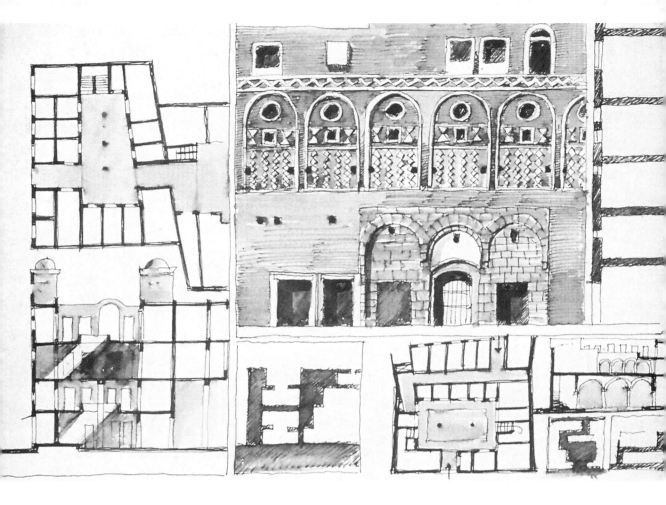

**Figure 3.45
Survey of Yemeni
window types. Rasem
Badran.**

the 100,000 square meters of housing he was asked to provide.
Using the same linear, vertically stacked organization he had seen
elsewhere, grouped around common gardens, he located housing
away from public streets for privacy, using shops, offices, and hotel
accommodations as a buffer. The mosque was used as an interme-
diary, linking the public and private areas. (Figs. 3.47 to 3.52)

Sustainable Architecture

Figure 3.46
Survey of Yemeni
window types. Rasem
Badran.

The result is contemporary in appearance, yet historically and culturally responsive and specific, as well as environmentally sensitive, serving as a vital example for those faced with the task of adapting to a specialized social and topographical context.

Figure 3.47
New housing proposal
for Sana'a. Rasem
Badran.

Figure 3.48
(opposite, top)
New housing proposal
for Sana'a. Rasem
Badran.

Figure 3.49
(opposite, bottom)
New housing proposal
for Sana'a. Rasem
Badran.

Sustainable Architecture

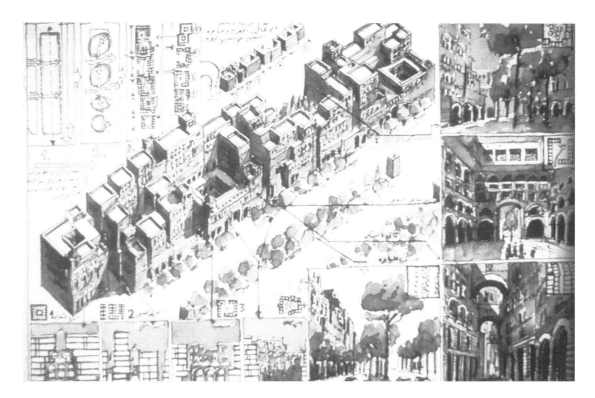

Figure 3.50
New housing proposal
for Sana'a. Rasem
Badran.

Figure 3.51
New housing proposal
for Sana'a. Rasem
Badran.

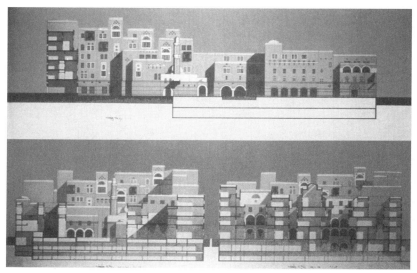

Figure 3.52
Courtyard sketch in new
housing complex. Rasem
Badran.

QASR AL HOKM; JUSTICE PALACE AND MOSQUE, RIYADH, KSA

Rasem Badran

By characteristically using the opportunity of a fortuitous commission to explore a wider vision, rather than just treating it as a singular, functional game, Rasem Badran has established significant design parameters in this large urban project. A first question was the reason for the isolation of a mosque within the contemporary city fabric, where it is now typically found in the midst of a large parking lot, and this was accompanied by a wish to clarify persistent debate about the proper attitude toward environmental controls and historical interpretation in this region. By researching rare old photographs of the 5-block site, which is laden with symbolic associations because of the proximity of the Musmak fort, which King Ibn Abdulaziz singlehandedly captured to return the al-Saud tribe to power, Badran was able to begin to confirm typological proportions. Not wanting to copy mindlessly the prevalent Najdi forms that had existed in the past, he approached the problem as a planning issue, testing for spatial interrelationships that still remain valid today. In the course of these typological studies, Badran found scale to be a key criterion of the previous architecture of the district in combination with environmental considerations related to an extremely hot, arid climate. In direct contrast to the current trend toward lightweight detached structures, he identified a consistent pattern of massiveness and clustering to reduce heat gain (and that mud brick helped a great deal in this respect). While realizing that this material would not be accepted as practical today, Badran was determined to recreate this aspect of density in his new complex, believing it to also be a far more effective way of approximating historical appropriateness and of establishing physical and symbolic connections between the disparate parts of this enormous project. (Figs. 3.53 and 3.54)

Figure 3.53
(opposite, top)
Aerial view of completed
Qasr al Hokm project in
Riyadh, Saudi Arabia.
Rasem Badran.

Figure 3.54
(opposite, bottom)
Detail of aerial view.

Rather than copying forms, Badran has employed symbolism in more general ways, such as by using a bridge between the mosque and the Justice Palace, which are the two major elements of the project. This represents the degree of accessibility that has traditionally existed between the government and the people in the Kingdom. This idea of openness carries over into the approach taken in the design of the Justice Palace, which is well integrated with the rest of the complex, with clusters of administrative buildings attaching to a new wall that the architect has created in several places and pulling away from it in others, to reinforce the analogy.

The mosque, however, is the primary focus of attention here. As the architect's exhaustive preparatory sketches show, many alternatives were considered before a final configuration was chosen. His approach of graphically testing options in an empirical, heuristic way, is what separates Badran's work from other contemporary architects seeking an appropriate expression of tradition today. Measuring his evolving graphic progress in the design at hand against his own exhaustive surveys of relevant monuments throughout the divergent parts of the Islamic world, Badran has demonstrated a sensitive approach that is attracting increasing attention and respect from an expanding following, which includes many students. Looking back to the hypostyle structure of the first mosque, generated from the trunks of palm trees which were used as columns, Badran developed a system in the state mosque that guides attention toward the *qibla*, (a niche indicating the direction of Makkah) rather than obstructing it, and naturally accommodates prayer rows instead of working against them, in addition to incorporating supplementary mechanical air delivery ducts. (Figs. 3.55 to 3.58)

Rows of towers on the roof, which correspond to the column spacing below, provide natural lighting and ventilation as a primary source, indicating the architect's emphasis on natural envi-

Figure 3.55
Background study sketch
for the Qasr al Hokm
complex. Rasem Badran.

ronmental systems. This is especially impressive because municipal regulations in this region, which were written in favor of artificial systems to reduce heat gain and wind-blown dirt, had to be challenged in this instance with proper safeguards proved to be effective. A visual bonus in the interior is that cumbersome horizontal duct work has been eliminated, as has the unsightly suspended ceiling that normally accompanies it.

No detail has been left to chance in this extraordinary complex, with each design decision subjected to a high degree of thorough, rational analysis. The minarets, for example, rather than following the trend toward public address systems, are treated with the symbolic power embodied in the traditional tower, and the architect determined that using a pair of them in this instance

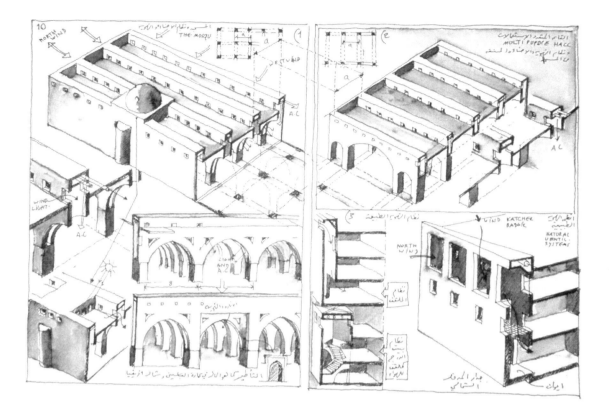

**Figure 3.56
Background study sketch
for the Qasr al Hokm
complex. Rasem Badran.**

would emphasize the stature of the building, based on local
precedents.

    A similar strategy was adopted in the Justice Palace, in
which building elements, materials, and details were used which
respond positively to the harsh climatic conditions of the area.
Ventilation towers were used in the main halls and offices, increasing air movement inside the building. These also provide indirect
lighting, which eliminates the need for windows on exterior walls.
This increases thermal mass as well as security and privacy. An
open water channel, which was often used in public buildings and
large houses in this region in the past, was introduced in the interior of the Palace to increase relative humidity in this arid climate.

Figure 3.57
Background study sketch
for the Qasr al Hokm
complex. Rasem Badran.

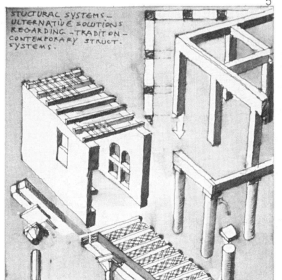

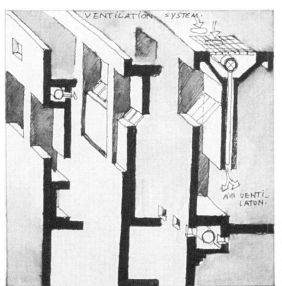

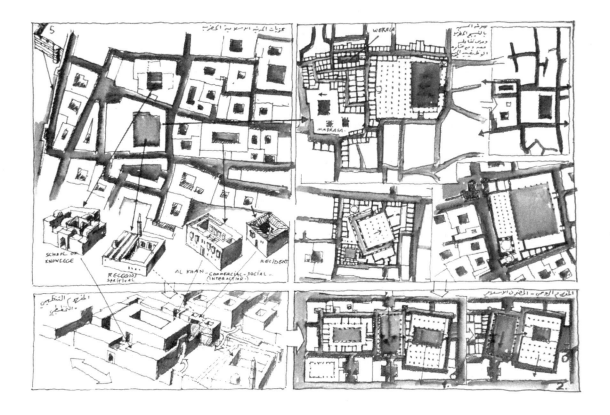

Figure 3.58
Background study sketch
for the Qasr al Hokm
complex. Rasem Badran.

Figure 3.59
(opposite, top)
Background study sketch
for the Qasr al Hokm
complex. Rasem Badran.

Figure 3.60
(opposite, bottom)
Background study sketch
for the Qasr al Hokm
complex. Rasem Badran.

It is strategically placed to delineate the various functions in the building, reminding all of the preciousness of water and the visible and audible delight just a small amount of it can offer. (Figs. 3.59 to 3.64)

The Jamea mosque and Justice Palace both have many planted courtyards which increase air movement and convective cooling, as well as being an essential component of the architect's strategy of linking complex to the urban fabric of the Riyadh city center. In the mosque, these courtyards are oriented toward the *qibla* direction and are used as prayer spaces on Fridays and during *Eid* (public celebrations following Ramadan, the month of fasting). The courtyards are planted with native species, in keeping with the architect's search for cultural and historical authenticity.

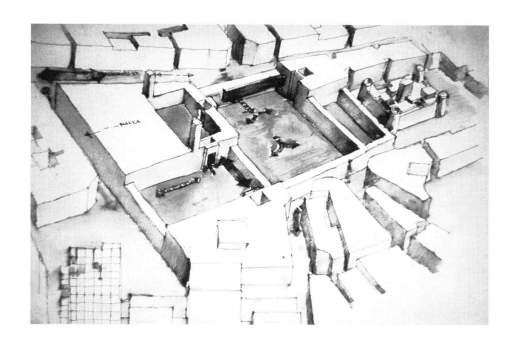

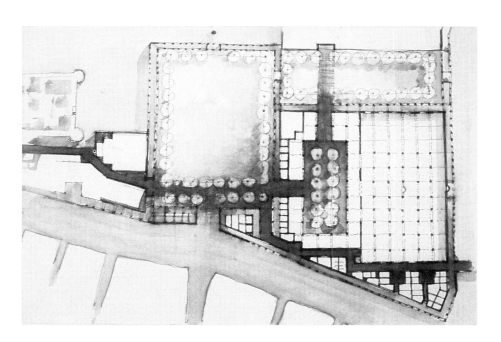

Figure 3.61
Background study sketch
for the Qasr al Hokm
complex. Rasem Badran.

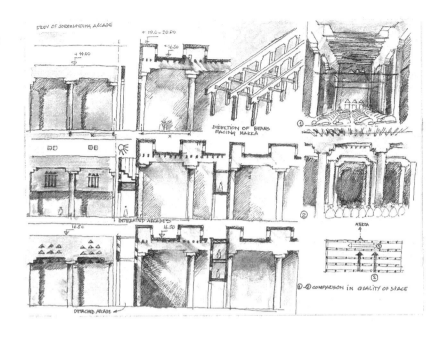

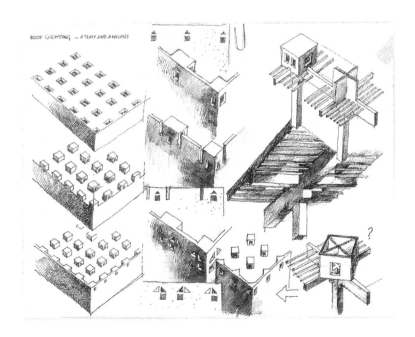

Sustainable Architecture

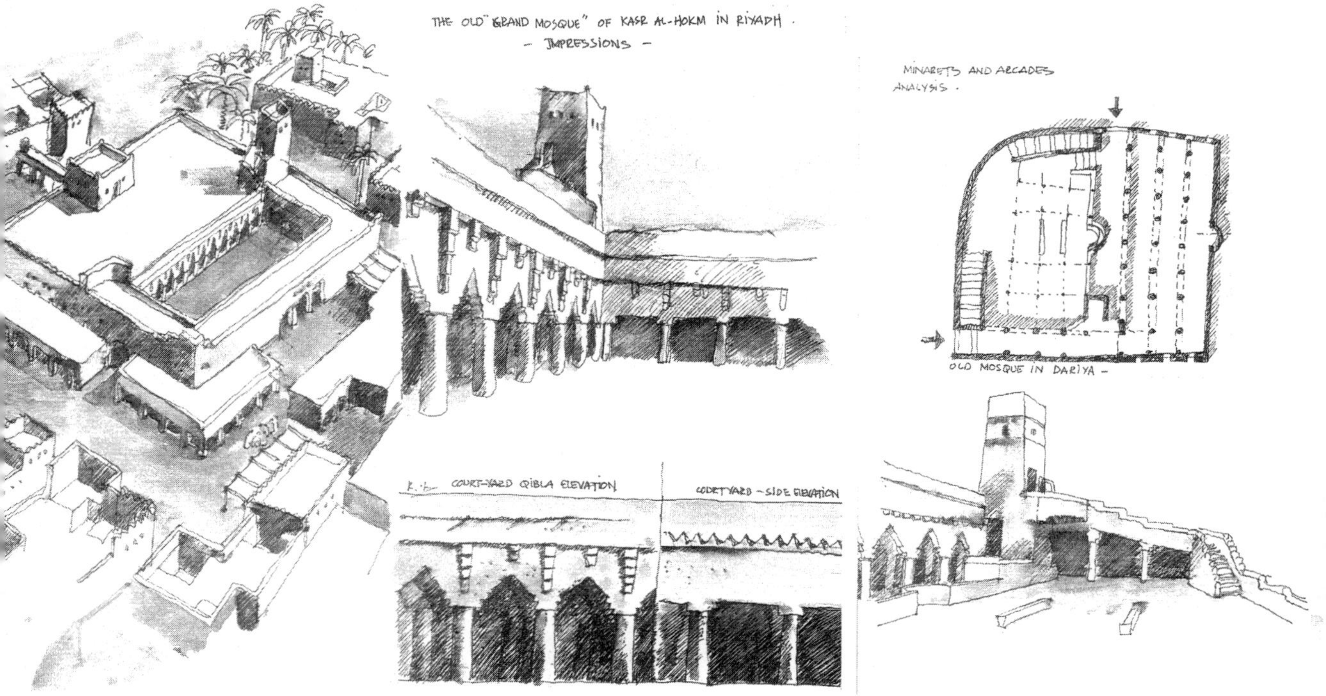
THE OLD "GRAND MOSQUE" OF KASR AL-HOKM IN RIYADH.
- IMPRESSIONS -
MINARETS AND ARCADES
ANALYSIS.
OLD MOSQUE IN DARIYA -
COURT-YARD QIBLA ELEVATION
COURTYARD - SIDE ELEVATION

Figure 3.62
Background study sketch for the Qasr al Hokm complex. Rasem Badran.

Figure 3.63
Background study sketch
for the Qasr al Hokm
complex. Rasem Badran.

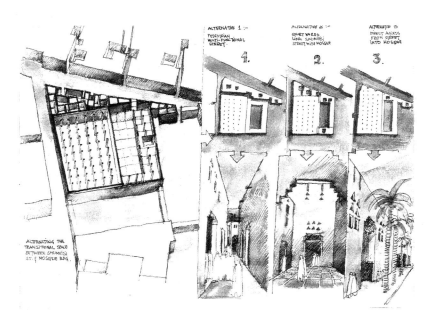

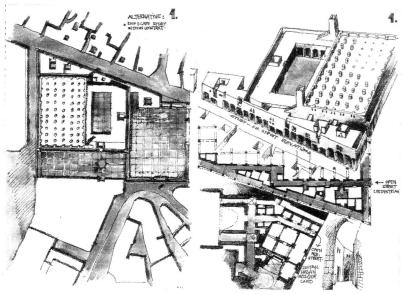

Figure 3.64
Completed project, Qasr
al Hokm. Rasem Badran.

PLAYA VISTA MASTER PLAN
Maguire Thomas Partners

As an intentional response to the low-density and highly negative environmental impact of suburban development, Maguire Thomas Partners has put forward a proposal with a different premise. Their alternative is for a community with a balanced mix of land uses, with higher densities to minimize damage to the site and regional infrastructure through a lower dependence on the automobile. Inherent in this premise is a desire to reduce the chronic traffic congestion caused by extensive commuting, air pollution, and endemic social isolation that have characterized life in the Los Angeles basin, especially since the end of World War II. (Fig. 3.65)

The master plan for Playa Vista is an alternative based on a system of streets that provide a framework for a series of distinct neighborhoods. In each of these there is a mixture of uses, ranging from institutional and civic through office, commercial, residential, and recreational, configured in a way that places the neighborhoods within walking distance of each other. In addition, these neighborhoods are joined by a low-emission internal transit system available to all residents, employees, and visitors. The basic intention behind this combination of alternative transportation system and mixed land use is to encourage walking and reduce dependency on the automobile. The plan also offers a wide variety of attached housing types meant to compete with suburbia, leaving nearly half of the 1087-acre Playa Vista site to be dedicated in common as open space, neighborhood parks, waterways, and habitat preserve. As part of this effort, Maguire Thomas has also committed to restore the 260-acre Ballona wetland, one of the region's few remaining wildlife sanctuaries. The restoration will include a freshwater marsh linked to a riparian corridor which extends over 2 mi along the base of the Westchester bluffs.

Figure 3.65
Aerial view of Playa Vista site. Courtesy Maguire Thomas.

Because of its significance to the plan, the direction of the restoration process and its possible repercussions require further elaboration. (Fig. 3.66)

About 187 acres of severely degraded fresh and saltwater wetlands now exist at the Playa Vista site (185.66 acres under the federal system of delineation and 188.35 acres under the California system). A program of wetland restoration and conversion of adjacent upland to wetland would result in a high-quality wetland system of about 260 acres (about a 40 percent increase over existing acreage). The program of wetland restoration and the provision for its implementation are embodied in a settlement agreement of a lawsuit brought against the previous owner of Playa Vista. This

PLAYA VISTA

MAGUIRE THOMAS PARTNERS

Figure 3.66
Playa Vista master plan.
Maguire Thomas.

agreement established the Ballona Wetlands Committee, an entity charged with formulating detailed plans for wetlands expansion and restoration. The Committee consists of representatives of the controller of California, the Sixth District Council Office, the Friends of Ballona Wetlands, and Maguire Thomas Partners—Playa Vista. The program embodied in the lawsuit consists of the following principal components:

> *Freshwater wetland system.* This approximately 51-acre system would be established primarily from upland acres and would provide rare habitat while ensuring a controlled source of fresh water for the optimum functioning of the adjacent salt marsh system. The freshwater system would, following the principles of ecology, also provide cleansing of urban run-off and flood control in addition to habitat functions. This system would be constructed as part of phase I of Playa Vista. Permits for constructing this system have been obtained from federal and state agencies.
> *Salt marsh wetland system.* This approximately 210-acre system would be centered on and would expand the existing deteriorated salt marsh. The two principal reasons for existing salt marsh deterioration, absence of tidal inunda-

Sustainable Architecture

tion and dumping of untreated urban runoff from offsite, would be eliminated by the program for wetlands and restoration and expansion. Tidal inundation would be provided, and urban runoff would be collected by the freshwater system. The salt marsh restoration and expansion would commence when Playa Vista project development in the coastal zone is approved and initiated.

Two approaches to salt marsh. The program in the settlement agreement calls for the pursuit of two approaches to salt marsh restoration. One approach would result in tidal inundation of about one-half the tide range. The other approach, which is preferred, would result in an inundation of the full range of the tide. The latter is more complex and costly, since extensive public infrastructure would have to be raised to avoid being inundated in a full tidal restoration. Funding for a full tidal restoration would have to be found. Expressions of interest in such funding have been made on a very preliminary basis by the Ports of Los Angeles and Long Beach, both of which require mitigation credits for their proposed facilities expansion. Approvals by an extensive number of federal, state, regional, and city agencies would be necessary both for the restoration plan as well as for any offsite credits for third parties. Such approvals are expected to require an extended time to obtain. (Figs. 3.67 to 3.71)

Wetlands fill. Of the approximately 187 acres of existing degraded wetlands, about 165 acres are contiguous, with the remainder scattered widely in a large number of small parcels. The scattered wetlands are unsustainable and are not feasible for restoration. Under the program of the settlement agreement, these scattered degraded wetlands would be filled and replaced by larger amounts of wetlands in the contiguous integrated system.

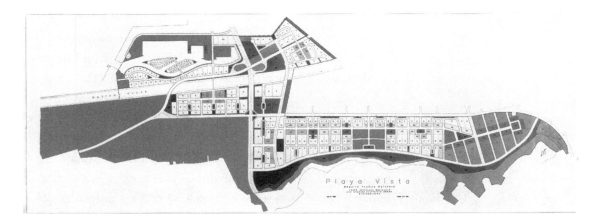

Figure 3.67
Playa Vista land-use
plan.

Figure 3.68
Playa Vista
neighborhood plan.

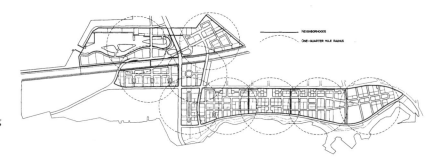

Figure 3.69
Typical layout of housing
in Playa Vista eastern
sector.

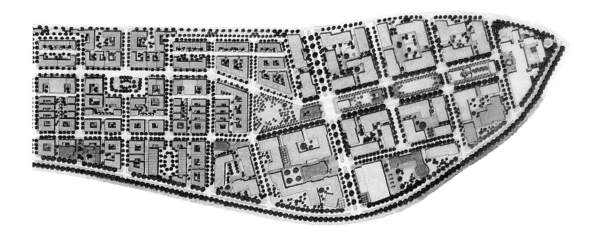

Sustainable Architecture

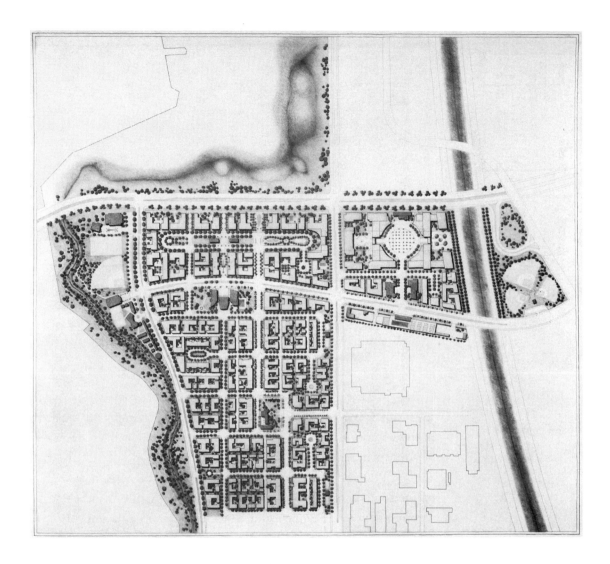

Figure 3.70
Typical housing layout in western sector of Playa Vista.

Associated habitat. In addition to the 260 acres of wetland in the total restoration system, about 90 more acres of upland habitat would be provided in association with the restoration. The resulting 350 acres of combined wetland and upland habitat would be the equivalent of about 75 percent of the UCLA campus and larger than downtown Los Angeles.

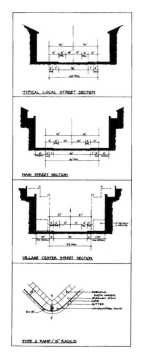

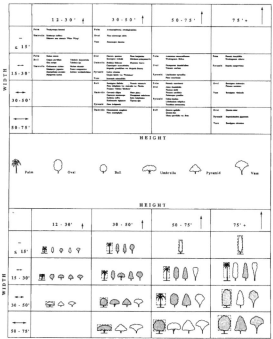

**Figure 3.71
Design guidelines for
Playa Vista.**

Each of these issues directly relates to that of general water quality in this region, which the Playa Vista master plan has been designed to address in specific ways.

Polluted urban runoff from over 265,000 acres is now drained into coastal wetland habitats and into Santa Monica Bay through concrete channels and pipes. Land use regulations of the past allowed and encouraged runoff from residential neighborhoods, commercial and industrial areas, and busy streets and freeways to be drained directly into habitats and the bay without protecting water quality. This past pattern is now being changed by regulations of federal, state, regional, county, and municipal agencies. (Figs. 3.72 to 3.76)

The wetland and terrestrial habitats at Playa Vista have suffered because of runoff. About 1140 acres of densely developed

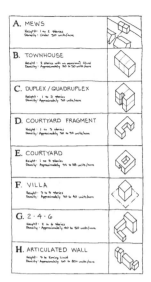

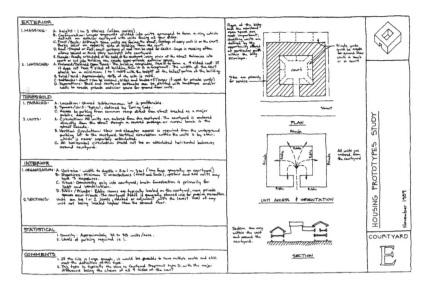

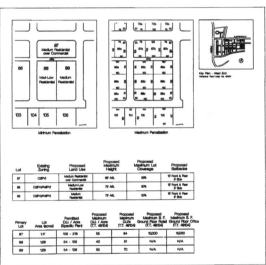

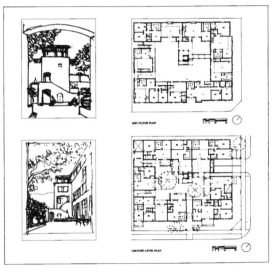

Figure 3.72
Design guidelines for Playa Vista.

lands surrounding Playa Vista dump their dry and wet weather polluted runoff onto the 1087-acre site. Because its soils are predominantly silts and clays with relatively low permeability, which do not readily absorb surface water, untreated urban runoff

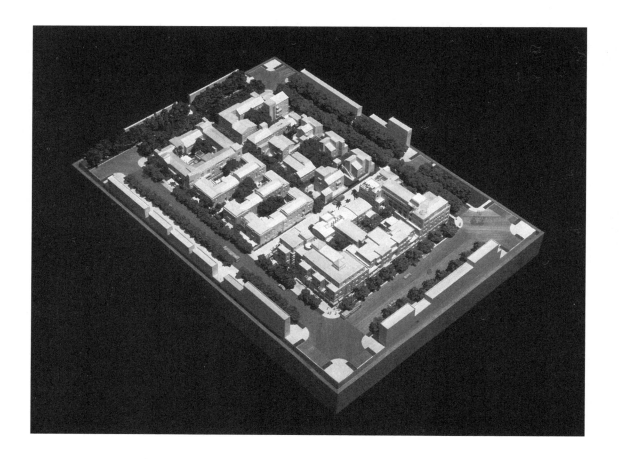

Figure 3.73
Typical courtyard cluster
in Playa Vista.

adversely affects native plant and animal life because it generally remains on the surface until draining into the Ballona flood control channel and Marina del Rey, where it is carried into Santa Monica Bay.

 Three principal strategies will be used to prevent polluted runoff from reaching aquatic habitats and Santa Monica Bay: (1) source control—prevention of pollutants from reaching the storm drain system by controlling them at their source; (2) targeted treatment control—treatment of flows going into the storm drain

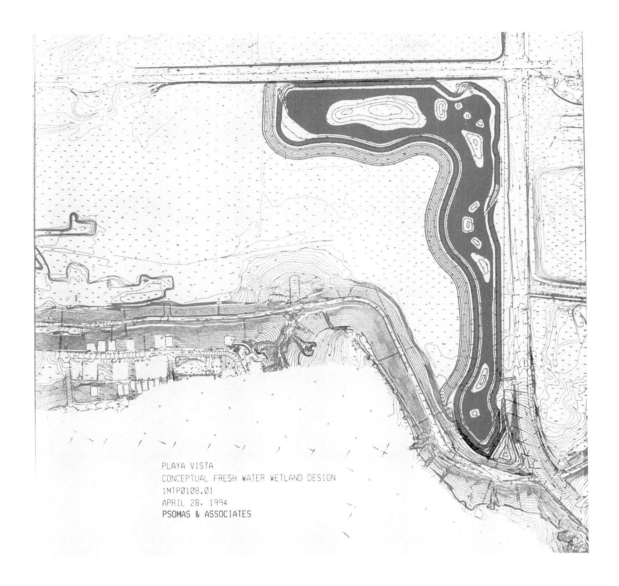

PLAYA VISTA
CONCEPTUAL FRESH WATER WETLAND DESIGN
1MTP0108.01
APRIL 28, 1994
PSOMAS & ASSOCIATES

Figure 3.74
Wetland restoration plan for Playa Vista.

system by filters, trash barriers, and other pollutant removal devices; and (3) sedimentation and/or polishing—stopping temporarily the flow of runoff at key locations so that pollutants can settle out as sediments or attach to vegetation and degrade.

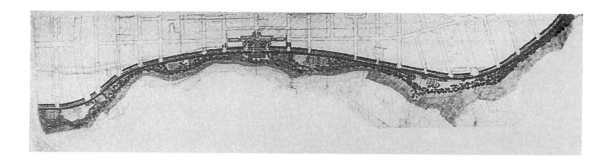

Figure 3.75
Riparian corridor
distribution for Playa
Vista.

These three actions are linked hierarchically to minimize pollutants from entering the storm drain system and then to remove pollutants from the system. All three strategies are needed to ensure effective cleanup of runoff.

Although large, Playa Vista represents less than 0.2 percent of the total watershed draining into the bay and less than 0.4 percent of the total developed area of that watershed. Even if Playa Vista were to be developed following inappropriate storm water practices of the past, the resulting increases in pollution would be undetectable in the bay because the site is such a small portion of the watershed. Playa Vista will, nonetheless, make a disproportionately large contribution to cleaning runoff entering the bay through a comprehensive storm water quality management plan.

This plan provides for programs to ensure effective implementation of the three strategies. The plan is being formulated in conjunction with various regulatory agencies and community groups, including Heal the Bay and the Friends of Ballona Wetlands. Implementation of the plan is projected to reduce post-development pollutant runoff from the site to about 15 to 30 percent below current levels. The three necessary steps for runoff pollutant prevention will include best management practices (BMPs), defined by Congress and the EPA as those practices which can reduce runoff pollutants to the "maximum extent practicable." In implementing these, the Playa Vista project has evaluated more than 36 potential technologies and techniques. More than 20 have been selected for implementation. Their implementation will enhance the effectiveness of the tiered linkage of the three stages of the plan: pollutant prevention, targeted treatment, and sedimenting and/or polishing of runoff. Through these steps the Playa Vista project will comply with all city, regional, state, and federal requirements for storm water management while reducing pollutant runoff from the site by about 15 to 30 percent.

The main components of these steps are:

1. Onsite and offsite source controls utilized to minimize pollutants entering the storm water system. Included will be household hazardous waste collection, landscape irrigation controls, street and catch-basin cleaning, signage warning against dumping in storm drains or catch basins, public education and information programs, and tracking and elimination of illegal dumping of pollutants.
2. Onsite and offsite targeted treatment control measures, including approximately 50 catch-basin filters onsite and about 10 offsite, will be used to remove pollutants from areas expected to have the highest pollutant potential, including busy streets and offsite parking lots, before they reach the runoff collection system. Emphasis on offsite catch basins is intended to reduce the amount of polluted runoff reaching the Playa Vista site.
3. A freshwater wetland system which ecologists and storm water management specialists believe is the best of all possible BMPs for maximizing pollutant removal and creating habitat. The wetland system includes pretreated areas at outfalls to isolate pollutants and allow the larger wetland to serve as a polishing area, rather than as the primary treatment.

The first phase of the Playa Vista master plan, approximately one-quarter of the total project, was approved by the Advisory Agency on July 8, 1993. The City Planning Commission subsequently upheld project approval on July 29, 1993. Total entitlements for the first phase include 3246 dwelling units; 1,250,000 ft² of office and light industrial space; 35,000 ft² of retail; 300 hotel rooms; and up to 120,000 ft² of community service space. This mix of uses is proportional to the total of such uses proposed for the master plan.

Approval of the entire master plan will require specific and general plan amendments to accommodate the mixed-use master plan concept and to reflect the reduction in intensity of the proposed project in comparison to potential development under existing zoning. However, the first phase of the plan is consistent with underlying zoning, occupying a portion of the site now zoned for mixed use. However, the existing zoning permits 2 million ft² of office development, and 1 million ft² of hotel and regional shopping mall development in an area which, under the new Playa Vista plan, will include only 400,000 units of office and light industrial space, 3246 dwelling units, and 35,000 ft² of neighborhood-serving retail uses. The first phase of the project, as defined in vesting tentative tract map 49104, is, therefore, consistent with existing zoning but substantially reduces the intensity of development as a first step in the realization of the overall master plan. The master plan, which emerged through a series of public workshops and community meetings, proposes to decrease office entitlement from that permitted under existing zoning by approximately 1 million ft²; decrease region-serving retail space by nearly 500,000 ft² and hotel space by 1350 rooms; and increase total housing by over 4200 units. The plan also prohibits buildings taller than the Westchester bluffs, in contrast to existing zoning which permits buildings of 20 stories or more. The project will expand the Ballona wetlands by 58 acres and commit $10 million toward the

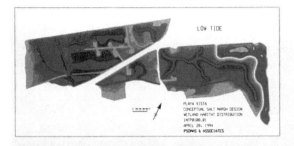

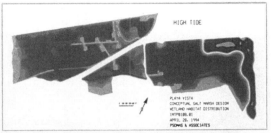

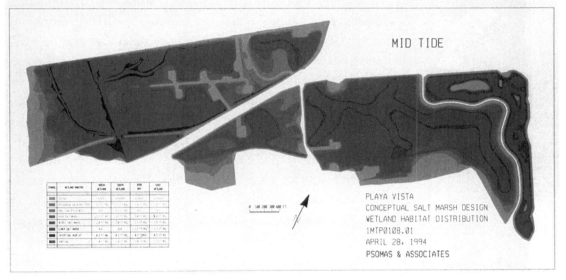

Figure 3.76
Freshwater drainage
scheme for Playa Vista.

wetland's restoration and maintenance, thereby achieving settlement of a longstanding lawsuit which challenged the legitimacy of the existing zoning for a significant portion of the property.

A final environmental impact report (EIR) for the first phase of the project, and an accompanying draft program EIR for the master plan project, was certified by the Advisory Agency on July 8, 1993. This documentation is perhaps the most exhaustive of its kind ever prepared for a development project in the City of Los Angeles. The environmental impact report for the first phase of the project, the only portion of the master plan for which approval is sought at this time, concludes that all project impacts are fully mitigated with the exception of 2 of the 103 intersections studied and of certain impacts regarding air quality, which has become a contentious issue, prior to the beginning of construction.

The final EIR concludes that Playa Vista will have significant air quality impacts in two categories: (1) impact from construction equipment exhaust, dust from grading the site, and emissions from architectural coating and building materials; and (2) motor vehicle emissions. In regard to the former, construction will be minimized by a mitigation program set forth in a Playa Vista air quality management plan. Although temporary, construction effects for the most part are categorized by Maguire Thomas as unavoidable.

Motor vehicle emissions will not have significant local effect because they will not exceed federal or state carbon monoxide standards at or near Playa Vista. Postconstruction motor vehicle emissions will, however, have a regionally significant impact, because low thresholds have purposely been established by regulators in order to enable local governments to impose mitigation measures which limit vehicle trips and vehicle miles traveled. Playa Vista and all other regionally significant projects would exceed regional air quality thresholds. However, Playa Vista will provide major air quality benefits to the basin due to its design as an integrated community whose goal is to reduce auto dependency. The EIR concludes that the project would reduce air emissions from motor vehicles by about 17 to 19 percent in contrast to conventional development patterns. Furthermore, this project's community-oriented plan complies with both the federal and state clean air acts and the regional air quality management plan.

On this issue it should further be noted that the Los Angeles basin has the worst air quality in the United States. The principal cause of air pollution is emissions from 9 million vehicles,

Sustainable Architecture

which account for almost two-thirds of the adverse air emissions in the basin, a situation aggravated by sprawling, low-density land-use patterns and the long-distance commuting that results. Despite continued poor air quality, significant progress has been made toward achieving clean air. Smog has declined about 56 percent over the past 37 years. During this period the basin's population has doubled and the number of motor vehicles has quadrupled. More important, the progress toward clean air is accelerating. Peak levels of ozone are reported to have declined by 25 percent in the last decade. Continued progress is ensured by standards for reduced motor vehicle emissions set by federal and state law and by the regional air quality management plan, which, among other provisions, will reduce vehicle trips and vehicle miles traveled as population growth continues to increase. Through these mandated requirements, air quality in the basin is projected to achieve federally established health standards by the year 2010 and state standards shortly thereafter.

Within the next 15 years, the population of the basin is projected to increase by about 30 percent. Most of that increase will be from children and grandchildren of those already living here. Accommodating this increase in population while reducing air pollution will require, among other initiatives, a significant change in the wasteful, sprawling land use patterns of the past, reductions in vehicle trips and vehicle miles traveled, acceleration of the use of low-emission vehicles, and reductions in energy consumption per capita.

The actual design of Playa Vista, which has taken a secondary position to the more integral, regional issues just discussed, is based on a thorough analysis of historical typologies. The design relies heavily on the regulation of urban form to promote a sense of community and to ensure that concepts such as mixed-use planning and a pedestrian environment have the best chance of success. Accordingly, the first phase of the plan has established as conditions of the vesting tract map a series of urban design guidelines which include the following:

Building heights. Each lot is assigned one of seven height zones which further restrict building heights to maximize view corridors. Other constraints, such as maximum lot coverage and required plan elements such as elevation setbacks, further regulate building massing. Existing zoning for the property permits building heights of up to 240 ft above sea level throughout most areas of the site, and for a portion of the site—up to 10 percent of the total building program—buildings would only be limited by FAA guidelines. Such zoning would have resulted in buildings of 20 stories or more, 8 stories higher than the adjacent Westchester bluffs, which now tower above the flat plain of the site on the south. Community reaction to these existing height zones reflected concerns not only with loss of available views from the bluff top, but with the potential impact to the character of the surrounding areas. Extensive discussion with the community resulted in the following guidelines which have been incorporated into the first phase of the Playa Vista plan:

> *Absolute height limits.* No portion of any building may exceed the average height of the Westchester bluffs, established as 140 ft above mean sea level.
>
> *Height zones.* In response to concerns about specific view corridors, each lot within the property is assigned one of seven height zones, which in most cases limits building heights to substantially below the height of the Westchester bluffs.
>
> *Building profiles.* To maximize view corridors, building profiles must be tapered, with smaller floor sizes required at upper floor locations.

Maximum lot coverage. To further regulate building massing and related potential view impacts, building footprints may only occupy between 45 and 60 percent of any given lot.

Building height definition. All building height restrictions are established in terms of height above sea level, to avoid ambiguities often associated with other standards, such as height above grade. Height restrictions include all rooftop-related elements (such as mechanical equipment, parapets, etc.) with the sole exception of ornamental building features (cupolas, spires, etc.), which are intended to enhance both the character and the appearance of the Playa Vista community.

Lot definition. The vesting map establishes a total of 147 lots, each with a prescribed set of development criteria which ensure reasonable increments of development consistent with the overall character of the plan.

Permitted land use. Each lot is designated with one of nine land-use categories, which limits development on a lot-by-lot basis to specific uses. Such uses are considerably more restrictive than those permitted by underlying zoning.

Density. Residential lots are designated with one of three density limits to ensure reasonable and appropriate residential development consistent with the character of individual neighborhoods and the overall concept of the plan.

Setbacks and lot coverage. Each lot is designated with required setbacks (generally more restrictive than city code) and limitations on the permitted lot coverage (not included in city codes) to ensure sufficient public and private open space.

These criteria, in concert with the street standards set forth in the vesting map, establish a well-defined array of building envelopes, which regulate all future building initiatives. These standards have been determined by the city Planning Department, Advisory Agency, and the city Attorney's Office to be of sufficient rigor to qualify the proposed subdivision as a vesting map, a determination upheld by the city Planning Commission.

The traffic caused by this new community has been a source of concern and intense study. An environmental impact review has analyzed street intersections over a 30-mi^2 area around the Playa Vista site. This study employs conventional traffic analysis methodology in which projected ambient growth during the buildout of the project is combined with largely unmitigated traffic from other potential new projects in the region and overlaid on the existing road systems. Playa Vista was then superimposed on this system to determine a worst-case traffic scenario, and feasible mitigation was then identified to mitigate Playa Vista's increment of the total impact. The final EIR sets forth an unprecedented array of such traffic mitigation measures comprised of the following:

Regional improvements and new secondary highways. Expansion of existing regional streets, and new connections between existing regional roads

Physical mitigation of intersections. Physical improvements, such as street widening, to increase intersection capacity

ATSAC. Extension of the city's automated traffic surveillance and control program—a computerized signalization system which optimizes traffic flow

Lincoln Boulevard transit enhancement program. Purchase, operation, and maintenance of five transit vehicles for the Lincoln Boulevard corridor

Transportation and management. Reduction of projected office traffic by 20 percent through ride-sharing programs, parking restrictions, and related measures

This program, which will cost in excess of $50 million, provides mitigation for 50 of the 52 impacted first-phase intersections. Of the two unmitigated intersections, one lies within the city of Culver City, and a satisfactory mitigation proposal measure is now being finalized with that jurisdiction. The lone unmitigated intersection in the city of Los Angeles—Sepulveda Boulevard at Howard Hughes Parkway—may be mitigated as part of the master plan project.

The housing mix in the Playa Vista Community is unprecedented and will serve as a model for similar communities in the future. The Playa Vista master plan commits to provide 15 percent of its overall housing program (a total of 1962 units) as affordable housing, as defined by City and County of Los Angeles criteria. This commitment includes not only required provision of affordable housing within the coastal zone but also a voluntary extension of this affordable housing program into the noncoastal areas of the plan, an initiative which will result in approximately 1000 additional affordable units. A total of 487 units, or 15 percent of the 3246 first-phase units, will be provided as affordable units. One-third of these units will be very low income units; one-third will be low-income units; and one-third will be moderate income units. In addition to these affordable housing commitments, the project will also provide a minimum of 10 percent of all units, a total of 347 units, as middle-income units for sale at a cost of $195,000 or below (in 1993 dollars, and adjusted periodically). Construction of affordable units will be phased to ensure concurrent availability of affordable units and market rate units according to a schedule set forth in the conditions of approval. To ensure that affordable units will function as effective components of an overall jobs and housing strategy, the number of such units which may be set aside for senior citizens is limited to 15 percent of the total first-phase affordable housing program. Affordable units will be distributed throughout the first-phase plan and will be compatible with market rate units in terms of exterior appearance, materials, and finished quality.

Jobs and housing balance, or the potential for people to live and work on site, and the effect the project may have on the existing subregional ratio of jobs and housing have also been analyzed. The Southern California Association of Governments (SCAG) has determined that the Playa Vista subregion is viable, and that new development should move the subregion toward a more balanced ratio of 1.72 jobs per dwelling unit. The first phase of the project contributes to this goal and encourages internal jobs and housing linkage.

For the 3246 dwelling units provided, the projected jobs-housing ratio is 1.52 to 1. This ratio may not be exceeded at any point during project buildout, thus ensuring that the creation of housing must either proceed or parallel the creation of jobs. To underscore the conviction that sound mixed-use planning will decrease commercial vehicle trips, and to provide incentive for on site jobs and housing linkage, the project includes a voluntary cap of 50 percent on peak-hour offsite office trips projected in the final EIR. To promote a full range of housing opportunities, and hence encourage linkage of onsite jobs and housing, 15 percent of all first-phase units will be "affordable" units. In addition, 10 percent of all units will be sold for $195,000 or less (in 1993 dollars adjusted periodically).

The final EIR does not recognize jobs and housing initiatives and calculates both traffic impacts and mitigation without regard to potential linkage. Walking is central to the success of the plan, to be encouraged with the following:

Pedestrian-oriented streets. Neighborhood streets within the Playa Vista plan have been carefully designed to establish a parity between vehicles and pedestrians. A street-width standard of 36 ft has been adopted for all local streets internal to the project (4 ft less than the typical city standard), along with a 15-ft curb radius at intersections (rather than the typical city standard of 25 ft). Both these initiatives will serve to reduce street crossing distances and slow traffic, thereby promoting pedestrian use.

Parkway design. All local streets will include a 7-ft planting strip and 5-ft sidewalk within a 12-ft right-of-way, 2 ft more than typically provided within city standards. The 7-ft parkway will be landscaped and will provide for the location of streetscape elements such as trees, street lighting, street furniture, signage, and so on and will serve as a buffer between pedestrians and adjacent traffic.

Land-use strategy. The project proposes development in a mixed-use pattern which distributes the land uses which constitute a variety of daily needs—shopping, recreation, cultural and civic needs—such that most of these needs may be satisfied within a walking distance of project residents and employees.

Internal transit system. The project will include a low-emission shuttle system which will operate on short headway, linking all areas of the community. The shuttle will function on a no-farebox basis for Playa Vista residents and employees.

To create a self-sufficient community, Maguire Thomas has also recognized the need for "community-serving" uses as fundamental elements of the plan. Although the precise nature of all such uses (which may include schools, fire stations, child care centers, libraries, police stations, churches and synagogues) must evolve with the growth of the community, sites have been identified and reserved to accommodate the needs of the community as it matures. The first phase of the project designates such sites in prominent locations, since the uses they will contain may often symbolize the community's values and may serve as the neighborhood's focal points.

MAJORCA DEVELOPMENT PROJECT

Richard Rogers Partnership

The climate of Majorca is typical of the Mediterranean, hot and dry in summer and mild in winter with little frost. The maximum rainfall takes place in autumn, typically accompanied by storms that cause localized flooding. Prevalent north and northwest winds are diminished by a mountain range running along the entire length of the island between Palma and the sea, and these winds cause turbulence along the inland foothills below.

The main development site, which is over 1.5 km^2, is 500 yards to the west of the University of the Balearic Islands, with an additional 50 hectares to the north designated as a protected natural habitat zone. The terrain is fairly flat but undulates gently in certain areas, creating two shallow valleys through which seasonal flooding periodically flows. An existing manor house is located in the center of the zone, at its highest point, framed by dense natural woodland behind it. (Figs. 3.77 to 3.97)

Because of the lack of rainfall in summer and the water shortages this causes, one of the first strategies proposed by the architect was to provide cisterns. These store approximately 10 percent of the flood water drawn from a 30 km^2 area around the site which would otherwise run straight into the sea. This is the amount required for both irrigation and drinking during the summer. Additional water is also diverted back into the ground to recharge the aquifer. Several methods are used to collect water in this scheme, including weir intakes and storage lakes. Open lakes are cheapest but need to be aerated to prevent infestation by mosquitos, and species of mosquito-eating birds and fish can be introduced in ways that do not conflict with the ecological balance of the island. Weirs, constructed alongside the seasonal flood torrent channel, are sized according to the daily variation in river level

Figure 3.77
Plan of
Majorca
project.
Courtesy
Richard
Rogers.

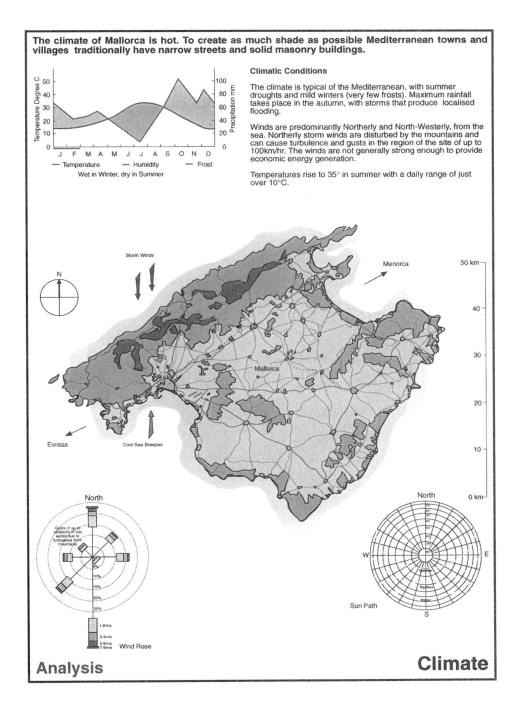

The climate of Mallorca is hot. To create as much shade as possible Mediterranean towns and villages traditionally have narrow streets and solid masonry buildings.

Climatic Conditions

The climate is typical of the Mediterranean, with summer droughts and mild winters (very few frosts). Maximum rainfall takes place in the autumn, with storms that produce localised flooding.

Winds are predominantly Northerly and North-Westerly, from the sea. Northerly storm winds are disturbed by the mountains and can cause turbulence and gusts in the region of the site of up to 100km/hr. The winds are not generally strong enough to provide economic energy generation.

Temperatures rise to 35° in summer with a daily range of just over 10°C.

Analysis

Climate

Figure 3.78
Phasing for
Majorca
master plan.

Development is Nodal. Each area is developed fully in turn to form an established succinct community. This avoids scattered growth without social focus.

Planning Phase

Years 1-5
Initial roads to the University are established. The earth sciences research unit is put in place so that it can begin to develop the irrigation and agricultural principles. The first water storage lake is constructed and prototypes for energy crops planted. A significant period is allocated to thorough design work and in depth research.

Phase 1

Years 3-7
The east node is developed around the university centre and lake. Agricultural terraces and energy crops are put in place. The main road South is constructed and the CentreBit control centre set up.

Phase 2

Year 6-11
The central node fills out around CentreBIT. The Second lake is constructed. When investments are high enough, roads are upgraded to take the public tram system.

Phase 3

Year 10-15 The third nodes fills out around the lake. Agricultural and energy systems come to fruition.

Assembly

Phasing

Sustainable Architecture

Figure 3.79
Urban
matrix study.

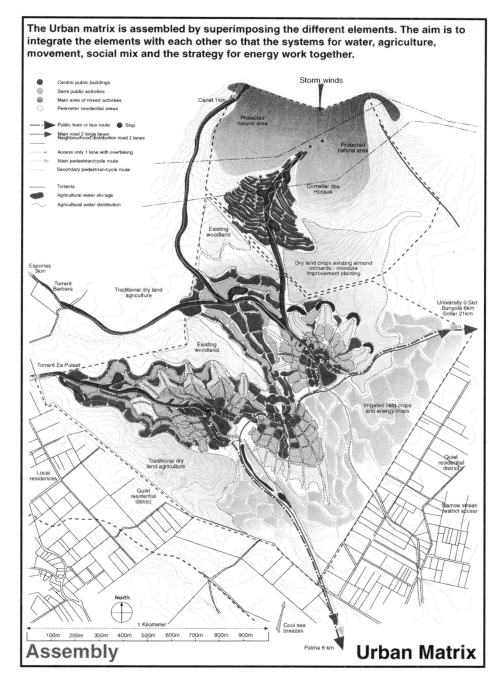

The Urban matrix is assembled by superimposing the different elements. The aim is to integrate the elements with each other so that the systems for water, agriculture, movement, social mix and the strategy for energy work together.

Central public buildings
Semi public activities
Main area of mixed activities
Perimeter residential areas

Public tram or bus route ● Stop
Main road 2 large lanes
Neighbourhood distribution road 2 lanes
Access only 1 lane with overtaking
Main pedestrian/cycle route
Secondary pedestrian/cycle route

Torrents
Agricultural water storage
Agricultural water distribution

Storm winds

Canet 1km

Protected
natural area

Protected
natural area

Comellar des
Hossos

Existing
woodland

Esporles
3km

Torrent
Barbera

Traditional dry land
agriculture

Dry land crops existing almond
orchards - moisture
improvement planting

University 0.5km
Bunyola 6km
Soller 21km

Existing
woodland

Torrent Es Puixet

Irrigated field crops
and energy crops

Quiet
residential
district

Local
residences

Traditional dry
land agriculture

Quiet
residential
district

Narrow streets
restrict access

North

1 Kilometer

100m 200m 300m 400m 500m 600m 700m 800m 900m

Cool sea
breezes

Palma 8 km

Assembly

Urban Matrix

Case Studies

147

Figure 3.80
Location
analysis plan.

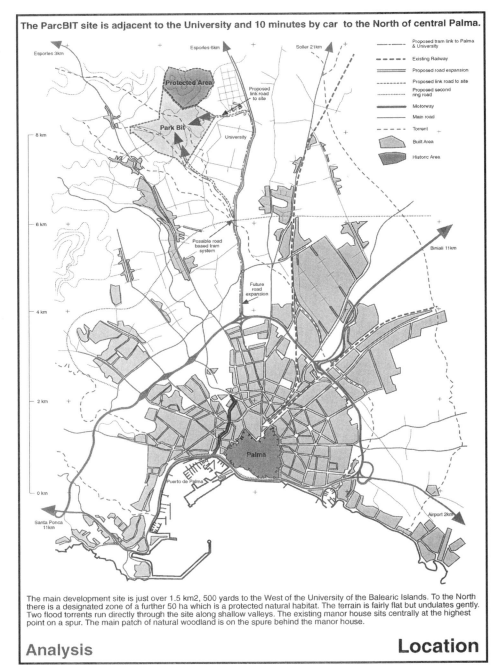

The ParcBIT site is adjacent to the University and 10 minutes by car to the North of central Palma.

Esportes 3km

Esportes 6km

Soller 21km

Protected Area

Proposed link road to site

Park Bit

University

Proposed tram link to Palma & University

Existing Railway

Proposed road expansion

Proposed link road to site

Proposed second ring road

Motorway

Main road

Torrent

Built Area

Historic Area

8 km

Possible road based tram system

6 km

Biniali 11km

Future road expansion

4 km

2 km

Palma

0 km

Puerto de Palma

Santa Ponca 11km

Airport 2km

The main development site is just over 1.5 km2, 500 yards to the West of the University of the Balearic Islands. To the North there is a designated zone of a further 50 ha which is a protected natural habitat. The terrain is fairly flat but undulates gently. Two flood torrents run directly through the site along shallow valleys. The existing manor house sits centrally at the highest point on a spur. The main patch of natural woodland is on the spure behind the manor house.

Analysis

Location

Figure 3.81
Majorca
neighborhood
plan.

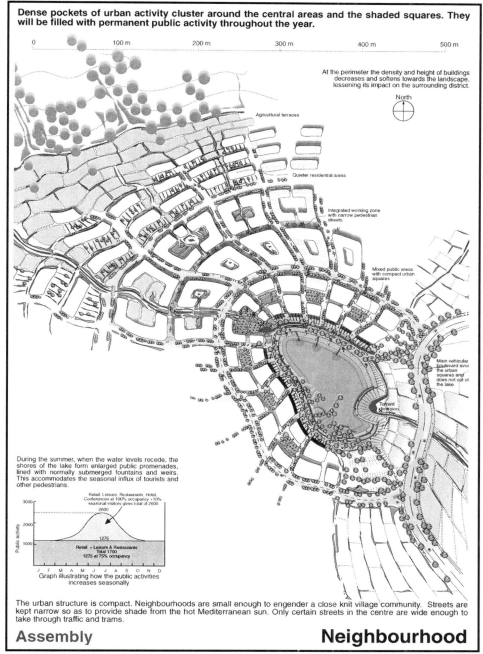

Dense pockets of urban activity cluster around the central areas and the shaded squares. They will be filled with permanent public activity throughout the year.

0   100 m   200 m   300 m   400 m   500 m

At the perimeter the density and height of buildings decreases and softens towards the landscape, lessening its impact on the surrounding district.

North

Agricultural terraces

Quieter residential areas

Integrated working zone with narrow pedestrian streets

Mixed public areas with compact urban squares

Main vehicular boulevard avoid the urban squares and does not cut of the lake.

Torrent diversion

During the summer, when the water levels recede, the shores of the lake form enlarged public promenades, lined with normally submerged fountains and weirs. This accommodates the seasonal influx of tourists and other pedestrians.

Retail, Leisure, Restaurants, Hotel, Conferences at 100% occupancy +10% seasonal visitors gives total of 2600
2600
1275
Retail + Leisure & Restaurants
Total 1700
1275 at 75% occupancy
J F M A M J J A S O N D
Graph illustrating how the public activities increases seasonally

Public activity 3000 2000 1000

The urban structure is compact. Neighbourhoods are small enough to engender a close knit village community. Streets are kept narrow so as to provide shade from the hot Mediterranean sun. Only certain streets in the centre are wide enough to take through traffic and trams.

Assembly

Neighbourhood

Figure 3.82
Majorca site
analysis.

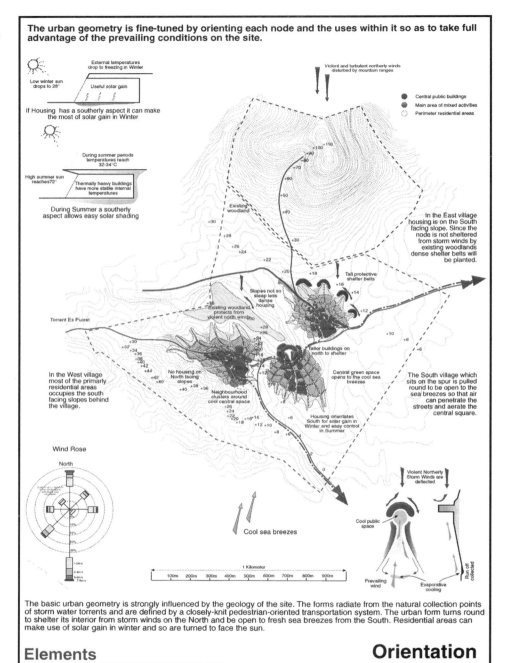

The urban geometry is fine-tuned by orienting each node and the uses within it so as to take full advantage of the prevailing conditions on the site.

External temperatures drop to freezing in Winter

Low winter sun drops to 28°

Useful solar gain

If Housing has a southerly aspect it can make the most of solar gain in Winter

During summer periods temperatures reach 32-34°C

High summer sun reaches 72°

Thermally heavy buildings have more stable internal temperatures

During Summer a southerly aspect allows easy solar shading

Violent and turbulent northerly winds disturbed by mountain ranges

● Central public buildings
● Main area of mixed activities
○ Perimeter residential areas

Existing woodland

In the East village housing is on the South facing slope. Since the node is not sheltered from storm winds by existing woodlands dense shelter belts will be planted.

Tall protective shelter belts

Slopes not so steep less dense housing

Existing woodland protects from violent north winds

Torrent Es Pulxet

Taller buildings on north to shelter

Central green space opens to the cool sea breezes

The South village which sits on the spur is pulled round to be open to the sea breezes so that air can penetrate the streets and aerate the central square.

In the West village most of the primarily residential areas occupies the south facing slopes behind the village.

No housing on North facing slopes

Neighbourhood clusters around cool central space

Housing orientates South for solar gain in Winter and easy control in Summer

Wind Rose

North

Cool sea breezes

Violent Northerly Storm Winds are deflected

Cool public space

Prevailing wind

Evaporative cooling

Run off collected

1 Kilometer

100m 200m 300m 400m 500m 600m 700m 800m 900m

The basic urban geometry is strongly influenced by the geology of the site. The forms radiate from the natural collection points of storm water torrents and are defined by a closely-knit pedestrian-oriented transportation system. The urban form turns round to shelter its interior from storm winds on the North and be open to fresh sea breezes from the South. Residential areas can make use of solar gain in winter and so are turned to face the sun.

Elements

Orientation

Figure 3.83
Urban
systems
study.

Each of the major urban elements needs to be analysed separately prior to coming together to form an interactive urban system.

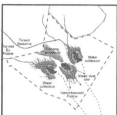

Social Fabric

The urban community is made up of three small villages. The size of each village is defined by the limits of easy walking distance from the centre to the furthest point. The mix of uses and social activities is gradually diffused from a vibrant publicly focused mix at the centre to the more peaceful predominantly residential areas.

The proposal maintains a balanced cycle of activities over the day, as well as throughout the week, to create a 24 hour urban community

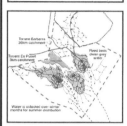

Plan for Water

The climate is dry in summer and very wet in winter. Water is collected in winter and distributed over the year for both irrigation and drinking.

The two torrents collect water from a 30km2 area which would otherwise run straight into the sea. Less than 10% of the flood water during the torrent season is used to fill the storage areas. This is sufficient for irrigation and drinking for the summer period. Additional water can be diverted back into the ground to recharge the aquifer.

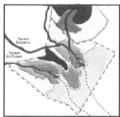

Agriculture

The agricultural strategy is to stimulate a fertile landscape that acts as a natural extension to the protected environmental zone to the North. The urban clusters are linked to the environmental zone by protected natural corridors.

Improved irrigation allows more diverse crops to be grown and increases the productivity of all crops. The diversity of crops creates a rich rural landscape.

Movement

The proposal is for a hierarchical transportation system which reduces vehicular congestion and pollution in the community by focusing on the public system. Walking and cycling are encouraged by limiting car movement to certain streets and creating protected pedestrian routes.

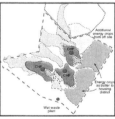

Energy

Demand is reduced by 70%, by ensuring that energy efficient buildings are built in conjuction with using locally generated power so that renewable sources of energy are used to generate power locally. This allows waste heat which comes from the process of generating electricity (35% electricity, 60% waste and 5% loss), to be used to heat residential areas.

Assembly

Urban Elements

Figure 3.84
Energy plan
for the entire
island of
Majorca.

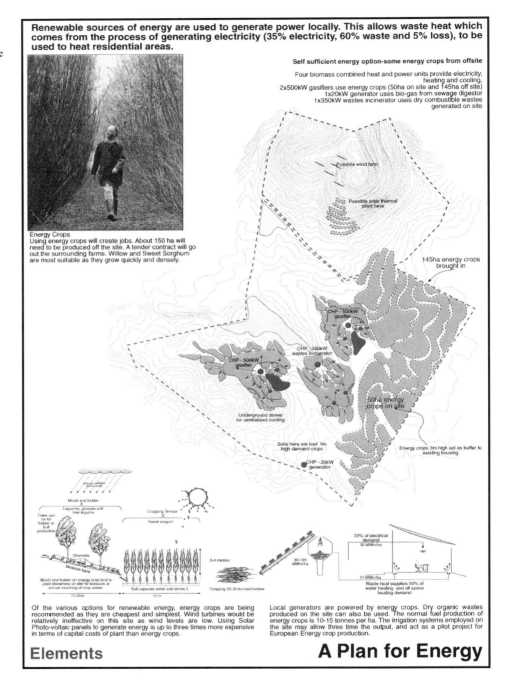

Renewable sources of energy are used to generate power locally. This allows waste heat which comes from the process of generating electricity (35% electricity, 60% waste and 5% loss), to be used to heat residential areas.

Self sufficient energy option-some energy crops from offsite

Four biomass combined heat and power units provide electricity, heating and cooling.
2x500kW gasifiers use energy crops (50ha on site and 145ha off site)
1x20kW generator uses bio-gas from sewage digestor
1x350kW wastes incinerator uses dry combustible wastes generated on site

Possible wind farm

Possible solar thermal plant here

145ha energy crops brought in

CHP - 500kW gasifier

CHP - 350kW wastes incinerator

CHP - 500kW gasifier

50ha energy crops on site

Underground stores for centralised cooling

Soils here are bad. No high demand crops

Energy crops 3m high act as buffer to existing housing

CHP - 20kW generator

Energy Crops
Using energy crops will create jobs. About 150 ha will need to be produced off the site. A tender contract will go out the surrounding farms. Willow and Sweet Sorghum are most suitable as they grow quickly and densely.

Mulch and fodder or
Legumes, grasses and tree legume
Trees can be for fodder or fruit production
Cropping Terrace
Sweet sorghum
Channels
Moisture bank
Mulch and fodder on energy crop land is used elsewhere on site for livestock or annual mulching of crop zones.
Soil captures water and stores it
3-4 metres
Cropping 25-30 tonnes/hectare
80-120 MWh/h/a
33% of electrical demand 35 MWh/h/a
70 MWh/h/a
Waste heat supplies 50% of water heating and all space heating demand
10-30m
10 m

Of the various options for renewable energy, energy crops are being recommended as they are cheapest and simplest. Wind turbines would be relatively ineffective on this site as wind levels are low. Using Solar Photo-voltaic panels to generate energy is up to three times more expensive in terms of capital costs of plant than energy crops.

Local generators are powered by energy crops. Dry organic wastes produced on the site can also be used. The normal fuel production of energy crops is 10-15 tonnes per ha. The irrigation systems employed on the site may allow three time the output, and act as a pilot project for European Energy crop production.

Elements

A Plan for Energy

Figure 3.85
Water
conservation
plan.

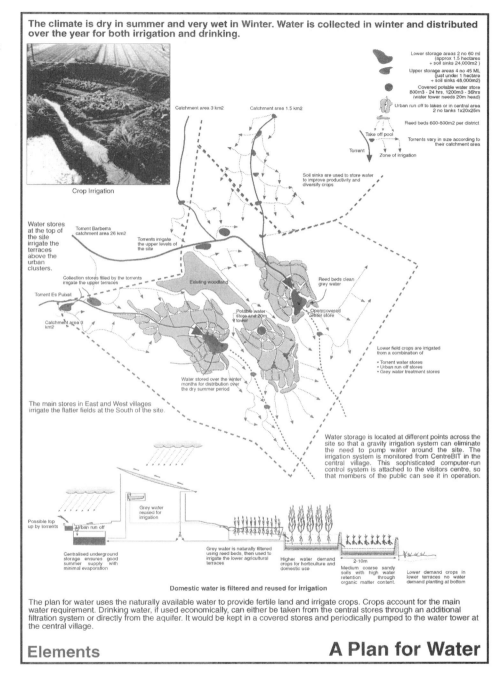

The climate is dry in summer and very wet in Winter. Water is collected in winter and distributed over the year for both irrigation and drinking.

Crop Irrigation

Lower storage areas 2 no 60 ml (approx 1.5 hectares + soil sinks 24,000m2)

Upper storage areas 4 no 45 ML (just under 1 hectare + soil sinks 48,000m2)

Covered potable water store 800m3 - 24 hrs, 1200m3 - 36hrs (water tower needs 20m head)

Urban run off to lakes or in central area 2 no tanks 1x20x25m

Reed beds 600-800m2 per district

Torrents vary in size according to their catchment area

Take off pool

Torrent

Zone of irrigation

Catchment area 3 km2

Catchment area 1.5 km2

Soil sinks are used to store water to improve productivity and diversify crops

Water stores at the top of the site irrigate the terraces above the urban clusters.

Torrent Barberra catchment area 26 km2

Torrents irrigate the upper levels of the site

Collection stores filled by the torrents irrigate the upper terraces

Existing woodland

Reed beds clean grey water

Torrent Es Puixet

Potable water store and 20m tower

Open/covered water store

Catchment Area 9 km2

Lower field crops are irrigated from a combination of

• Torrent water stores
• Urban run off stores
• Grey water treatment stores

Water stored over the winter months for distribution over the dry summer period

The main stores in East and West villages irrigate the flatter fields at the South of the site.

Water storage is located at different points across the site so that a gravity irrigation system can eliminate the need to pump water around the site. The irrigation system is monitored from CentreBIT in the central village. This sophisticated computer-run control system is attached to the visitors centre, so that members of the public can see it in operation.

Grey water reused for irrigation

Possible top up by torrents

Urban run off

Centralised underground storage ensures good summer supply with minimal evaporation.

Grey water is naturally filtered using reed beds, then used to irrigate the lower agricultural terraces

Higher water demand crops for horticulture and domestic use

2-10m

Medium coarse sandy soils with high water retention through organic matter content.

Lower demand crops in lower terraces no water demand planting at bottom

Domestic water is filtered and reused for irrigation

The plan for water uses the naturally available water to provide fertile land and irrigate crops. Crops account for the main water requirement. Drinking water, if used economically, can either be taken from the central stores through an additional filtration system or directly from the aquifer. It would be kept in a covered stores and periodically pumped to the water tower at the central village.

Elements

A Plan for Water

Figure 3.86
Water
collection
plan.

The two torrents collect water from a 30km2 area which would otherwise run straight into the sea. Less than 10% of the flood water during the torrent season is used to fill the storage areas. This is sufficient for irrigation and drinking for the summer period. Additional water can be diverted back into the ground to recharge the aquifer.

Monthly Torrent Volume

Month	Rainfall (mm)	Temp. (Deg.C)	Evaporation & Evapotransporation (mm)	Soil Moisture Requirement (mm)	Torrent Volume (mm)	Torrent Volume (ML)
JAN	106	8	17.6	0	58.6	1753
FEB	80	9	23.6	0	34.8	1044
MAR	82	10	30.8	0	30.8	927
APR	53.4	11	39.8	0	2.7	81
MAY	69.6	15	68.8	0	0	0
JUN	48.2	19	102.4	54	0	0
JUL	50	23	133.4	137	0	0
AUG	60	23	124.7	202	0	0
SEP	110	22	106.4	198	0	0
OCT	170	16	58.8	87	75.9	2277
NOV	120	13	38.4	0	53.7	1611
DEC	130	9	20.7	0	74.5	2235

Calculations for the Torrent Catchment (30 SQ.KM)

Monthly Water Demand

Month	Runoff (ML)	Torrent Volume (ML)	Torrent + Runoff (A)	Potable Water (ML)	Storage for Vegatation Requirements RS1 (ML)	Storage for Vegatation Requirements RS2 (ML)	Potable + Storage For Vegatation Requirements RS2 (B)	(A -B)
JAN	10.38	2346	2356.38	23.75	0	0	23.75	2333
FEB	7.56	1392	1399.56	23.75	0	0	23.75	1376
MAR	6.90	1236	1242.9	23.75	0	0	23.75	1219
APR	7.02	108	115.02	23.75	0	0	23.75	91.27
MAY	4.98	0	4.98	23.75	0	4.7	28.45	-23.47
JUN	3.18	0	3.18	23.75	0	86.8	110.55	-107.4
JUL	0.96	0	0.96	23.75	120	139.4	163.15	-162.2
AUG	3.66	0	3.66	23.75	128	128.6	152.35	-148.7
SEP	8.88	0	8.88	23.75	74.5	74.5	98.25	-89.37
OCT	16.02	0	16.02	23.75	19.6	19.6	43.35	-27.33
NOV	10.62	0	10.62	23.75	4.4	4.4	28.15	-17.53
DEC	11.64	2979	2990.64		213	100	123.75	2867

Estimated Water Supply and Demand

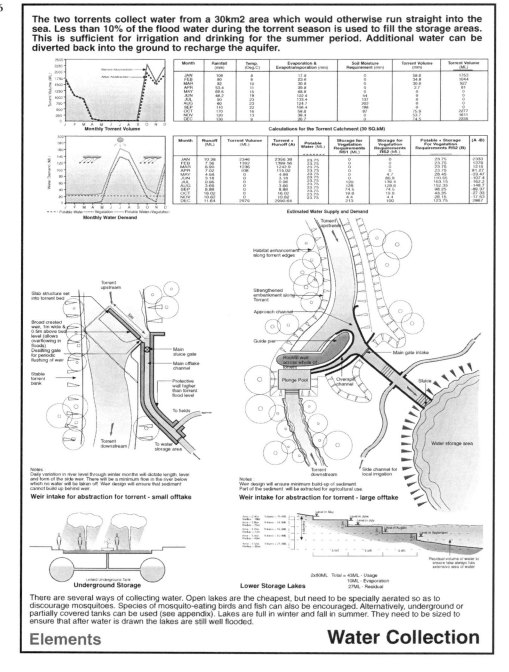

Torrent upstream

Habitat enhancement along torrent edges

Strengthened embankment along Torrent

Approach channel

Slab structure set into torrent bed

Torrent upstream

Broad crested weir, 1m wide & 0.5m above bed level (allows overflowing in floods) Desilting gate for periodic flushing of weir

Stable torrent bank

Main sluice gate

Main offtake channel

Protective wall higher than torrent flood level

To fields

Torrent downstream

To water storage area

Guide pier

Rockfill weir across whole of torrent

Plunge Pool

Overspill channel

Main gate intake

Sluice

Water storage area

Torrent downstream

Side channel for local irrigation

Notes
Daily variation in river level through winter months will dictate length, level and form of the side weir. There will be a minimum flow in the river below which no water will be taken off. Weir design will ensure that sediment cannot build up behind weir.

Weir intake for abstraction for torrent - small offtake

Notes :
Weir design will ensure minimum build-up of sediment
Part of the sediment will be extracted for agricultural use.

Weir intake for abstraction for torrent - large offtake

Underground Storage

Linked Underground Tank

Lower Storage Lakes

2x80ML Total = 43ML - Usage
10ML - Evaporation
27ML - Residual

There are several ways of collecting water. Open lakes are the cheapest, but need to be specially aerated so as to discourage mosquitoes. Species of mosquito-eating birds and fish can also be encouraged. Alternatively, underground or partially covered tanks can be used (see appendix). Lakes are full in winter and fall in summer. They need to be sized to ensure that after water is drawn the lakes are still well flooded.

Elements

Water Collection

Figure 3.87
Study of
possible
social fabric.

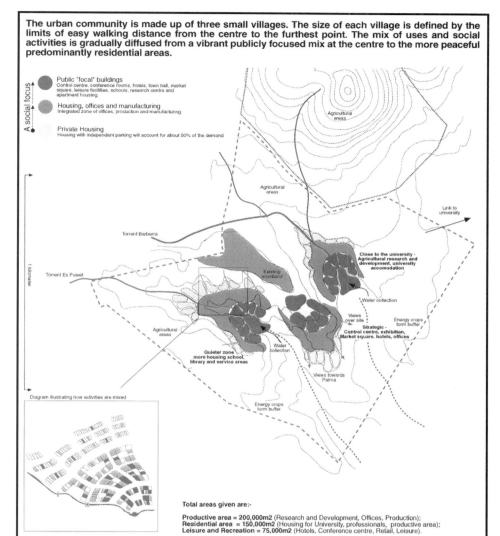

The urban community is made up of three small villages. The size of each village is defined by the limits of easy walking distance from the centre to the furthest point. The mix of uses and social activities is gradually diffused from a vibrant publicly focused mix at the centre to the more peaceful predominantly residential areas.

A social focus

Public "focal" buildings
Control centre, conference rooms, hotels, town hall, market square, leisure facilities, schools, research centre and apartment housing.

Housing, offices and manufacturing
Integrated zone of offices, production and manufacturing

Private Housing
Housing with independant parking will account for about 50% of the demand

Agricultural areas

Link to university

Torrent Barberra

Close to the university - Agricultural research and development, university accomodation

Torrent Es Puixet

Existing woodland

Water collection

Views over site

Energy crops form buffer

Agricultural areas

Strategic - Control centre, exhibition, Market square, hotels, offices

Water collection

Quieter zone more housing school, library and service areas

Views towards Palma

1 kilometer

Energy crops form buffer

Diagram illustrating how activities are mixed

Total areas given are:-

Productive area = 200,000m2 (Research and Development, Offices, Production);
Residential area = 150,000m2 (Housing for University, professionals, productive area);
Leisure and Recreation = 75,000m2 (Hotels, Conference centre, Retail, Leisure).

At the centre of each village occurs the most dynamic mix of uses, including public activities as well as offices and housing. A ring of integrated offices and housing encircles the centre, in turn giving way to a predominantly residential area on the outskirts of each village. Although quieter, each residential zone is still within easy walking distance of the village centre.

The public focus of the central village is based around the farm and 'Centre BIT', and includes a hotel, conference and exhibition facilities. Centre BIT is the main control centre for the water, energy and agricultural systems.

The centre of the Eastern node accommodates a branch of the nearby University's Earth Science Department and nursery gardens for crop research.

The West village is the quietest, so more residential. It includes a school, kindergarten and library.

Elements   **Social Fabric**

Figure 3.88
Energy
conservation
proposal.

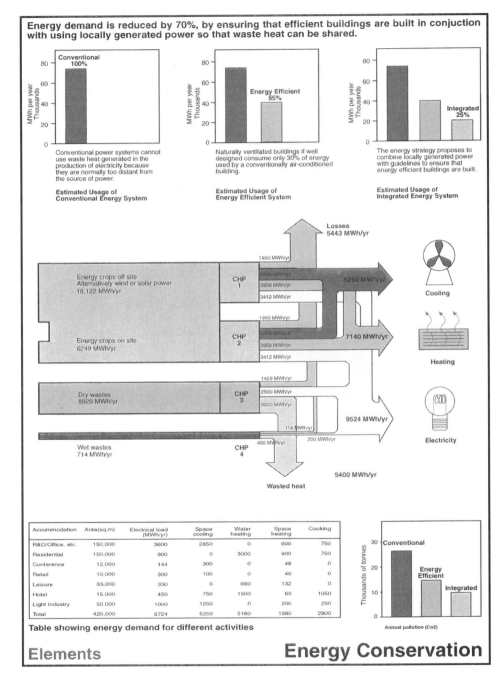

Energy demand is reduced by 70%, by ensuring that efficient buildings are built in conjuction with using locally generated power so that waste heat can be shared.

Conventional 100%

Conventional power systems cannot use waste heat generated in the production of electricity because they are normally too distant from the source of power.

Estimated Usage of Conventional Energy System

Energy Efficient 55%

Naturally ventilated buildings if well designed consume only 30% of energy used by a conventionally air-conditioned building.

Estimated Usage of Energy Efficient System

Integrated 25%

The energy strategy proposes to combine locally generated power with guidelines to ensure that energy efficient buildings are built.

Estimated Usage of Integrated Energy System

Losses 5443 MWh/yr

Energy crops off site
Alternatively wind or solar power
18,122 MWh/yr

CHP 1

1950 MWh/yr
3958 MWh/yr
3412 MWh/yr

5250 MWh/yr

Cooling

1950 MWh/yr

Energy crops on site
6249 MWh/yr

CHP 2

3958 MWh/yr
3412 MWh/yr

7140 MWh/yr

Heating

1429 MWh/yr

Dry wastes
8929 MWh/yr

CHP 3

2500 MWh/yr
5000 MWh/yr

9524 MWh/yr

114 MWh/yr

Electricity

400 MWh/yr   200 MWh/yr

Wet wastes
714 MWh/yr

CHP 4

5400 MWh/yr

Wasted heat

Accommodation	Area(sq.m)	Electrical load (MWh/yr)	Space cooling	Water heating	Space heating	Cooking
R&D/Office, etc.	150,000	3600	2850	0	600	750
Residential	150,000	900	0	3000	900	750
Conference	12,000	144	300	0	48	0
Retail	10,000	300	100	0	40	0
Leisure	33,000	330	0	660	132	0
Hotel	15,000	450	750	1500	60	1050
Light Industry	50,000	1000	1250	0	200	250
Total	420,000	6724	5250	5160	1980	2800

Table showing energy demand for different activities

Conventional

Energy Efficient

Integrated

Annual pollution (Co2)

Elements

Energy Conservation

Sustainable Architecture

Figure 3.89
Transporta-
tion plan.

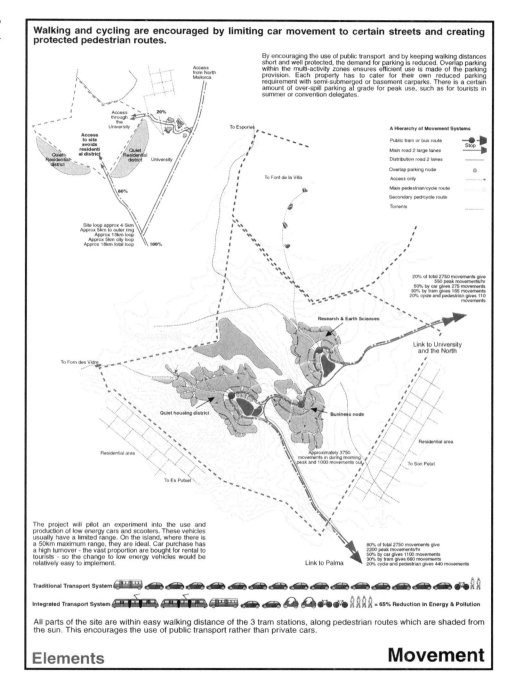

Walking and cycling are encouraged by limiting car movement to certain streets and creating protected pedestrian routes.

By encouraging the use of public transport and by keeping walking distances short and well protected, the demand for parking is reduced. Overlap parking within the multi-activity zones ensures efficient use is made of the parking provision. Each property has to cater for their own reduced parking requirement with semi-submerged or basement carparks. There is a certain amount of over-spill parking at grade for peak use, such as for tourists in summer or convention delegates.

Access from North Mallorca

Access through the University

20%

Access to site avoids residential district

Quiet Residential district

University

Quiet Residential district

80%

Site loop approx 4-5km
Approx 5km to outer ring
Approx 13km loop
Approx 5km city loop
Approx 18km total loop

100%

To Esporles

To Font de la Villa

A Hierarchy of Movement Systems

Public tram or bus route — Stop
Main road 2 large lanes
Distribution road 2 lanes
Overlap parking node
Access only
Main pedestrian/cycle route
Secondary ped/cycle route
Torrents

20% of total 2750 movements give 550 peak movements/hr
50% by car gives 275 movements
30% by tram gives 165 movements
20% cycle and pedestrian gives 110 movements

Research & Earth Sciences

Link to University and the North

To Forn des Vidre

Quiet housing district

Business node

Residential area

Residential area

Approximately 3750 movements in during morning peak and 1000 movements out

To Son Pelat

To Es Putxet

The project will pilot an experiment into the use and production of low energy cars and scooters. These vehicles usually have a limited range. On the island, where there is a 50km maximum range, they are ideal. Car purchase has a high turnover - the vast proportion are bought for rental to tourists - so the change to low energy vehicles would be relatively easy to implement.

80% of total 2750 movements give 2200 peak movements/hr
50% by car gives 1100 movements
30% by tram gives 660 movements
20% cycle and pedestrian gives 440 movements

Link to Palma

Traditional Transport System

Integrated Transport System = 65% Reduction in Energy & Pollution

All parts of the site are within easy walking distance of the 3 tram stations, along pedestrian routes which are shaded from the sun. This encourages the use of public transport rather than private cars.

Elements

Movement

Figure 3.90
Transporta-
tion systems
study.

The proposal is for a hierarchical transportation system which reduces vehicular congestion in the community by focusing on the public system and encouraging pedestrian movement.

Transport System		Passenger Capacity	Energy Consumption KJ/person km	Pollution g/person km
Tram		150/unit 5 units/hr peak	580	15.3
Bus		50/unit 6 units/hr (first phase)	590	146.5
Electric Car	Electric	2/unit	1600	41.5
Electric Scooter	Electric	1	1200	30.0
Bicycle/ Pedestrian		1	0	0

Reduction in private transport reduces the energy consumption and pollution emitted.

Traffic Congestion

Excessive surface parking should be avoided

Trams are a traditional transport solution for Mallorca and ease vehicular congestion in the narrow streets.

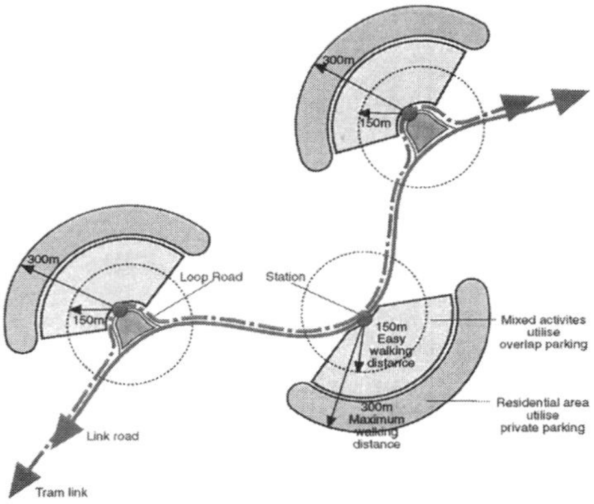

Diagram illustrating transport link & comfortable walking distances

A road based tram system is proposed that will serve 7,000 people on the site and a further 4-5,000 people on the University Campus, so as to distribute the running costs. In the early stages buses can be used in place of trams which will avoid an initial capital outlay for the tramlines. Only after investment has reached sufficient levels will roads be upgraded to take trams.

Alternatively powered cars are increasingly available.

New scooters consume very little energy

Cycles and Pedestrians are encouraged by protected routes

Electric fuel points allow easy recharging

Elements

Transportation Systems

Figure 3.91
Agricultural
strategy.

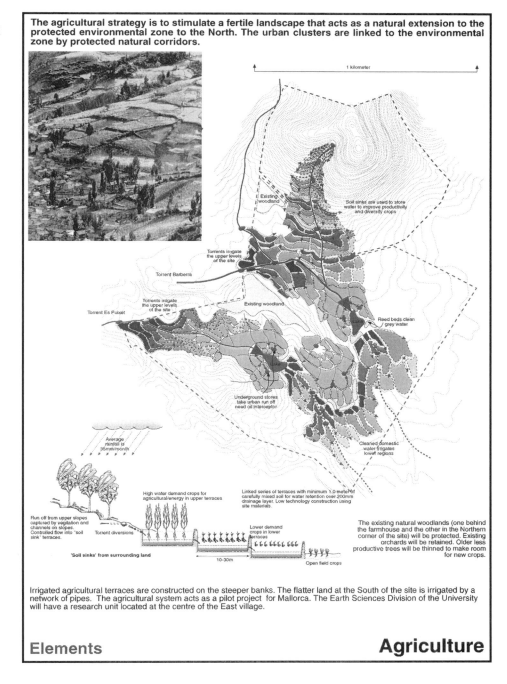

The agricultural strategy is to stimulate a fertile landscape that acts as a natural extension to the protected environmental zone to the North. The urban clusters are linked to the environmental zone by protected natural corridors.

1 kilometer

Existing woodland

Soil sinks are used to store water to improve productivity and diversity crops

Torrents irrigate the upper levels of the site

Torrent Barberra

Torrents irrigate the upper levels of the site

Existing woodland

Torrent Es Puixet

Reed beds clean / grey water

Underground stores take urban run off need oil interceptor

Cleaned domestic water irrigates lower regions

Average rainfall is 35mm/month

High water demand crops for agricultural/energy in upper terraces

Linked series of terraces with minimum 1.0 meter of carefully mixed soil for water retention over 200mm drainage layer. Low technology construction using site materials.

Run off from upper slopes captured by vegetation and channels on slopes. Controlled flow into 'soil sink' terraces.

Torrent diversions

Lower demand crops in lower terraces

The existing natural woodlands (one behind the farmhouse and the other in the Northern corner of the site) will be protected. Existing orchards will be retained. Older less productive trees will be thinned to make room for new crops.

'Soil sinks' from surrounding land

10-30m

Open field crops

Irrigated agricultural terraces are constructed on the steeper banks. The flatter land at the South of the site is irrigated by a network of pipes. The agricultural system acts as a pilot project for Mallorca. The Earth Sciences Division of the University will have a research unit located at the centre of the East village.

Elements

Agriculture

Figure 3.92
Irrigation
plan.

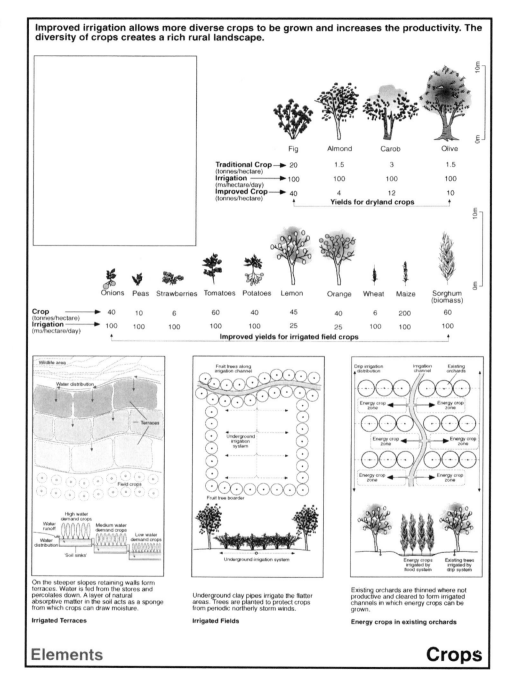

Improved irrigation allows more diverse crops to be grown and increases the productivity. The diversity of crops creates a rich rural landscape.

	Fig	Almond	Carob	Olive
Traditional Crop (tonnes/hectare)	20	1.5	3	1.5
Irrigation (m3/hectare/day)	100	100	100	100
Improved Crop (tonnes/hectare)	40	4	12	10

Yields for dryland crops

	Onions	Peas	Strawberries	Tomatoes	Potatoes	Lemon	Orange	Wheat	Maize	Sorghum (biomass)
Crop (tonnes/hectare)	40	10	6	60	40	45	40	6	200	60
Irrigation (m3/hectare/day)	100	100	100	100	100	25	25	100	100	100

Improved yields for irrigated field crops

Wildlife area
Water distribution
Terraces
Field crops
High water demand crops
Water runoff
Medium water demand crops
Water distribution
Low water demand crops
'Soil sinks'

On the steeper slopes retaining walls form terraces. Water is fed from the stores and percolates down. A layer of natural absorptive matter in the soil acts as a sponge from which crops can draw moisture.

Irrigated Terraces

Fruit trees along irrigation channel
Underground irrigation system
Fruit tree boarder
Underground irrigation system

Underground clay pipes irrigate the flatter areas. Trees are planted to protect crops from periodic northerly storm winds.

Irrigated Fields

Drip irrigation distribution
Irrigation channel
Existing orchards
Energy crop zone
Energy crops irrigated by flood system
Existing trees irrigated by drip system

Existing orchards are thinned where not productive and cleared to form irrigated channels in which energy crops can be grown.

Energy crops in existing orchards

Elements

Crops

Sustainable Architecture

Figure 3.93
Community
activity plan.

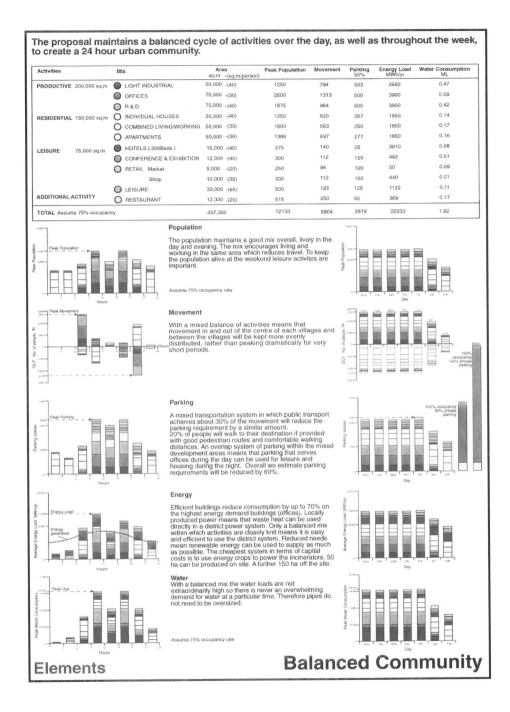

Figure 3.94
Majorca
master plan
economic
strategy.

Planning to create a proper infrastructure by phasing the construction over a long term period. This stimulates long term prosperity and vitality for the community.

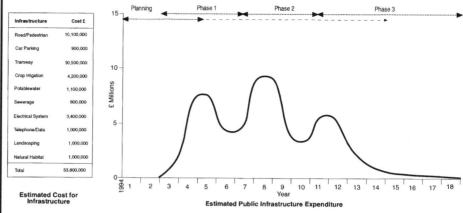

Infrastructure	Cost £
Road/Pedestrian	10,100,000
Car Parking	900,000
Tramway	30,500,000
Crop Irrigation	4,200,000
Potablewater	1,100,000
Sewerage	600,000
Electrical System	3,400,000
Telephone/Data	1,000,000
Landscaping	1,000,000
Natural Habitat	1,000,000
Total	53,800,000

Estimated Cost for Infrastructure

Estimated Public Infrastructure Expenditure

Infrastructure Investment

Public infrastructure will be implemented as investment occurs. A certain amount of it will need to be placed in advance of private building work to encourage investment. The major item of infrastructure is the tram system. This will be implemented as part of phase 2 when investment reaches sufficient levels. Wherever possible systems will be built node by node. The advantage of the nodal phasing is that the infrastructure need only be laid as each node is developed.

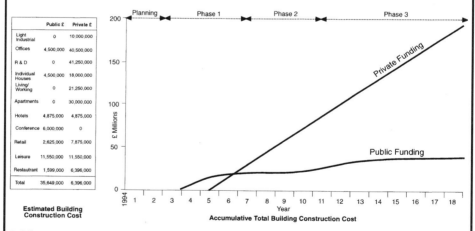

	Public £	Private £
Light Industrial	0	10,000,000
Offices	4,500,000	40,500,000
R & D	0	41,250,000
Individual Houses	4,500,000	18,000,000
Living/Working	0	21,250,000
Apartments	0	30,000,000
Hotels	4,875,000	4,875,000
Conference	6,000,000	0
Retail	2,625,000	7,875,000
Leisure	11,550,000	11,550,000
Restaurant	1,599,000	6,396,000
Total	35,649,000	6,396,000

Estimated Building Construction Cost

Accumulative Total Building Construction Cost

Building Investment

A certain amount of key public focus buildings should receive public support so as to act as catalysts to stimulate private investment. Private building investment will be more secure in the long term if the proper infrastructure is laid from the onset.

The figures above do not represent a definitive plan for finance. They simply illustrate The importance of phased planning so as to distribute finace and achive firm and sufficient urban infrastructure.

Assembly

Economics

Figure 3.95
Section showing
proposed underground
habitat. Photo by
Eamonn O'Mahoney.

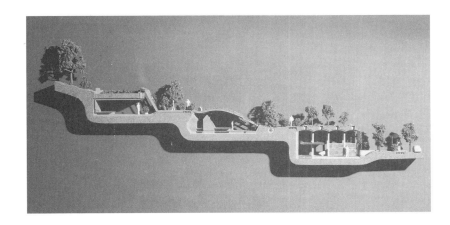

Figure 3.96
Commercial area and
courtyard configuration.
Photo by Eamonn
O'Mahoney.

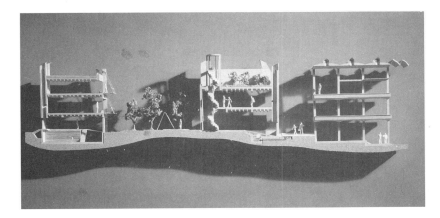

Figure 3.97
Mixed-use area near tram
station. Photo by
Eamonn O'Mahoney.

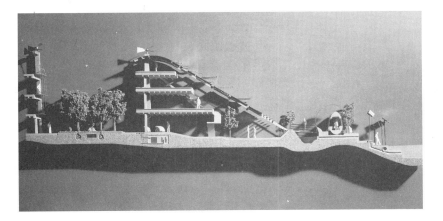

throughout the winter, when rainfall is abundant, with a minimum level established below which no water is taken off. Water storage is located at different points across the site so that a gravity irrigation system eliminates the need to pump water, and this system is constantly monitored. A computer-run control system is attached to a visitors center in a local village so that members of the public can see it in operation. To better utilize this water for irrigation, agricultural terraces have been built on the steeper slopes of the study area. The flatter land at the south of the site is fed by a network of pipes. This entire system has been approached as being prototypical, a pilot project for the entire island. The earth sciences division of the university, near the site, has taken advantage of this opportunity by establishing a research group that will monitor the performance and progress of the project, which will include inventories of a diverse range of new crops which irrigation will make possible as well as improved yields of traditional crops, which are expected as a result of the availability of a constant source of water. These yields are expected to double in most cases and rise as much as tenfold in several instances. Judicious planting of trees along the edges of terraces are intended to protect crops from excess wind and storms, indicating the extent to which landscaping has been integrated into the master plan. This integration extends to the use of crops for energy production. Quick growing crops, such as willow and sweet sorghum, will provide renewable sources of energy to generate power locally, based on an estimated fuel production of 10 to 15 tons per hectare.

The architectural component of the plan, envisioned as only one, superimposed part of a complex system including water and agricultural management as well as energy strategies and social mix, takes advantage of the gentle slope of the site. Based on a neighborhood concept, the idea was to create a compact community, with streets kept narrow to provide shade and reduce travel distances. Inserting building forms into the hillside, with heavy structure used for roofing, has allowed terracing to be extended over enclosed spaces. Vents for light and ventilation, placed between rows of deciduous trees, which allow maximum solar gain in the winter, provide the only clue that there is habitation below the planted surface. The scale of buildings increases toward the town center, reaching its highest point at a tram line which runs along the lake's edge. This growth relates to bands of use, from agricultural terraces on the perimeter of the zone, through quiet residential areas and a working, or office zone, to a mixed-use public area, including small plazas around the lake. During the summer, when water levels recede, cascading terraces around the lake perimeter are sequentially revealed, becoming stepped public promenades to accommodate residents' desire to walk near the water, as well as the seasonal influx of tourists.

By making densities high and encouraging the use of public transport, the demand for parking is reduced. Each property is expected to accommodate a semisubmerged carpark, and overspill parking is provided for peak summertime use, when tourists arrive. The project is intended as a pilot experiment in the use of low-energy cars and motorcycles, which have a limited range of 50 km. An energy reduction of 65 percent is anticipated.

SHANGHAI DEVELOPMENT PROPOSAL
Richard Rogers Partnership

The brief presented to the architect requested proposals for the redevelopment of the western district of Shanghai which will be known as Lu Jia Zui. This is intended as a business center with a minimum of 4 million m² of mixed-use accommodations to act as a link between the historic part of Shanghai and a new spine of growth to the southeast. Lu Jia Zui is expected to play a key role in promoting economic growth, and the architects used this opportunity to reexamine accepted concepts of town planning to arrive at a prototype for a futuristic city based on environmental principles. To this end, the criteria set for Lu Jia Zui were that it should be integral to, not isolated from, Shanghai, based on the idea of the street, rather than singular object buildings related to the context of the riverside site, and energy efficient. In creating this new urban prototype the architects began with the premise that the circulation of people and goods is a problem cities are grappling with worldwide. In the center of London, for example, traffic speeds have now fallen to an average of 10.3 mph—the same average speed as in the nineteenth century when horses and carts were used.

Increasingly draconian measures are being applied by municipalities in Europe and North America to try to reduce congestion, improve public transportation, and redress the damaging effects of vehicular pollution. The redevelopment of Shanghai Lu Jia Zui provides an opportunity to design an urban center which incorporates the key elements of a coordinated transportation strategy, involving the efficient layout of buildings, the management of vehicular circulation, and the provision of an efficient and reliable public transportation system. (Figs. 3.98 to 3.101)

A number of different modes of transport have been incorporated into the strategy, including, in order of importance, sub-

Figure 3.98
Lu Jia Zui,
Shanghai
expansion
proposal.
Richard Rogers.

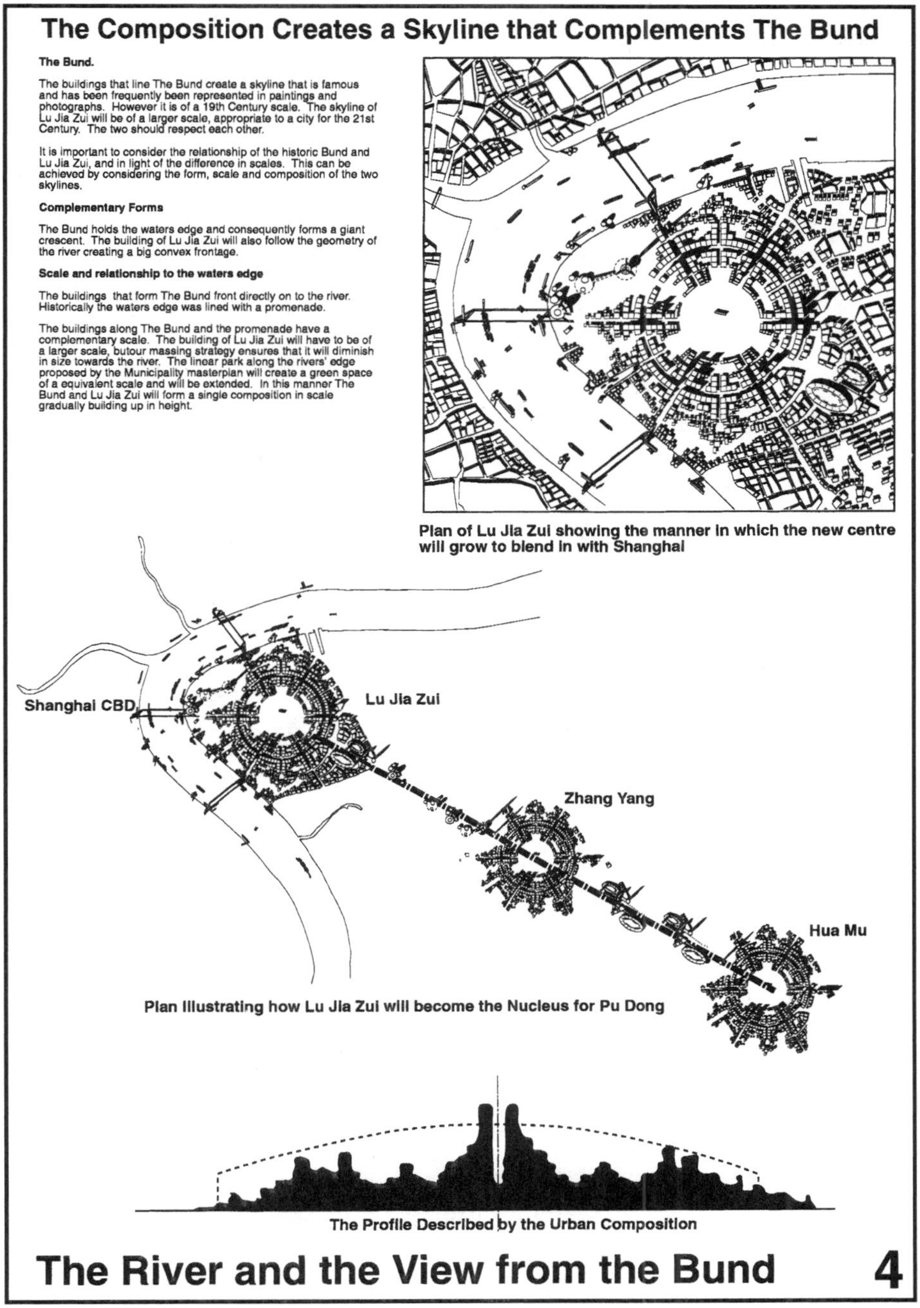

The Composition Creates a Skyline that Complements The Bund

The Bund.

The buildings that line The Bund create a skyline that is famous and has been frequently been represented in paintings and photographs. However it is of a 19th Century scale. The skyline of Lu Jia Zui will be of a larger scale, appropriate to a city for the 21st Century. The two should respect each other.

It is important to consider the relationship of the historic Bund and Lu Jia Zui, and in light of the difference in scales. This can be achieved by considering the form, scale and composition of the two skylines.

Complementary Forms

The Bund holds the waters edge and consequently forms a giant crescent. The building of Lu Jia Zui will also follow the geometry of the river creating a big convex frontage.

Scale and relationship to the waters edge

The buildings that form The Bund front directly on to the river. Historically the waters edge was lined with a promenade.

The buildings along The Bund and the promenade have a complementary scale. The building of Lu Jia Zui will have to be of a larger scale, butour massing strategy ensures that it will diminish in size towards the river. The linear park along the rivers' edge proposed by the Municipality masterplan will create a green space of a equivalent scale and will be extended. In this manner The Bund and Lu Jia Zui will form a single composition in scale gradually building up in height.

Plan of Lu Jia Zui showing the manner in which the new centre will grow to blend in with Shanghai

Shanghai CBD

Lu Jia Zui

Zhang Yang

Hua Mu

Plan Illustrating how Lu Jia Zui will become the Nucleus for Pu Dong

The Profile Described by the Urban Composition

The River and the View from the Bund 4

Figure 3.99
Lu Jia Zui, Shanghai
expansion proposal.
Richard Rogers.

ways, rapid light rail, trams, pedestrians, taxis, buses, bicycles, and cars. The approach to the transport issue is an overlapping system of separate but interrelated networks. An important feature of the transportation strategy within Lu Jia Zui is the light rail loop which forms the major space of the development area. A maximum walking distance of 350 m has been determined as the maximum depth of the development zone from the light rail loop and a network of centralized parking structures which helps minimize vehicular movement.

A business center composed of a series of discrete and separate buildings will not successfully contribute to the economic growth of Shanghai. For the new business center to function as an integral part to the economic life of the city, it must be integrated within the physical form of the city. To do this, the architects created a discrete and separate community with a physical form that is distinct from the other parts of the city, not allowing the communities to grow into one another; otherwise, Lu Jia Zui cannot function as a social focus for Shanghai and Pu Dong.

Achieving a mix of activities also has significant environmental advantages. A good balance between commercial and residential activities evens out demands on the infrastructure, for example, power generation and transport. Three key elements are required to create a vital community: a plan based on the street, as the existing CBD is; a plan that establishes a critical density to the development; a plan that provides a mix of activities throughout the Lu Jia Zui district by dividing the center into six segments.

The drawings illustrate a strategy for the mix of activities: a focus for commercial development (offices, hotels, etc.) along the light rail loop, cultural and social facilities concentrated around the open spaces, housing clustered at the subcenter, shopping located along the primary routes leading to the river crossings. This strategy achieves a mix of activities within each of the six sectors of the city.

The layout of the development zone is defined by the transportation system. The height and profile of buildings within the zone will be defined by two complementary objectives: to maximize aspect to all the buildings and to maximize daylight to all the buildings. To maximize the daylight admitted to the building a model was made and tested for both summer and winter conditions. The following sun angles were used:

Winter solstice	27.5°
Summer solstice	74.5°

Lighting of buildings typically consumes 30 percent of the total energy used by buildings. Maximizing daylight admission can reduce dependence on artificial lighting, thereby resulting in an approximate 15 percent savings in energy costs. By introducing a series of peaks and troughs in the building massing, daylight can be admitted to buildings from more than one orientation. The resultant profile to the buildings will be similar to a series of overlapping waves. This concept was incorporated into a contour drawing which defines the maximum building envelope. Buildings can be constructed to any height or form within this envelope without compromising the basic objectives in the scheme.

An important element in the proposal is a large central park at the focus of the project. This will supplement the linear park that runs parallel with the Huang Pu proposed in the master plan by the municipality of Shanghai. These two open spaces represent the key elements in the open space plan. Green space will be located at the heart and at the perimeter of the development area. All areas of Lu Jia Zui will be within easy reach of open space. The community and cultural activities already planned by the municipality and additional facilities included in this proposal will be located around the edges of the central park. The central park and the linear park will be connected by a major link located at the base of the new television tower. Smaller neighborhood parks and squares will be located within each segment of the plan. All major cities of the world have major urban parks, the name of which is often synonymous with the city, such as London's Regents Park or Hyde Park, New York's Central Park, and Chapultapec Park in Mexico City. The Rogers partnership has proposed an open space of a scale and design appropriate for their vision of Lu Jia Zui.

The parks will also provide the "lungs" to help the city breathe. Large open spaces introduce an air movement that can help dispel pollution. Trees and, in particular, certain species of trees, can consume significant amounts of CO_2 and replace it with oxygen. In addition to open spaces, the environmental strategy uses a number of strands: an efficient transportation strategy, a system of parks designed in conjunction with the design of the built

Figure 3.100
Proposed park
system for Lu
Jia Zui.

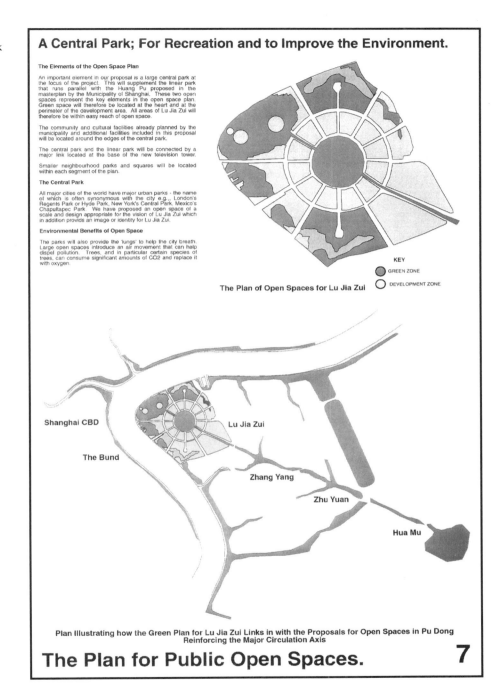

A Central Park; For Recreation and to Improve the Environment.

The Elements of the Open Space Plan

An important element in our proposal is a large central park at the focus of the project. This will supplement the linear park that runs parallel with the Huang Pu proposed in the masterplan by the Municipality of Shanghai. These two open spaces represent the key elements in the open space plan. Green space will therefore be located at the heart and at the perimeter of the development area. All areas of Lu Jia Zui will therefore be within easy reach of open space.

The community and cultural facilities already planned by the municipality and additional facilities included in this proposal will be located around the edges of the central park.

The central park and the linear park will be connected by a major link located at the base of the new television tower.

Smaller neighbourhood parks and squares will be located within each segment of the plan.

The Central Park

All major cities of the world have major urban parks - the name of which is often synonymous with the city e.g., London's Regents Park or Hyde Park, New York's Central Park, Mexico's Chapultapec Park. We have proposed an open space of a scale and design appropriate for the vision of Lu Jia Zui which in addition provides an image or identity for Lu Jia Zui.

Environmental Benefits of Open Space

The parks will also provide the 'lungs' to help the city breath. Large open spaces introduce an air movement that can help dispel pollution. Trees, and in particular certain species of trees, can consume significant amounts of CO_2 and replace it with oxygen.

KEY

⬤ GREEN ZONE

◯ DEVELOPMENT ZONE

The Plan of Open Spaces for Lu Jia Zui

Shanghai CBD

The Bund

Lu Jia Zui

Zhang Yang

Zhu Yuan

Hua Mu

Plan Illustrating how the Green Plan for Lu Jia Zui Links in with the Proposals for Open Spaces in Pu Dong Reinforcing the Major Circulation Axis

The Plan for Public Open Spaces.

7

Figure 3.101 (opposite)
Lu Jia Zui master plan
model. Photo by
Eamonn O'Mahoney.

area, a coordinated energy strategy. The overriding concept for the layout of the city is to facilitate easy and efficient circulation between all areas. The urban plan is defined by the major movement system, specifically the light rail loop. All areas of Lu Jia Zui will be within easy walking distance of the stations on this loop. This layout reduces the amount of traffic movement and makes travel by public transport very easy. This, in turn, reduces demand and need for the private car. Vehicular movement can, therefore, be carefully controlled. The energy requirements of seven different types of building have been calculated. These are offices, housing, hotels, conference, shopping, cultural, and leisure centers. The development area has been split into six zones. The building types have been split among the zones to give an even mix of space coverage, energy usage and compatible uses. One energy center will provide the energy of two zones. The energy required has been split between thermal energy required for heating, energy required for cooling (electrical), and electrical energy for lighting and the like.

The objective has been to provide sensible and achievable targets for energy consumption to enable the sizing of the energy supply. Two methods have been used to achieve reductions in energy requirement compared with traditional usage. Instituting energy use standards and using combined heat and power (CHP) both will produce reductions in the energy required for traditional buildings.

Traditional energy use is taken to be that required for current buildings. Much energy is wasted through lack of awareness among building users and because energy efficiency is a low priority with building designers. Buildings should be designed to be naturally ventilated where possible, and where not possible buildings should have energy-efficient air conditioning systems using free cooling. The total energy required for the development area if traditional buildings were built would be 212 MW. This is divided

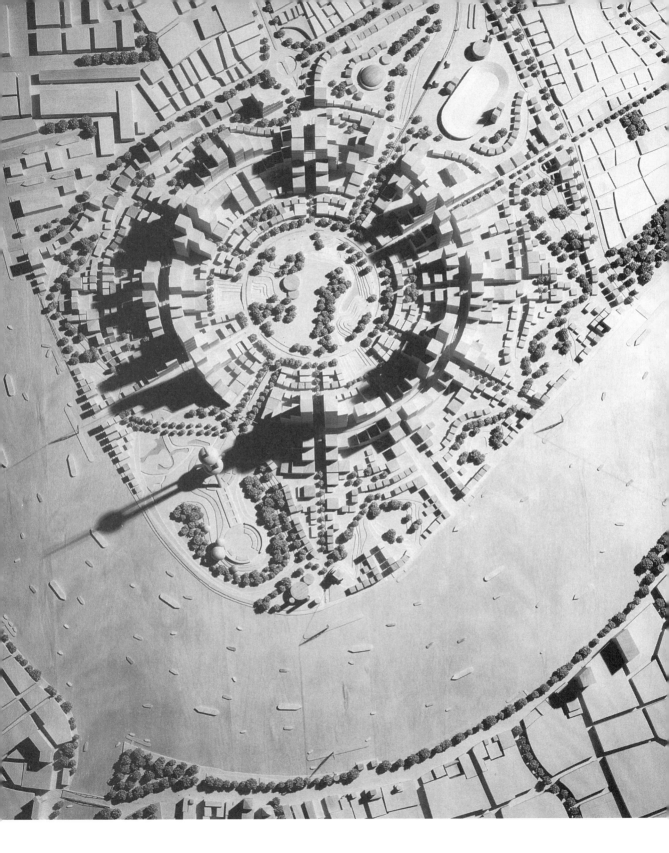

between 123 MW for heating, 22 MW for cooling (electrical), and 67 MW for electricity generation. Instituted standards should ensure that buildings are built with good thermal properties, that energy-efficient electrical equipment is selected, that buildings are fitted with energy-saving controls—CO_2 detectors, thermostats, sensible lighting controls. Building systems should be regularly maintained so that systems operate at optimum levels. The total energy required for the development area, if energy-efficient buildings were built, would be 136 MW. This is divided between 61 MW for heating, 14 MW for cooling (electrical), and 60 MW of electricity. Electricity generation produces nearly twice as much thermal energy (in the form of hot water) as electrical energy. CHP allows the thermal energy to be used for heating rather than being wasted. Using a district heating scheme, the thermal energy can be distributed to each of the buildings; hot water can also be used for cooling, using absorption chillers. Thus energy needs to be provided only for the generation of 60 MW of electricity. The hot water and cooling will be generated from this. The energy requirement for energy-efficient buildings supplied by CHP is the same as above except that the 61 MW for heating, 14 MW for cooling, and 60 MW of electricity can all be provided by the 60 MW of electrical generation. Therefore, the energy requirement of the area would be just 60 MW of electrical generation.

Sustainable Architecture

THE SECOND REGIONAL VOCATIONAL SCHOOL IN FREJUS

Norman Foster and Partners

Figure 3.102
Site plan of the Lycee Polyvalent in Frejus. Norman Foster.

The design for this vocational school near Frejus, France, was guided by climatic considerations, primarily the hot summers of the Cote d'Azur. Won by competition in 1991, the commission allowed Sir Norman Foster and Partners, who are typically identified as being at the forefront of the high-tech movement and, therefore, supposedly antithetical to sustainability, to expand on themes established in the Willis Faber, Sainsbury, and Hong Kong Shanghai Bank buildings. In each of these previous projects Foster has succeeded in separating himself from other practitioners in the genre by paying attention to context and environmental factors, rather than ignoring them. This contradiction in his work, of a cel-

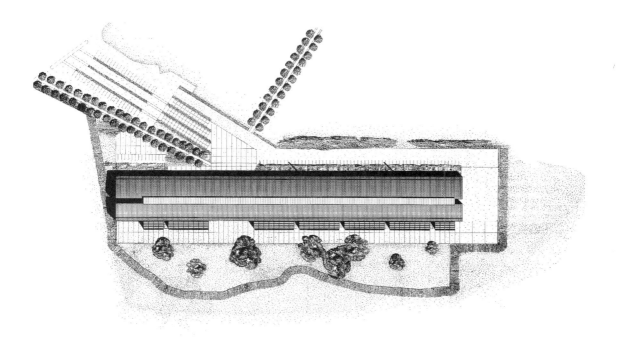

ebration of the most advanced and admittedly energy- and resource-intensive industrial materials on the one hand, and a sensitivity to site and climate on the other, makes this project valuable as a case study, not the least because it demonstrates the extent to which environmental considerations have penetrated into corporate consciousness. Foster has been determined to finally reconcile Mies van der Rohe's mandate that architecture should "reflect the technology of the time," with Modernism's failed attempt to do so and to realize the intentions of the visionary phase of that idiom, in conforming to physical laws. Best expressed in the axiom "high-tech equals low energy," in building performance rather than in the extraction and manufacture of its materials and in the method of its construction, Foster's approach is evidenced by the deep plan of the Willis Faber headquarters in Ipswich, the computer-driven louvres providing a "smart" response to solar gain in the Sainsbury Center as well as an emphasis on natural rather than mechanical ventilation and careful orientation, and stack effect for cooling in the Hong Kong Shanghai Bank.

The Vocational School in Frejus follows this pattern. The linear site straddles a hill, which suggested a building of similar form, oriented to maximize southern exposure and splendid views in that direction. This led to an internal arrangement of classrooms branching off a central "street" which is now the social heart of the Lycee. The long profile was also derived from a decision to use primarily natural ventilation for cooling. Taking the history of Provence into account acknowledged that "the method of ventilating the building in this hot climate relies on techniques familiar from traditional Arabic architecture. This led to the use of a concrete structure to provide thermal mass in order to absorb temperature variations. It also led to the choice of a building form which would enhance natural ventilation using stack effect, thus avoiding the need to mechanically ventilate the building: the lofty internal street creates a solar chimney to induce the flow of air." (Figs. 3.102 to 3.111)

Sustainable Architecture

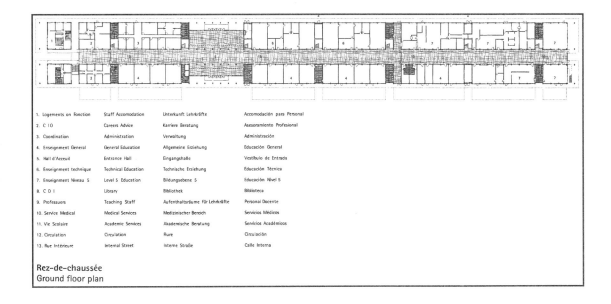

1. Logements on Fonction	Staff Accomodation	Unterkunft Lehrkräfte	Accomodación para Personal
2. C 10	Careers Advice	Karriere Beratung	Asesoramiento Profesional
3. Coordination	Administration	Verwaltung	Administración
4. Enseignment General	General Education	Allgemeine Erziehung	Educación General
5. Hall d'Acceuil	Entrance Hall	Eingangshalle	Vestíbulo de Entrada
6. Enseignment technique	Technical Education	Technische Erziehung	Educación Técnica
7. Enseignment Niveau 5	Level 5 Education	Bildungsebene 5	Educación Nivel 5
8. C D I	Library	Bibliothek	Biblioteca
9. Professuers	Teaching Staff	Aufenthaltsräume für Lehrkräfte	Personal Docente
10. Service Medical	Medical Services	Medizinischer Bereich	Servicios Médicos
11. Vie Scolaire	Academic Services	Akademische Beratung	Servicios Académicos
12. Circulation	Circulation	Flure	Circulación
13. Rue Intérieure	Internal Street	Interne Straße	Calle Interna

Rez-de-chaussée
Ground floor plan

Figure 3.103
Plan of the Lycee Polyvalent.

Figure 3.104
Elevation showing climatic controls.

A simple, repetitive structural system to minimize fabrication and maximize efficiency on site allowed the 243-m long, 14,500 m² school to be completed in less than a year. Construction cost and time were reduced so effectively that the building was produced for 5 million francs less than originally estimated. Foster's decision, to rely on natural rather than mechanical cooling will also greatly reduce life-cycle costs.

The use of concrete is undoubtedly arguable, as it is not the only material that would have provided the amount of thermal mass required, and local stone is abundant and readily available. The Foster office contends that it was chosen to correspond with

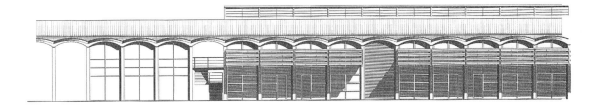

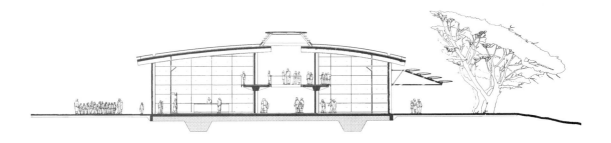

local construction techniques, with the structure designed to utilize French expertise in the fabrication of good quality in-situ concrete. The glazing system as well as internal finishes are all standard components chosen for durability and low maintenance, and floors are tiled throughout. Seismic concerns, as well as a desire to fit into the landscape, dictated a low-profile, two-story building, and vaulted concrete shells serve to tie it visually to the ground. The double-height circulation space, or "street," between the classroom blocks provides ventilation and allows daylight to reach the interior. A canopy over the street has remote-controlled louvres which can be opened to allow air to be drawn upward by thermo-siphoning, as the canopy is heated by the sun. The classrooms are also equipped with large operable and adjustable windows on both external and internal facades so that outside air can circulate through them, into the street, and then up through the canopy louvres as it is heated. High ceilings allow warmed air to stratify, rising to the highest part of an occupied space before it is pulled

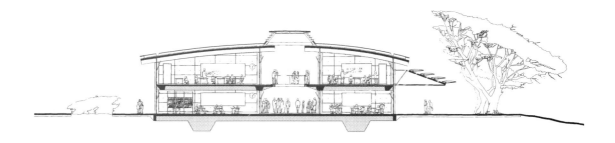

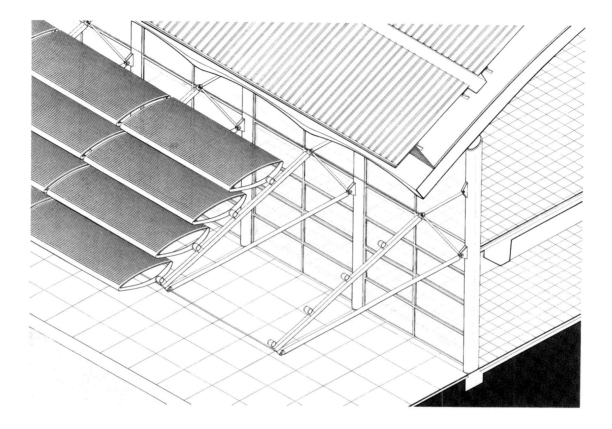

Figure 3.107
Detail of a shading
device.

into the central zone and exhausted, by natural convection. A thin outer metal roof, layered over the inner concrete shells, creates an air space, reducing solar gain through the largest surface that the sun strikes, for the longest period, during the day. Mechanical ventilation is supplied only in spaces where it is absolutely necessary, such as kitchens and laboratories.

The energy-saving features of this design were largely responsible for its being selected by the client, and a rigorous financial analysis by the architect weighted each potential saving in energy cost against the capital outlay necessary for each component of the solution. Although it may be criticized as an "object

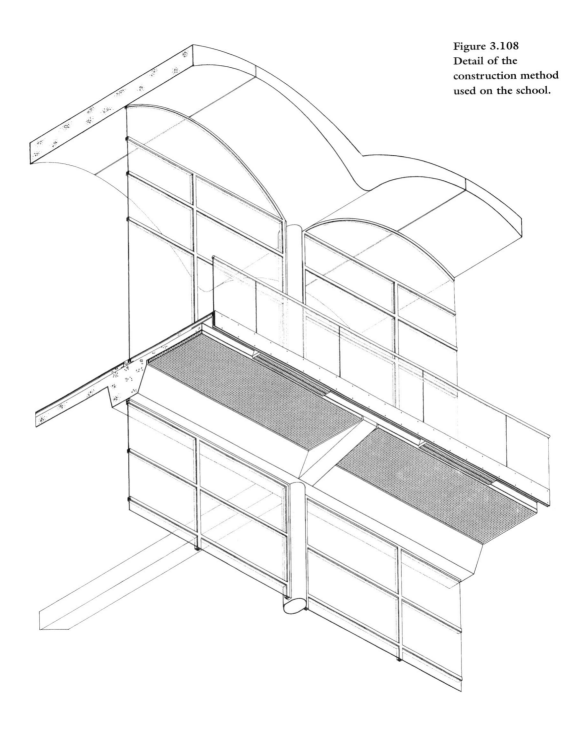

Figure 3.108
Detail of the
construction method
used on the school.

Sustainable Architecture

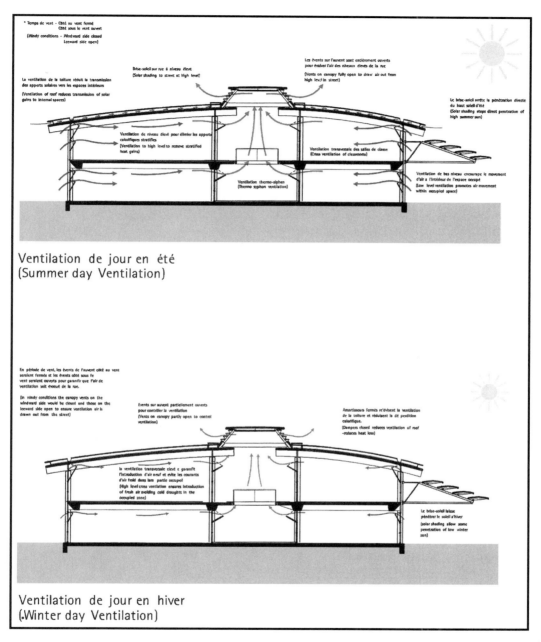

Ventilation de jour en été
(Summer day Ventilation)

Ventilation de jour en hiver
(Winter day Ventilation)

Figure 3.109
Seasonal daylight natural ventilation patterns.

Case Studies

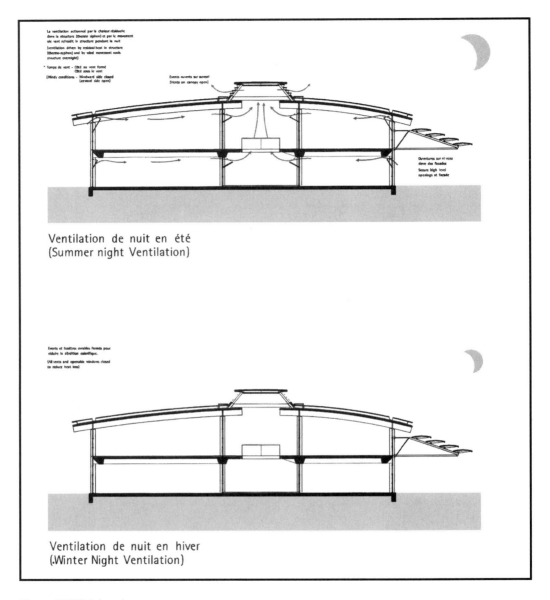

La ventilation actionnée par la chaleur résiduelle
dans la structure (thermo-siphon) et par le mouvement
ole vent refroidit la structure pendant la nuit

(ventilation driven by residual heat in structure
(thermo-syphon) and by wind movement cools
structure overnight)

* Temps de vent - Côté au vent fermé
           Côté sous le vent

(Windy conditions - Windward side closed
           Leeward side open)

Events ouverts sur auvent
(Vents on canopy open)

Ouvertures sur ni veau
élevé des facades
Secure high level
openings at facade

**Ventilation de nuit en été
(Summer night Ventilation)**

Events et fenêtres ovrables Fermés pour
réduire la déédtion calorifique.

(All vents and openable windows closed
to reduce heat loss)

**Ventilation de nuit en hiver
(.Winter Night Ventilation)**

Figure 3.110 (above)
Seasonal night-time ventilation patterns.

Figure 3.111 (right)
Exterior view of the Lycee Polyvalent in Frejus; Norman Foster. Photo by Dennis Gilbert.

Sustainable Architecture

building" utilizing industrial, energy-intensive materials, this example is instructive on several levels. First, it demonstrates a growing client awareness about energy-related issues, along with a parallel, continuing preference for a high degree of finish, if possible, and a singular image. Second, it suggests an equal degree of interest by an architect who represents an ongoing commitment to high technology as a means of architectural expression. This stems from a belief that exemplary architecture has historically utilized the most advanced materials and techniques available in each age, and that high-tech architecture, also in the best British tradition of the Crystal Palace and Palm House at Kew, represents that aspiration today. This modest exercise, regardless of all the reservations listed, is encouraging as an indication of the extent of influence of a new sensibility.

GRAMEEN BANK HOUSING PROJECT, BANGLADESH

Rural Economics Program

The Grameen Bank prototype offers an insight into the dramatic changes that can occur when adjustments are made in institutional policy. Begun in 1976 in the village of Jobra by Dr. Mohammed Yunus, who was then the director of the rural economics program of Chittagong University, this new system of credit involves providing loans to the landless poor in Bangladesh. This segment, representing nearly 60 percent of the Bangladeshi population at the time the program was instituted, had previously been excluded from receiving bank loans because of their lack of collateral, in spite of the critical contribution they make to the economic system through agricultural production and small-scale endeavors. The concept was to offer small loans equivalent to a maximum of $350 to the rural poor without requiring any collateral, in direct contradiction to the customary practice of the financial community in the past. Although this may not seem like a significant amount, note that the estimated annual per capita income in Bangladesh is $140. The implicit position of the bank has been that all human beings, regardless of social position, deserve lives of dignity and should have the opportunity to care for themselves if they have the determination to do so. Personal commitment, rather than financial resources, becomes the main criterion in determining creditworthiness, and the expectation is that this new group would repay their debt through their individual commercial activities. The only conditions the bank imposed was that communal groups be organized to ensure repayment, making it difficult for an individual to default. Participation in the program is limited to families whose total assets do not exceed the market value of an acre of land in their area, and to get the loan, which is issued in the name of one family member

Figure 3.112
Grameen Bank housing
scheme, Pakistan. Photo
by Anwar Hossein for
the AKAA.

Figure 3.113 (opposite)
Grameen Bank housing
scheme, Pakistan. Photo
by Anwar Hossein for
the AKAA.

only, that person must sign up a minimum of five other members
in similar circumstances, from which a chairperson and secretary are
elected. (Figs. 3.112 to 3.114) Each loan is given for 1 year only
and paid back in weekly installments, with an obligatory deduction
of 5 percent placed in a group fund account, which can be used by
any member in difficulty, with common consent. At present, more
than 80 percent of Grameen Bank members are women. Within 5
years of its founding in 1983, as a joint venture in which the government of Bangladesh held 60 percent of the capital and 40 percent was held by bank members, the program had 535,170 partici-
pants spread through 11,793 villages in nine major zones throughout the nation, and the loan recovery rate averaged 98.35 percent.

Sustainable Architecture

Figure 3.114 Grameen Bank housing scheme, Pakistan. Photo by Anwar Hossein for the AKAA.

The housing loan portion of the program, which was begun in 1984, has been particularly successful, making it possible for members to receive funds for building new houses or rehabilitating old ones. The loan amounts are larger, and the payback period, to a maximum of 15 years, is longer, making it necessary to implement procedures that are more involved, although the basic theoretical principles of the program still apply. Two types of loans for a "basic house" or "standard house," are offered, with the bank itself providing the components for each. The basic house occupies 20 m², structurally defined by four prefabricated reinforced concrete columns at each of the four corners of a rectangular slab. Because of endemic termite problems, concrete has replaced the original wooden columns provided by the bank, and corrugated metal is also preferred over wood for the same reason. Intermediate structural members, as well as enclosing partitions, provided by each family, are typically of bamboo, or jute, but bamboo is now becoming scarce and must be imported from India, increasing its cost. Earth floors are typical. The standard house is larger, but the materials are the same. The bank also provides a prefabricated concrete latrine for each house, but beyond supplying these, the columns and the corrugated iron sheets, which are distributed by 34 different production yards throughout the country, it does not get involved in siting, orientation, subsidiary materials, or the internal organization of the house.

The basic house loan of 10,000 taka (Tk), given at 5 percent interest, breaks down as follows:

1. Four reinforced concrete columns = Tk 1300
2. Two bundles of corrugated iron sheets = Tk 5000
3. Sanitary latrine = Tk 500
4. Other materials to frame roof = Tk 3200

Because of monsoons, flooding, and humidity, the lifespan of the bamboo frame and jute siding is only 2 years on average, but these are relatively easy to replace, compared to the basic structural components of column and roof, which they supplement.

Follow-up surveys have been far from comprehensive, based on a small sample. The responses received, however, indicate that the significance of the houses made possible by the Grameen Bank greatly exceeds their scale, making it possible for many poor families to literally raise themselves out of the mud. Working in close conjunction with their earlier incentive loans to help increase income, the longer-range housing subsidies have made it possible for the quality and quantity of work to increase, providing protection from the elements for the occupants and their personal possessions and lowering the incidence of disease.

The simplicity of this project, and the startling results that have obtained from it, present a stark contrast to expectations in the West, showing just how greatly values can differ and how important the most minimal materials can be.

ENVIRONMENTAL ECONOMICS

Each of the segments that make up the intricate kaleidoscopes of sustainable development are inevitably becoming subspecialties, the rapidly increasing literature replete with yet another extensive study of some aspect of the subject. For those trying to make sense of the entirety, such fragmentation is initially distracting, but eventually, a pattern begins to emerge, as rich in its own artificial way as the natural world it attempts to reflect. The field of environmental economics, which its practitioners insist is not "sustainable" or "ecological" economics, is one such arena, generating everything from studies on natural capital and the proper calculation of income from depletable natural resources to articles about the connection between population and poverty or loans and ecological problems.

Putting together a descriptive, rather than purely analytical, narrative that adequately prescribes the entire endeavor is a daunting, and risky, but necessary, task, since those involved with the built environment at all levels must eventually interact with environmental economics, if they are serious about understanding all of the ramifications of sustainability.

THE DEBT CRISIS

Discussions with environmental economists, as well as a sequential historical overview, most logically begin with the international debt crisis, which was triggered by the rise of oil prices in 1973. In that instance, the attempt by a cartel of countries in the developing world to control access to one of the most precious nonrenewable resources not only created repercussions in the eurocurrency market but also focused attention on the worth of resources in a general sense, as well as on inequities in pricing them. One immediate result of the first oil price rise was that the account deficits of the non-oil-producing countries of the developing world, on loans liberally offered in the flush of postwar prosperity, could no longer be carried by banks on surpluses generated by the oil exporters, and the burden was shifted to the borrowers themselves.[1] This significant shift was accompanied by a dramatic growth in international banking, and in the decade following the oil embargo the eurocurrency market expanded from $300 billion to $2000 billion (in US dollars). A recession in 1980, following soon after a second oil embargo, prompted higher interest rates to curb inflation. This rapid rise in debt service responsibility caused many nations in the developing world to delay payments, eventually caused a massive rescheduling of debt, involving 30 countries. By 1983, the long-term external debt of all developing countries was nearly $650 billion, with 85 percent of that total made up by non-oil-producing nations.

The negative effect of the world-wide recession at the beginning of the 1980s cannot be overemphasized, since between 1980 and 1983 the debt of the non-oil-producing developing countries was nearly 100 times their aggregate increase in export earnings, particularly due to depressed commodity prices, which caused what has tersely been described as a "forced transition from trade deficits financed by net capital inflows to net capital outflows, made possible by running trade surpluses."[2] The real impact of this "transition" was staggering, with purchasing power of exports declining by as much as 20 percent in many low-income countries in Africa and by 10 percent in Asia.

Threatened default by Mexico at this time caused the formation of a different kind of cartel, the commercial banks with the International Monetary Fund as leader, to enforce structural changes in debtor countries that included currency devaluation, severe reductions in social programs, and the end of government subsidies on commodities such as sugar and flour. In return for compliance with these changes, nations received new loans to bring interest payments current. In February 1987, President José Sarney declared that Brazil intended to suspend interest payments, and 2 months later Citibank shocked the banking community by setting aside $3 billion in loan loss reserves in anticipation of default; many other banks, who had also been creditors to Brazil, followed Citibank's lead. Structural economic changes were once again enforced, this time through the device of withholding short-term trade credits, and the once unthinkable disaster of a national bankruptcy was, once again, averted.

This sad litany of the relatively rapid fall from a time of innocence and readily available money in the 1970s to today's condition of intrusive control of national governments by international lending institutions as a direct consequence of indebtedness is tragic but also incontrovertible. What is more contentious, however, is the environmental impact that this shift has had; one view, now known as the *exports promotions hypothesis,* has been consistently put forward by those favoring the left side of the sustainable equation. The hypothesis is based on the idea that, in order to produce the foreign exchange necessary to repay its international debts, poor countries in the developing world are forced to concentrate on the production of commodities for export instead of on goods for the domestic market. These commodities, it is claimed, typically include nonrenewable resources, which are concentrated in the developing world, involving more energy-intensive and environmentally destructive processes than domestic production would require.

THE CONNECTION BETWEEN DEBT AND ENVIRONMENTAL DAMAGE

In rebuttal to this argument, others claim that the hypothesis is "anecdotal and speculative," based on equivocal evidence, pointing out that although there are clear instances of the diversion of funds from public service to debt service, the connection to environmental degradation has yet to be proved. The opposite, these researchers note, is often the case, since countries lacking liquidity have postponed or cancelled huge capital projects, such as dams and highways, which have proved to be so destructive in the past, just as often as they have shelved plans to curb pollution or improve sanitation. The same dichotomy extends to the structural adjustments increasingly required by international lending institutions as a condition of further loans to developing countries, frequently configured as destructive to national sovereignty and natural resources. Analysis of specific instances of such conditionality by the World Wildlife Fund in Mexico, the Ivory Coast, and Thailand, however, shows that structural adjustment programs have on balance benefitted the environment, with the caveat that "whether the consequences for the environment are good or bad seems to depend a great deal on the particular provisions of the loan agreement and on the individual circumstances of a country or even a region within a country."[3] The removal of agricultural subsidies, for example, which is typically a feature of conditionality, can be shown to have been an important factor in slowing deforestation and subsequent degradation of topsoil on the forest floor by erosion in Brazil, which encouraged cattle ranchers to clear the rain forest by offering financial incentives that covered nearly 75 percent of the cost of developing a property. In other instances, such as in Indonesia, direct cause-and-effect relationships have been established between deforestation and debt service, indicating the difficulty with drawing superficial conclusions when dealing with complex socioeconomic environmental issues.

Cognizant of the heavy responsibility implicit in conditionality, as well as the adverse public opinion arising out of the funding of environmentally damaging capital projects of little real social value in the past, and charges of causing "debt slavery," international lending institutions have really been a primary driving force behind sustainability. In an initiative referred to internally as the "greening of the bank," The World Bank, for example, has instituted a department of environmentally sustainable development (ESD), and at the first conference on the subject held at the Bank in the fall of 1993, Sven Sandstrom made it clear that environmental assessment was then and would continue to be integral to "the preparation and the implementation of all the projects that we finance."[4] He also said that "lending for environmental purposes is the fastest growing segment in our portfolio, amounting to some $2 billion during our 1993 fiscal year…environmentally sustainable development is being mainstreamed."[5]

The World Bank has provided considerable leadership in establishing new techniques in environmental economics, which has grown especially rapidly between 1990 and 1995. The changes that have taken place in this forced marriage between development and the environment, pronounced as an inherent part of sustainability at the Rio Conference, are best appreciated in contrast to conventional economic theory, based on a model involving the producers of goods and services on the one hand (the firms) and the purchasers of this output on the other (the households), who interact in a market. In this idealized cycle of production and consumption, or closed economy, interaction is unfettered and self-interest rules supreme, guided by the desire to consume and to make a profit from the commodities that are consumed. Prices are set by striking a balance between these two desires. Further refinements, such as deductions from the cycle by the households for savings, and a comparable withdrawal by the firms for investment, up through the Keynesian insight that interest represents the return for forfeiting liquidity on both sides, are all secondary to this basic cycle, which optimizes the distribution of resources and is considered to be most efficient when "the benefits of participating in the market exceed their costs by the maximum possible amount."

VALUES BEYOND VALUE

The difficulty with considering environmental factors as part of this neoclassical cyclical model, which is a prima facie requirement of sustainability, is that they have typically been considered valueless at worst, or beyond price at best—common property for which there should be no charge.

Environmentalists have considered the entire exercise of attempting to attach economic value to characteristics of the natural world nothing less than sacrilege. Economists, who look at this world as capital stock with a potential for productivity as a benefit to human welfare, are essentially inimical to them. Environmentalists are subjective and normative, both seeing and describing the world as they think it should be. Economists are relative and dimensionless. Time and place are irrelevant to them. The dynamic ecological system, full of imagery for the environmentalist, is simply a source of tabulated data for the economist, a matrix that is populated or unpopulated, an algorithmic function. Because architects also deal with imagery, time, and place, and tend to be more empirical than rational, with notable exceptions, the concept that a beautiful forest is simply a resource to be produced into either timber or cropland is equally antithetical to them, as is the basis for the idea of sustainability, which derives from such views.

Environmental economists attempt to resolve this basic conflict to defuse the tension between these two opposing views. Ecology, they note, is very similar to neoclassical economic theory because both deal with the processing of energy and matter in the most efficient way and "as with communities of living organisms, the fraction of each year's mass energy intake that is actually embodied in the growth increment as new biomass, is typically very small compared to the fraction that is used for metabolic activities."[7]

VALUATION

The age-old dilemma, of how to put a price on something that we know to be beyond a price, is the most critical task faced by environmental economists today and is yielding slowly to a barrage of concentrated research. Similar in many ways to the problem of fixing costs to the human misery caused by crime, which economists view as dichotomous choices that can be affected by punishment, environmental problems have thus far proved to be impervious to the cost-benefit analysis methods that have attached values of $2.4 million for a human life, $60,000 for a rape victim, and $20,000 for a life disrupted by robbery, at 1993 rates. Value as a part of sustainability has been identified as instrumental in its capacity to satisfy want or intrinsic, with inherent characteristics that make something precious. Instrumental value has been further subdivided into direct, indirect, option, and quasi-option value, which are all related to use. Direct value is a function of production, indirect value corresponds to ecological processes, option values relate to willingness to pay, and quasi-option values are those that derive after the choice to develop, or not to develop has been made.[8]

Of all these, the assessment of option values, bound up in the concept of willingness to pay, has been one of the easiest to establish, since it involves dichotomous choice. In several developing countries in Africa, for example, people have been given a choice between having water delivered to their houses by vendors, of collecting it at a central location in the village, or collecting it at a well, with the choices decreasing in cost, from most to least expensive. People were essentially being asked how much convenience and their time spent in collecting water was worth to them with results typically showing that it is worth a great deal.

Partha Dasgupta, following the work of Tjalling Koopmans on optional economic growth, has warned against expecting decisive ethical judgments when dealing with such difficult environmental questions as resource use, since various scenarios can be constructed which make each claim seem to have equal validity. Dasgupta has noted that the discount rates used in social cost-benefit analysis are "consumption discount rates," similar to income discount rates. These are frequently confused with "social discount rates," which are percentage rates of change of relative shadow prices, dependent upon a *numeraire* that has been adopted. Following Koopmans, Dasgupta argues that consumption rates of discount, which are essential in cost-benefit analysis, are derived and do not reflect primary value judgments. Rather than using a constant discount rate in evaluating critical environmental issues, such as global warming, for example, which when relentlessly applied indicates negligible change, Dasgupta argues for the use of negative, rather than positive, consumption rates of interest (where sigma is set to 0) to amplify real dangers in current simulation models.

SYSTEM OF NATIONAL ACCOUNTS

The starting point for environmental economists has been the system of national accounts (SNA), established by the United Nations in 1968 as a comprehensive means of recording the economic "flows and stocks" of each nation. Although this record includes such categories as agriculture, mining, fishing, forestry, and transportation, natural resources are not specifically covered and can only be partially extrapolated from the cost of land as a part of gross capital formation. At the Conference for European Statisticians, held 5 years after the system of national accounts was established, it was determined that sufficient information did not then exist to develop a system of environmental statistics that would complement the SNA.[9] Work on environmental statistics at the United Nations continued through the 1980s with the holy grail there as elsewhere continuing to be the search for an appropriate common *numeraire,* such as the monetary unit used in the system of national accounting, which could be used to aggregate economic values. While that search, equivalent to finding a single cure for cancer or AIDS, goes on, however, there is a growing realization that finding a single aggregate probably is not possible. As Ismail Serageldin, the vice president of the Department of Environmentally Sustainable Development at The World Bank, has said, "What we have now is inadequate and whatever we do, no single number will be sufficient. We may have to look at wealth accounting as well as income accounting. We may have to look at physical accounting as Karl Goran Maler and others have advocated, stock and flow analysis as well, but we surely cannot capture everything and boil it down to a single number no matter which methodology will be adopted and it would be a mistake to try to do so."[10] The total initial expenditure for natural resources that are traded commercially, such as timber, are counted as capital formation in the SNA, and further changes are not recorded there but are dealt with in "reconciliation accounts." Some feel these changes may be useful as one measure of environmental degradation. In 1986, a system of environmental satellite accounts was developed in France to augment the SNA to measure environmental outlays, reflecting the inability of the SNA to do so. All this activity is indicative of what Peter Bartelmus has described as "a new interest in accounting for selected resources in physical accounts and has also revitalized attempts to assign monetary values to the stocks and flows of these accounts."[11] This is the search for an environmentally adjusted national income account.

GROSS NATIONAL PRODUCT AND A GREEN EQUIVALENT

Government and institutional policy in the past has been closely geared to gross national product, which measures annual aggregate value of a national economy. Depreciation of this stock of capital, deducted from the gross national product, yields net national product, but both of these well-known indicators fail to reflect environmental degradation. The financial gain realized in exchange for goods or services that is the basis for the aggregation of the gross national product may have been partially realized by cutting down a first-growth forest or draining a wetland to build condominiums, but such damage to the environment will register a positive gain in the GNP, as timber sold and houses built. Much research is now being concentrated on the problem of how to adjust the GNP to reveal such degradation. Based on the economic principle that beneficial income is that which leaves capital untouched, environmental economists define sustainable income as "that flow of income that leaves the capital stock of the economy intact," and that is certainly not the case with GNP, which measures the exhaustion of national assets. Various proposals have been put forward for an "environmental impact coefficient" (EIC) or a "green net national product" (GNNP) that would redress this imbalance; this task is very critical because national and international development policy is predicated on existing methods of measurement, but no alternative method has gained wide acceptance.[12]

MULTICRITERIA ANALYSIS

Because of the difficulty of expressing costs and benefits in monetary measurement in many of the issues related to the environment, a nonmonetary method called *multicriteria analysis* has been developed. The goal of this method is to rank attributes according to their importance and to eliminate those which are marginal. Using an X-Y-Z axis, with social, economic, and environmental attributes assigned to each of the three legs of the graph, a determination is first made about the position of existing conditions on the graph, with the location being an admittedly subjective decision. Options representing the fullest extent of each leg on the graph are then plotted. The final evaluation representing a win-win situation is then determined, typically falling roughly halfway between the existing and optimal triangles on the graph.

WATCH POINTS FOR ARCHITECTS

As all these investigations continue, architects need not feel like irrelevant bystanders, waiting in the wings for the results before being able to implement them in their work. The information that is available, particularly related to the resources which make up the architect's primary palette of building materials, is definitive enough. A review of any of the major sources, such as the *World Resources Guide* produced annually by the World Resources Institute, shows that global consumption of primary metals and minerals, such as iron ore, copper ore, tin ore, zinc ore, bauxite for aluminum, lead ore, nickel ore, manganese, and phosphate, has increased by more than 120 percent between 1960 and 1990, with half of that increase taking place at the beginning of that 30-year period. The majority of this increase took place in middle- and low-income countries, and consumption in the postindustrial North began to decrease significantly after 1970. (Figs. 4.1 and

Figure 4.1
The Energy Resource Center in Los Angeles is a 44,572 ft² facility that
showcases leading edge energy-efficient and environmental technologies in its
design and construction and exhibits in its halls. It is a national clearinghouse
for information on energy conservation and environmental technology. This
former gas company building was first dismantled and then replaced with
materials that were either recycled or reused in some way including asphalt,
concrete, metal, glass, wood, brick, and porcelain plumbing fixtures. Among
the recycled materials used are steel from a melted-down retired Navy attack
submarine; used in the frame are weapons confiscated by the Los Angeles
Sheriff's Department, which were also melted down to be used as reinforcing
bars. All suppliers were required to use recycled, toxinfree materials and
equipment. Photo courtesy of the Gas Company.

**Figure 4.2
The Energy Resource
Center, Los Angeles.
Photo courtesy of the
Gas Company.**

4.2) The most marked increase in that 30-year period took place in low-income countries, in which consumption doubled, from 7 to 14 percent, and the gradual reduction of such use in the North. An overview of much of the new architecture that has been built in this same sector, as a result of expansionist policies and the desire to modernize, indicates a regeneration of the international-style anonymity that took place in the developed world soon after World War II, with steel, glass, and concrete predominating. Although it would be hypocritical to criticize this second energy-intensive wave of building and the kinds of materials used in it on the grounds that we now realize that the resources that supply such materials both are energy-intensive to process, frequently resulting in pollution when manufactured, and are increasingly in short supply, it does put a burden on all architects in all parts of the world to reclaim the leadership role that they have lost, or abdicated, especially in advocating a more sensible approach toward material use.

For architects in the North, that will require restraint both in work at home and in their increasing involvement in international practice as prime practitioners, or consultants, where they are still looked to for advice on general national direction. Recommending a return to more sustainable, historical, and cultural precedents using indigenous, natural materials and traditional methods that may be updated to conform to contemporary practice, or the reusing or recycling of materials, will invariably invite a critical or negative response and holds the risk of losing an important commission. For the architects in the developing countries, such attitudes will almost certainly result in charges of being retrogressive, romantic, unrealistic, and against national progress. Knowing the numbers of resource depletion, chapter and verse, as well as the consequences of such depletion for future generations, and refuting such arguments is an important weapon in changing patterns that now lead to environmental degradation.

Reading as much literature in this area as possible and keeping track of progress being made toward a green index as part of the gross national product, particularly as it relates to resources, is one way to increase such knowledge, which architects today can ill afford to do without. This should extend to such critical techniques as life-cycle costing, which is proving to be a much more accurate measure of the relative financial burden of resource processing into building materials.

Life-cycle costing is an internationally recognized method of examining the total environmental burden associated with a product and its use. It is the only legitimate way of determining actual environmental cost, or burden, and the most credible means by which "green" product claims can be validated. Life-cycle inventory (LCI) provides a quantitative assessment of environmental inputs and outputs associated with a product, beginning with extraction of the resource and continuing through manufacturing, distribution, use, and disposal. Quantified inputs include raw material resources as well as energy consumed in the form of fossil fuels and electricity to process them. Outputs include air and water emissions such as carbon dioxide, carbon monoxide, nitrogen oxides, hydrocarbons, suspended solids, hazardous chemicals, and solid wastes generated from production as well as the cost of disposal.

Dr. Ian Boustead, a British physicist, pioneered the science of life-cycle assessment in his work at the Open University in Sussex, England, in the early 1970s. His life-cycle methods, involving extensive data review, onsite inspection, record auditing, and complex computer calculations, have evolved over the past 20 years into a comprehensive assessment system. The British life cycle methods are widely used throughout Europe, where life-cycle inventories are beginning to provide a basis for decisions and regulations related to building materials selection.

Life-cycle modeling is a relatively new endeavor in the United States but is rapidly gaining acceptance as a reliable method of determining true cost. Late in 1992, in an effort to establish common criteria for life-cycle scientists and practitioners, the Environmental Protection Agency drafted guidelines for life-cycle methodology for the United States, which have yet to be widely accepted.

A review of the most frequently used materials and the energy required to produce them will help to clarify the sustainable mindset in this regard, which considers cradle-to-grave costs and environmental impacts in judging the appropriateness of any construction process.

THE RELATIONSHIP BETWEEN SUSTAINABILITY AND BUILDING MATERIALS

The materials favored by advocates of sustainability are natural and renewable. Without covering the energy required to produce all materials available, the following brief overview of a selected palette will give some idea of the hidden labor and embodied energy required to produce some of the preferred materials most architects use today. In spite of knowledgeability, architects must reacquaint themselves with these hidden energy requirements.

ALUMINUM

Aluminum has come to symbolize the essence of the idea of progress in architecture due to its promotion by such pioneers of the modern movement as Otto Wagner, Albert Frei, and Buckminster Fuller. In Wagner's work alone, aluminum bolts connecting thin marble sheets to buildings such as the church on Steinhof and the post office in Vienna were intended to represent a new, honest approach to materials, as embodied in his transitional lecture *On Modern Architecture*. The futuristic, freestanding aluminum heating elements, far advanced even by current standards,

Figure 5.1
Clay crusher used in the
manufacture of clay tile
block. Photo by James
Steele.

continue this honesty in the interior hall of the post office, in which the roof is sheathed in a veil of glass.

Upon closer inspection, however, aluminum production may now be seen to represent one of the most extreme forms of resource abuse. Made from bauxite ore, aluminum is the product of a finite commodity, calculated as a world reserve of little more than 24.0 billion metric tons. The majority of this resource, other than the 4.44 billion metric tons found in Australia, is located in the developing world, primarily in Guinea (5.6 billion metric tons), Jamaica (2.0 billion metric tons), India (1.0 billion metric tons), and Brazil (2.8 billion metric tons). Bauxite is extracted primarily by strip mining, which scars the landscape and creates general environmental disruption. On the north shore of Jamaica, for example, at the opposite side of the island from the majority of the tourist resorts, bauxite mining has deforested much of the slope above the sea. After mining, the bauxite ore is crushed, mixed with caustic soda, and kiln dried at temperatures up to 2000°F, which, obviously, requires additional energy depletion. This process yields aluminum oxide, or "alumina," which can then be fabricated into metal, the ratio being 6 lb of bauxite to produce 2 lb of alumina, or 1 lb of aluminum, all requiring approximately 85,000 to 103,500 BTUs per pound.

The Hall-Heroult electrolytic reduction process, which is the main way of manufacturing the metal, takes place in a smelter, where alumina powder is dissolved in long narrow carbon-lined vats containing molten cryolite, or sodium-aluminum fluoride. An anode lowered into the bath transfers up to 250,000 A of electricity through it, separating the alumina molecules into aluminum, which falls to the bottom of the vat, and oxygen. The aluminum is periodically drawn out of the vats during the process, which never stops. After processing, the aluminum is fabricated through various techniques, including casting, extrusion, and rolling, and may be painted or anodized.

As opposed to the highly energy intensive smelting process, involving an electrolytic interaction reaching temperatures up to 3000°F, an 80 percent reduction can be realized by recycling, where the metal is melted at much lower heat. Recovery of scrap aluminum has now reached about 30 percent of the total supply in the United States due to aggressive campaigns initiated in the western part of the country, but there has yet to be an efficient system devised for recycling material from demolished buildings, and estimates are that less than 20 percent of all available scrap aluminum is retrieved from this source. Even recycling, however, is not without problems, since impurities typically created by various castings rise to the top when the metal is remelted, and this waste, which is substantial, must be disposed of.

In general, then, aluminum is one of the most easily assessed materials of the industrial age in terms of its considerable environmental effects. The sources and amount of its ore and trade dependency of the limited number of predominantly poor countries in which it is located are precisely known, as are the detrimental effects of extracting it. The extensive amount of energy needed to process it, as well as the substantial amount of toxic wastes produced are also known, as is the extensive requirement for fresh water, which is another resource acknowledged by many to be under severe and growing stress. Although one of the best performers in the recycling mode, aluminum is not problemfree in this phase either. The United States, Japan, the countries of the former Soviet Union, and Germany, respectively, have been the largest annual consumers of aluminum products.

CONCRETE

Concrete consists of hydrated Portland cement, water, sand, and gravel or crushed rock called "aggregate" and sometimes contains admixtures used to increase workability. Cement, which makes up to 10 to 20 percent of this mixture, is the most energy-intensive component to produce. It is manufactured by heating limestone with clay. The materials are fed into a long sloping rotary kiln, which has progressively hotter zones, eventually reaching 2700°F (1480°C). As it rotates, the kiln slowly mixes the contents moving through it, generating the necessary chemical reaction, through hydration. Although water was once added, most new kilns use a dry process. One result of the reaction that occurs is the calcinating of the limestone (calcium carbonate) into lime (calcium oxide). This takes place in the cooler portion of the kiln, where temperatures average 1650°F (900°C), creating carbon dioxide (CO_2) as a result. The second reaction is the bonding of calcium oxide and silicates to form dicalcium and tricalcium silicates. Small amounts of tricalcium aluminate and tetracalcium alumina ferrite are also produced. The high temperatures in the kiln convert all ingredients into a molten state. When they cool, they solidify into pellets called clinkers. This is subsequently ground with a small amount of gypsum, and the resulting powder is bagged. Nearly 3500 lb of limestone and clay, or shale, are required to produce 1 ton of finished cement. (Fig. 5.2) Including the direct fuel consumption required for the mining and transporting of the raw materials used in cement production, it is estimated that nearly 6 million BTUs are required per ton. (See Tables 5.1 and 5.2.) A great deal of CO_2, as well as nitrous oxide, sulphur, and other pollutants, are

Figure 5.2
Cyprus Parliament by Panos Koulermos. A concrete structure with central courtyards and roof fin windcatches.

Table 5.1

U.S. LABOR AND ENERGY SURVEY — SUMMARY REPORT

All Plants

Industry

Clinker production: 53,632,536 tons
Finish cement production: 58,025,257 tons
Shipments of cement: 58,810,841 tons
Annual practical clinker capacity: 62,011,568 tons
Capacity utilization rate: 86.5%

Labor

	Number of Employees	Employee Hours	Tons per Employee Hours
Raw material handling	1,275	2,536,916	21.40
Production	2,841	5,906,055	9.19
Distribution	984	2,002,198	27.12
Maintenance	3,734	7,753,518	7.00
Total direct labor	8,834	18,198,687	2.98
Overhead labor	2,147	4,411,447	12.31
Total labor	10,981	22,610,134	2.40
Hourly labor	8,209	16,934,254	3.21
Salaried labor	2,338	4,756,356	11.41
Contract labor	434	915,824	59.28

Energy

Fuel Type	Quantity	BTUs (billions)	BTUs per Ton
Coal (tons)	6,261,911	146,274.72	2,709,596.28
Gasoline (gallons)	1,242,086	154.97	2,870.59
LPG (gallons)	265,236	25.11	465.13
Middle distillates (gallons)	15,746,017	2,176.30	40,313.89
Natural gas (gallons)	29,493	30,316.50	561,583.54
Petroleum coke (tons)	1,181,976	34,056.51	630,863.63
Residual oil (gallons)	4,266,159	640.97	11,873.35
Wastes		20,068.87	371,756.13
Total fossil fuel		233,713.94	4,329,322.58
Electricity (1000 KWH)	7,493,901	25,569.19	473,644.26
Total BTUs		259,283.14	4,802,966.85

From November 1993, by Market and Economic Research Department, Portland Cement Association.

Sustainable Architecture

Table 5.2

ENERGY CONSUMED IN CONCRETE PRODUCTION*

	Weight	Materials	Hauling	Concrete	Percent
Cement	12%	5,792,000	504,000	1,574,000	94.0
Sand	34%	5,000	37,000	29,000	1.7
Crushed stone	48%	46,670	53,000	100,000	5.9
Water	6%	0	0	0	0.0
Concrete	100%	6,400,000			100

Fuel Use for Cement Production

Fuel	Thousands BTUs per Ton of Cement	Percent
Petroleum product	63	1.1
Natural gas	476	8.2
Coal and coke	3524	60.8
Waste fuel (recycled motor oil, scrap tires, etc.)	286	4.9
Electricity (including primary energy to generate)	1443	24.9
Total	5792	100

*BTUs of a typical batch, assuming concrete hauled 50 miles to ready mix plant. Aggregate hauled 10 miles, concrete hauled 5 miles to building site. Concrete mix 500 lbs. cement, 1,400 sand, 2,000 lbs. crushed stone, 260 lbs. water per yard.

Source: Environmental Building News, March/April 1993, p. 8.

generated by the coal used to heat the kiln. Nearly 250 kg of coal, or 187 m³ of natural gas are burned for each ton of cement produced. (Fig. 5.3)

The amount of CO_2 produced, both in the chemical reaction in the kiln itself and from the burning of coal to fuel it, is not insignificant. According to the World Resources Institute, which has monitored these emissions, 9.8 million metric tons of CO_2 were generated from the production of 76 million metric tons of finished concrete in the United States. It is important to understand, then, that there are two sources of carbon dioxide emission during cement production: those from the fossil fuels used to fire the kiln and those from the chemical process of calcinating the lime.

Alex Wilson, writing in the *Environmental Building News*, has put the question of carbon dioxide and energy production in the concrete industry in clearer perspective, especially as it relates to the United States, by calculating that the United States used 0.5 quadrillion BTUs in 1992 to produce 80 million tons of cement, which is "roughly .6% of total U.S. energy use, a remarkable amount given the fact that in dollar value, cement represents only about .06% of the gross national product. Thus, cement production is approximately ten times as energy intensive as our economy in general. In some Third World countries, cement production accounts for as much as two thirds of total energy use."[1]

Industry literature generally acknowledges this aspect of the product, as well as the fact that little can be done to improve carbon dioxide release. To offset this, industry spokespeople point to singular advantages such as high thermal mass, low maintenance and life-cycle costs, low emissivity, fire resistance, and speed of construction. As bad as the figures are related to energy consumption and carbon dioxide release, the arguement is, they are 60 times less than those required for steel, and the advantages of the material alone should be enough for it to be considered "green." Because of the various construction methods used, such as in-situ placement, precasting and concrete masonry units, as well as the variety of structural systems available, precise life-cycle costing has been difficult to achieve, however, and the issue of thermal mass has also been contested, most eloquently by the late Egyptian architect Hassan Fathy, who was a staunch advocate of mud brick construction. His extensive criticism of the poor performance of the material in the Nubian relocation program carried out in Egypt in the late 1960s as a result of the construction of the Aswan High

Figure 5.3
Cyprus Parliament by
Panos Koulermos.

Dam related primarily to comparisons with the superior climatic performances of the mud brick houses the refugees had left behind. Citing a number of infant deaths from overheating in the new concrete houses provided for relocated families by the Egyptian government, Fathy condemned the planners' choice of material as inappropriate for the context involved because it cannot "breathe" and required the use of expensive imported ingredients when a free, time-proven alternative was literally available under foot. Although his condemnation must be considered in the light of his own nationalistic and personal agenda, it should also be objectively judged along side the myopic tendency of architects, who, in the tradition of Le Corbusier at Chandigarah, Oscar Neimeyer in Brasilia, and Louis Kahn in Bangladesh, specify a material simply because its malleability accentuates creativity and it is symbolic of Western progress, without considering economic or microclimatic impact. Claims of universal applicability for this material are as unspecified as the international style with which it is historically associated and must now be adapted to changing conditions, as regional interaction increases.

Several interesting developments indicate that this adaptation is beginning to occur. One of the most significant of these is the substitution of fly ash in the mix for either the silica or sand portion, or for a part of the cement itself, which replaces the amount of solid waste in production and cuts down on the energy required. Naturally existing sand, such as beach sand, is typically unacceptable as an aggregate for concrete. The sand that is used must be mined, graded, screened, and washed prior to use. The fly ash is the residue from the coal used to fire the kilns, a suitable recycled replacement that requires little prior preparation before reuse. In addition to use as a substitute for sand, fly ash can also replace between 15 to 35 percent of the cement itself, and experiments with this new mix, called *autoclaved cellular concrete,* are now being explored in conjunction with precasting methods throughout Europe. Fly ash reacts with the free lime left after the chemical reaction of hydration to form calcium silicates similar to those formed during cement curing. A technical journal has elaborated on its virtues by describing that "fly ash increases concrete strength, improves sulfate resistance, decreases permeability, reduces the water ratio required and increases the pumpability and workability of the concrete." This additional savings in water use at a time when future supplies of this essential commodity are causing increasing concern make this alternative especially attractive, as does its lightness, which means that foundations can be more modestly sized and less intrusive.

Another initiative, also just beginning in the United States as of this writing, but more advanced in Europe, has been the recycling and reuse of waste concrete with metal used for reinforcing separated from rubble, which is then used as aggregate.

PLYWOOD

Plywood is composed of several thin layers of wood, *veneers,* bonded together by an adhesive. Each layer is placed at right angles to that of the adjacent layer, which is called cross-lamination. This gives plywood strength along and across its grain. Cross-lamination permits thin, lightweight panels to be substituted for boards that are twice as thick and gives plywood panels dimensional stability.

Plywood is made up of an odd number of layers. A layer may consist of one veneer or two or more, laminated parallel to each other. In its usual form, plywood has three-ply panel face and back veneers glued to each side of core veneer; the grain of the core is laid at right angles to that of the outer plies. To produce thicker panels, the thickness of veneers can be increased to a limited degree, or additional plies and layers may be added. By regulating veneer thickness and the number of plies, plywood panels of almost any thickness can be manufactured. However, three-ply, four-ply, five-ply and six-ply panels are most commonly produced in thicknesses ranging from ¼ to ¾ in.

Logs received at the plywood plant are either stored in water or stacked. Soaking in hot water softens the wood fibers, making it easy to strip them into veneers. They are then transported to either a pond saw or deck saw, where they are debarked and cut into lengths that fit the plant processing equipment. Lengths of 8 to 10 ft are most common. The cut sections of logs are now referred to as *blocks*. Removal of the bark is an important step in log preparation. This prevents damage to the lathe knife by rocks or other matter imbedded in the bark and is usually performed before a log is cut into blocks. Debarking occurs when a log is pushed through an enclosure that contains a power driven ring of knives. These adjust to various diameters and scrape away the bark as the log passes through.

The block-conditioning process is usually performed after debarking. The blocks are placed in large concrete vaults usually located between the log storage area and the lathe operation. These are closed so that steam penetrates the wood at a controlled temperature for a long period. The time and temperature requirements for softening the wood fibers varies according to wood species and desired depth of heat penetration. When properly performed, this process results in smoother veneers, with less checking or fracturing of wood fibers.

The most common method of producing veneers is by rotary cutting on a massive lathe. Rotary lathes are equipped with chucks attached to spindles. These spin large blocks against a knife which is bolted to a movable carriage.

From the debarking and wood-softening process, blocks are moved to the lathe charger. These machines rapidly position individual blocks to receive the lathe chucks. Many chargers now use computerized scanners that determine the maximum diameter of solid wood cylinder in a block. The block ends are then automatically adjusted so that the block will be chucked to yield the maximum volume of usable veneer.

Once in place, the chucks revolve the block against the knife, and the process of *peeling* begins. To maintain a constant veneer thickness as the block diameter decreases, a gear from the main drive feeds the knife carriage toward the center of the block at a set rate. Recently, electric digital drives and hydraulic digital drives have replaced the gear box and feed screw method of regulating the knife carriage.

The veneer emerges between the cutting edge of the knife and an adjustable pressure bar called a *roller bar.* The veneer length is regulated by small scoring knives which are forced into the block ahead of the cutting knife.

The function of the pressure bar is to prevent the wood from tearing or spreading due to the cutting action of the knife. The best veneer is produced when substantial pressure is exerted on the pressure bar. Insufficient pressure results in lower-quality veneer that is extremely rough and severely checked.

Accurate alignment of the pressure bar in relation to the knife edge and proper knife angle, or pitch, are important for a good peel. The pitch of the knife, as determined by the angle which the bevel of the knife makes with a perpendicular line through its cutting edge, must be initially set to suit the particular species and thickness of veneer to be cut. In addition, the pitch will vary according to the diameter of the block being peeled. Most lathes are equipped with inclined pitchways that slope downward toward the block and automatically make this latter adjustment.

At first contact with the lathe knife, the veneer produced is not whole or full length, since blocks are never absolutely round. It is necessary to *round up* the block before full veneer begins. Usable pieces of round-up veneer, at least 50-in long, are salvaged and used for plywood core or cross-band stock. Once the block is rounded up, the veneer unrolls in a continuous sheet. The highest-grade veneer comes from the early cutting, for as the block diameter is reduced, knots become more frequent and larger in size. Various thicknesses of veneer are produced according to the type and grade of plywood desired, ranging from $\frac{1}{16}$ to $\frac{5}{16}$ in.

The drying of veneer is necessary to reduce the moisture content of the stock to a predetermined percentage and to produce flat and pliable veneer. Modern veneer dryers carry the stock through the dryer between a series of rolls. Numerous pairs of rolls positioned at close intervals are enclosed in a shell of sheet metal which is divided into sections, each containing a door. These sections often range from 5 to 7 ft in length.

The shell also contains fans, ducts, and baffles for circulating and directing heat to the various lines. The heat for drying is supplied either by steam lines piped into the dryer or by the combustion of fuel such as natural gas, wood waste, or propane in a chamber inside the dryer. The combustion reaches temperatures up to and exceeding 5000°F, but the most common maximum temperature seldom exceeds 4000°F.

As water is given up by the heated veneer, it is converted into steam, which, when mixed with air, makes an excellent drying medium. The amount of moisture in the dryer is controlled by dampers in venting stacks which allow excess steam to escape. Moist air inside the dryer is essential to uniform drying as this keeps the surface pores of the wood open and allows the veneer to dry more evenly.

Fans keep the air-steam mixture in constant circulation. The flow may be longitudinal or cross-circulating. Cross-circulating dryers have fans in each section along one side of the dryer. The "jet" circulating dryer has gained wide acceptance in the industry. The jet dryer has numerous tubes, closed at one end, located above and below each drying line. Each tube has a narrow slit or slits along the length facing the nearest line. The hot, moist air is forced into the tubes by the fans and then pressured through the slits and onto the veneer.

Dryer temperature and speed of travel through the drying chamber can be controlled by the operator to regulate the amount of moisture to be removed and the final remaining moisture content desired. Veneer thickness, heartwood or sapwood, and wood species all play an important part in determining this amount. Feeding veneer into the dryer is usually performed manually in conjunction with automatic feeding equipment. However, fully automatic dryer-feeders, utilizing suction lifts are used in some mills.

After leaving the dryer, the veneer travels through a cooling chamber and is then discharged onto a table or a belted conveyor called a *dry chain*. In most mills, outfeed conveyors receive the veneer as it leaves the dryer and carry it first through an electronic *moisture detector*. This machine is set to detect any part of the veneer that contains more than a given percentage of moisture. If the electronic field is disturbed, a colored dye is sprayed on the sheet. The marked veneer is accumulated separately to be taken back to the dryer for redrying or stacked for a period to permit the remaining moisture in the wood to equalize.

Dry veneer must be manually graded and stacked according to width and grade. Veneer graders must be able to readily gauge the size of defects, the number of defects, and the grain characteristics of the various veneer pieces. Grades such as "B," "C," and "0" allow defects of specified size and, in some instances, of specified number.

Several basic substances are used as adhesives in plywood manufacture. The most common are blood, soybean, and phenolic resins. Other adhesives such as urea and resorcinot are used to a lesser degree for edge gluing, panel patching, and scarfing. *Soybean glue* is a protein type made from soybean meal. This glue is usually blended with blood and used in both cold pressing and hot pressing. *Blood glue* is another protein type made from animal blood collected at slaughter houses. The blood is spray dried and supplied to the plywood plant in powder form. Blood and blood-soy blends may be cold pressed or hot pressed. Protein glues are not waterproof and therefore are used only in the production of interior use plywood. *Phenolic resin* is synthetically produced from phenol and formaldehyde. It hardens, or cures, under heat so must necessarily be hot pressed. When curing, phenolic resin goes through a chemical change which makes it waterproof and resistant to attack by microorganisms. For these reasons, it is used for the production of plywood that may be subjected to permanent exterior exposure. Phenolic resin is also used in the production of interior plywood. Resin syrup contains a certain percentage of resin solids. After mixing with water and other ingredients, the resin solids in the finished glue mix are generally reduced to a safe level for exterior use plywood. *Extended resin* is a phenolic resin mix which has been extended out to reduce the resin solids content below the safe level for exterior application and therefore is classified for interior use plywood only. These basic glue substances are mixed with other chemicals to the exact proportions listed on a formula sheet supplied by the adhesive manufacturer. Deviations from the formula or mistakes in mixing can produce expensive waste or poorly bonded panels.

Assembly of veneers into plywood panels takes place immediately after adhesive application. The techniques for applying adhesive vary, but the most common application is at a precision machine called a *glue spreader*. This machine has two large steel rolls, usually covered with rubber, into which grooves have been cut. The grooves are engraved uniformly around the roll to a prescribed depth. The rolls are positioned to rotate in troughs which contain an adhesive. The adhesive clings to the rolls; in order to remove the excess, additional steel rolls are used. The rolls are adjustable and are set a distance corresponding to the amount of glue film desired.

Semiautomatic layup lines for gluing panels have replaced manual gluing in recent years. In most of these systems, adhesive application is accomplished by either spraying or curtain coating. In all cases, veneers to construct the panels are transported by conveyor belts under the adhesive applicators and then stacked, usually manually.

Spray layup lines may have from one to seven separate spraying stations, each enclosed to accumulate overspray. Adhesive, under pressure, is supplied to the spray heads and is dispersed onto the veneer sheets in the form of globules which generally spread out under pressure to fill the surrounding areas. Some spray systems are designed to fan the pattern the length of the veneer sheets, but most are operated to cover the 4-ft width.

Curtain coater layup lines have one machine per line. These are usually positioned to cover the 8-ft length of veneer. The machine is composed of an enclosed reservoir to hold glue and a pair of stainless steel knives located beneath the reservoir. When the knives are slightly open, the glue drops through the opening as a continuous film or curtain. As veneer is transported under the curtain, it is completely coated with adhesive. The knife opening determines the velocity of the glue film. Glue spread rates are governed by the speed of the conveyor system and the speed at which the pump can supply adhesive to the reservoir. Certain factors, such as gap opening, height of the reservoir head, pump speed, and line speed, will govern the quality and quantity of adhesive application.

A recent development in adhesive application is the *foam glue extruder*. The extruder layup line is similar to that of a spray line. The extruder head contains tubes spaced approximately ⅜-in apart with each tube having an opening approximately 0.150 in or slightly larger. The foamed glue, under pressure, is forced through the openings and onto the veneer in continuous beads. Following placement of the top sheet, the veneers that comprise a panel pass under a roll that applies sufficient pressure to flatten the beads so they uniformly cover the surfaces to be bonded.

Prior to hot pressing, most mills prepress loads when they are discharged from the gluing operation. This is performed in a cold press which is a stationary platform connected to hydraulic rams. A load of panels is transported into this press, and pressure is applied at a lower pressure than that used in the hot press. The load is held under pressure for several minutes to develop consolidation of the veneers, to allow the wet adhesive to "tack" the veneer together to permit easier, faster press loading, and to eliminate breaking and shifting of veneers when loading.

The hot press has numerous steam-heated plates with openings between them. The number of openings is an indication of the press capacity, with 20 to 30 opening presses being the most common sizes, although 40 and 50 opening presses are used. In general, one or two panels can be inserted into each opening depending on the thickness; however, in some cases, three thin panels can be handled.

In some mills, the panels are hand-fed directly into the hot press one opening at a time. In others, the panels are hand fed into a loading mechanism which automatically places all panels into the press simultaneously. Unloading is sometimes manual but often automatic.

When the press is fully loaded, hydraulic rams push the plates together exerting a pressure of 175 to 200 psi. The temperature of the plates is set between 2300°F and 3300°F, depending upon the type of adhesive to be cured, the thickness of the panels, and the number of panels per press opening. The length of time the panels are subjected to heat and pressure depends on the same factors. When the pressing cycle is complete, the panels are removed. In most mills, the press loads are then stacked and allowed to cure and cool.

Plywood, besides being produced in varying thicknesses, is also produced to varying widths and lengths. The most common size is 48 x 96 in, or 4 by 8 ft. To produce these panels, precision sawing equipment is necessary. Panels are first passed through the "skinner" saws, where both long edges are cut simultaneously. To accomplish this, a metal straight edge is used to guide panels in line with the saws—the long straight edge of the panels goes against this guide. Spring-loaded feed rolls hold the panel firmly in line and transfer it through the saws. A cut of ¾ to 1 in is usually taken off the panel straight edge.

Once the panels have been cut for width, they next pass through the trim saws, which remove the end edges and determine the length. Panels are fed through the trim saws by motorized chains with attached lugs.

Certain panel grades, mainly those classed as sheathing are sold and used in an unsanded or "rough" state. Therefore, after sawing, these panels require only grading and grade marking before loading for shipment.

Unsanded panels are usually graded at the sawing operation after coming from the trim saws and before stacking.

Many mills use automatic gradelines with two or more storage bins to aid in observing and separating panels. In the case of sheathing panels, the gradeline conveyor belts transfer single panels directly from the trim saws to the grader where they are automatically turned over so he or she may see both sides and the edges. After determining the grade quality of the panel, the grader activates a particular limit switch which, in turn, causes the moving panel to be dropped into the appropriate bin.

Many panel grades must be sanded to fulfill grading requirements. When panels require complete sanding, they are usually constructed $\frac{1}{16}$-in heavier in thickness to allow for removal of $\frac{1}{32}$ in from each side.

For many years, drum sanders were used most extensively in the plywood industry. These usually have eight drums, 48 to 60 in wide, double decked with four upper and four lower drums. In some cases, fewer drums are used or a machine may have only a single deck. Each drum is cylindrical, about 11 in in diameter, and covered with sandpaper. Each "stacked" pair of drums has a paper of particular grit or cutting capability. The first upper and lower drums on the infeed end are equipped with a more coarse paper than their counterparts on the outfeed end. Each set of drums must be aligned to remove a uniform portion of a panel's two surfaces. Metal feed rolls, located between drums, hold the panel in line and transfer it through the machine.

A more common type of sanding machine now in use is the wide belt sander. These machines come in various combinations of one, two, four, or six belts and operate on the same principle as a drum sander with regard to purpose and manner of transferring panels through the machine. On the drum sander, the sandpaper is securely fastened to each drum, whereas the wide belts are tension-held and driven by several drums. Machines equipped with one or two belts are usually used when only a minor amount of cutting is necessary, such as for resanding or touch sanding.

This laborious production process, along with the extensive amount of energy required and the various kinds of glues and chemicals used to bind the veneers, are not uppermost in the minds of the architects who specify this material, which is one of the most popular staples of American residential construction. This detailed description is intended to raise such awareness, to serve as a reminder that knowledge of *how* materials are made is just as important, or more so, than how they perform when considering sustainability. This detailed account, if extended across the entire palette of materials used by architects, would be most revealing.

STEEL

Unlike aluminum, which has other primary uses not directly related to construction, such as containers, the building industry is the largest customer for steel products, and iron ore, from which steel is produced, is found mostly in the developed world. Reserves, estimated at approximately 65 billion metric tons, are found as follows: 4.6 in Canada, 3.8 in the United States, 2.5 in South Africa, 1.6 in Sweden, and 10.2 in Australia. Otherwise, there is a significant portion of this total in the developing sector, with 6.5 billion tons in Brazil, 1.2 in Venezuela, 3.5 in China, and 3.3 in India. Steel is another relative newcomer to construction technology due to economical mass production made possible by the Bessemer process of blasting air through molten iron in a large furnace, perfected in 1896. The manufacture of steel has become one of the most important indicators of the economic prowess of an industrialized nation. The basic ingredients in steel production—iron ore, limestone, and coal—are each produced in complicated processes of their own, making this the most energy-intensive of all construction materials. To appreciate the degree of this use, it will be helpful to describe the process in brief sequential detail. Iron ore is extracted by either open pit or shaft mining, with open pit removal by power shovel and truck being the most prevalent method. There is a great deal of waste in this process, and the amount of material mined is more than five times greater than the ore actually retrieved. Pit mining also leads to erosion, toxic runoff, and dust, and a great deal of energy is consumed in the process. Coal, for the production of coke (which is coal from which most of the gases have been removed by heating), is of the bituminous variety, which, unlike anthracite, does not lend itself to strip mining. After being removed from the shaft, the coal is transported to a coking facility, where it is crushed, sieved, preheated, and then fed into a series of oxygenfree ovens, where it remains until all volatile gases are removed and recycled to heat the ovens. After the lengthy process is complete, the hot coke is transported by open rail car; it is quenched with water and dried before use in the blast furnace. Limestone, which is the third major ingredient in steel making, is also primarily quarried from open pit mines. After blasting, the rock is removed by bulldozer or power shovel and taken by truck for crushing and sizing.

In the most time-honored method of steel making, derived from the Bessemer process, which first made the material commercially viable and widely available at the end of the nineteenth century, the iron ore, limestone, and coke derived from these three mining and reductive processes are fed into a blast furnace. This furnace is a cylindrically shaped 10-story high steel tower lined with heat-resistant brick. Once the furnace is fired, it remains in production until the brick lining is spent.

These brief descriptions indicate the extensive energy consumption issues that architects must be aware of. These issues are now being addressed by the American Society for Testing Materials (ASTM) and the American Institute of Architects' Environmental Resources Guide.

THE CASE FOR CHANGE AND A SUSTAINABLE ARCHITECTURE

Since the much heralded, but in retrospect premature, pronouncements about the death of Modernism at the beginning of the 1970s, which coincided with the first oil crisis and the start of the ecological movement, the half-lives of subsequent movements seem to have diminished radically. Although exact dates are hard to determine, Modernism lasted from the final decade of the nineteenth century until the coup de grace administered by Robert Venturi in *Complexity and Contradiction in Architecture* in 1966, which took about 5 years to register in the public consciousness. Following as yet unexplained ties to changes in critical theory, Modernism's architectural successor lasted less than half that time, with the postmortem on Post-Modernism issued in the late 1980s by none other than Robert Venturi, who is frequently credited with also starting it. His article, "Plus, ça change, plus la même chose," is a scorchingly lucid indictment of what went wrong with a movement that began with several intentions that sound similar to those that are integral to sustainable architecture, among them the desire to be inclusive rather than exclusive, to utilize historical typologies, to relate to context, to seek community involvement.

Venturi's analysis in "Plus ça change" criticizes the self-indulgence that finally emerged in the movement, following a purer heroic phase with parallels to its predecessor. Those parallels, he claimed, also extended to the tendency of architects to want to speak only to other architects in their work, all claims of inclusivity to the contrary, leading them to finally abandon any pretext of appropriate relationship to context and historical typologies in a search for ever more arcane references. The result, Venturi charges, was pure pastiche and superficiality, with no connection to people's physical or psychological wants and needs, a parody of an initial ideology that stressed communication as much as its structuralist theoretical parallel did, even though it was understood from the start that the basis for that communication was ironic and somewhat flawed.

Following its 25-year run, Post-Modernism was replaced, or more accurately overlapped, by Deconstructivism, equally linked to critical theory in Post-Structuralism and equally hyped by the media as the style of the movement. Following observations by Jacques Derrida, Jacques Lacan, and Michel Foucault which attacked the written and, therefore, historical, basis of culture and knowledge, as opposed to the optimistic structuralist semantics of Ferdinand de Sassure, Deconstructionism disclaimed communicative priorities as well as the primacy of space, functionalistic concerns, contextual relationships, and historical references. Rather than finally falling into the category of architects talking to each other, as Post-Modernism eventually did, this movement became an isolated, introspective exercise of architects talking to themselves and not getting an answer, since the author had supposedly died with the possibility of any truth in the word. Architects literally began drawing with their eyes closed, the seismographic subconscious results deemed by them to be as valid as any rational exercise in design, the ultimate negation of personal, conscious thought; nominal comparison with Constructivism was also intentional, the ideology of a new social order replaced in this reincarnation with a nihilistic, self-destructive urge. Further permutation of that urge, named mirrored Suprematism, the weightless parallel to Constructivism, sought to deny the historical limitations of gravity itself, the architect's age-old enemy. The apologists for this movement, sensing a critical change in direction and the onset of media ennui, also began to jump ship less than a decade after the movement was christened, in this instance. Seventy-five years reduced to ten.

It would be an overstatement to suggest that the public now waits with bated breath for the next architectural movement of the moment to be launched, and the media, which was so bedazzled by the audacity and pyrotechnics of Deconstructivism, is reluctant to see it go. Denial that it has already gone is endemic in some quarters, since it has helped sell so many magazines and books, but the clues are unmistakable. Another, as yet unnamed, change has taken place in critical theory once again, and the critics, who usually have their noses in the wind, are now scrambling to identify its architectural equivalent, looking to mathematical folding theory, chaos, and the possibility of a jumping universe as possible paragons. The theory in this case, however, supported by philosophers such as Jurgen Habermaus and Edward Said, has little to do with abstract mathematical concepts or disorderly order and is based instead on a retreat from nihilism and a return to the structuralist belief in communication.

A significant difference in this new philosophical initiative, however, is the thought that although there is a belief that communication *can* work, that belief is tempered by the understanding that intractable social and cultural differences *do* exist, making this communication imperfect and difficult, at best. Trying to achieve it, however, is seen as our last, best hope in a rapidly fragmenting world. The paradox predicted by futurists at the end of the 1980s, of a global village increasingly connected by transport and electronic communication in which each of its members desperately struggles to retain individual identity in the face of the onset of a suffocating, homogenous culture, has now come to pass.

In a recent lecture given at the Royal Academy in London in July 1995, Japanese architect Arata Isozaki made the poignant and inspired observation that the history and traditions of his country are as intellectually distant from him as they are from those in the West, who claim to revere them so much. The image that many outsiders, who have not visited Japan, still have of that country no longer has a real counterpart there, since the Japanese have been dismantling the physical remnants of their past as rapidly as they can. One result of this ethnic destruction has been mass nostalgia, a longing for the way things used to be, symptomized by the popularity of anything, such as books about the Edo period that tell the story of what they consider to be a high point of their culture. This same sort of dismantling may be seen to be endemic in many neighboring countries in that region, almost as if an inexorable leveling process is at work and a long-held image of progress cannot be fulfilled until that process runs its tragic course. It would be too facile to blame the media for that process, as well, although a considerable body of literature does so.[1]

Beyond Asia, in the Middle East, a dynamic similar to that in Japan is at work, particularly at the epicenter of Islam, in Saudi Arabia. (Figs. 6.1 and 6.2) After a parallel commitment to modernization and the implementation of basic infrastructure on a Western model, the same syndrome could be identified there, beginning about 1985. Suddenly there was a resurgence of interest in traditional architecture, accompanied by a growing awareness of the built heritage that had been lost. New initiatives, such as that by Rasem Badran in his design of the Qasr al Hokm Justice Palace and mosque in Riyadh described in Chap. 3, were welcomed in an attempt to replace that lost heritage.

Elsewhere throughout the world similar attempts to recapture a past identity, now all but lost to the ravages of a ubiquitous

Figure 6.1
The Ruwais Mosque in Jeddah, Saudi Arabia by Abdel Wahed El Wakil. The elevation was generated by the need for natural ventilation and patterned after the market in New Bariz designed by Hassan Fathy.

Figure 6.2
Ruwais Mosque.

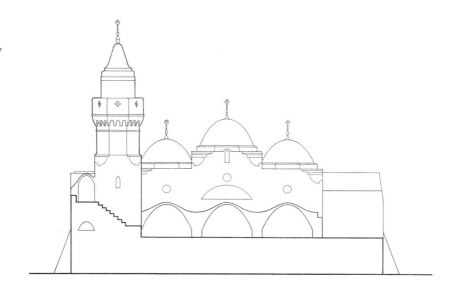

global culture, are now under way; the human need for a sense of self and of belonging inevitably prevails over the seductive convenience that technology can offer, with anonymous architecture, fast food, movies, syndicated TV shows, faxes, modems, internet, fashions, trends and fads proving insubstantial substitutes in the end.

This is the unity in diversity that Habermas and Said address, a global community made up of individuals who increasingly insist on retaining their personality in spite of being increasingly thrown together by the force of the future and the communication it requires.

Sustainable architecture, variously called ecological, biological, green, or Gaia architecture by others, aligns with this critical response to a perceived global imperative but differs from its predecessors. Pushed not only by many pundits and the press, sustainable architecture will also *be forced upon architects by an overwhelming confluence of ecological, social, and economic forces unless architects reach out to embrace and take control of it first*. The temporal half-life that seems to have become an integral part of architecture since the release of *Complexity and Contradiction* stands a good chance of being superseded in this instance, because these forces are real and not a contrived, intellectual construct. One clue to the atemporal aspect of the initiative, in fact, has been the difficulty, or reluctance, in naming it, in the fear that in doing so, it too will become a "style," doomed to its proscribed 15 minutes of fame. And yet, the consensus that there is a sustainable architecture afoot continues to grow daily.

What is sustainable architecture? A basic definition extends that of sustainability itself, an architecture that meets the needs of the present without compromising the ability of future generations to meet their own needs. Those needs differ from society to society and region to region and are best defined by the people involved. Unlike previous movements, which all eventually revealed a complete distrust of popular involvement, both sides of the political equation in this instance affirm a basic trust in human wisdom, with the caveat that communal size threatens to erode and distort it, leading to the sense of detachment and selfishness that Garrett Hardin describes in the "Tragedy of the Commons." That tragedy, in the sense of an inexorable process that carries characters along with it in spite of themselves, has been identified by sociologists as a function of scale, predicted in a parable written by Egyptian architect Hassan Fathy during his period of self-exile in Greece between 1956 and 1963, after the debacle at New Gourna. The parable entitled "Land of Utopia," was never published, but describes a preindustrial paradise of the kind envisioned by arts and crafts advocates such as John Ruskin, William Morris, and Thomas Carlyle, 100 years earlier. Containing unmistakable parallels with his visionary project at New Gourna, which was finally derailed by human greed and official corruption, Fathy's communal paradise is destroyed by population growth and the substitution of technology for human instinct. These ideas now reoccur in proposals for "pedestrian pockets" by Peter Calthorpe and Playa Vista by Maguire Thomas Partners, both for self-sufficient communities of optimum size designed with maximum size for effective social interaction in mind. Traditional communities relied upon self-regulation of the commons and the opprobrium that would inevitably result from a violation of public trust. Contemporary examples of such regulation and community cooperation in societies of maximum size abound, and the *johad* built in Rajastan (discussed in Chap. 2) is a perfect case in point. Nongovernmental organizations throughout the developing world offer overwhelming evidence that people, left to their own devices, are capable of self-regulation for the common good and instinctively seek a community if one does not exist. If Los Angeles is one urban paragon for the future, its several satellites in search of a center, originally resulting from the range provided by the freeway and the car, now confirm this impulse as people identify more with one of the seven subcenters that make up the urban entity, such as Venice or Pasadena, than they do with the idea of Los Angeles itself. The size of these communities is more comprehensible, and the issue of the degree of control exercised by outside agencies, either government or institution, protecting and "managing" the environment as part of the sustainable ethos remains contentious. The role of the architect as expert advisor rather than isolated aesthete does not. It is significant, in this regard, that Charles Moore, who has also become identified as one of the initiators of Post-Modernism, which he found amusing and not quite accurate, sought to establish this kind of connection with his clients, but he has been one of the few architects to do so. In many of the case studies included here, such as Bariz and Playa Vista, that function has admittedly only been partially realized, revolving around a framework provided by the architect to be filled out by the individuals who constitute the community. This extension of the impetus toward community involvement, initiated by Charles Moore, continues the comparison between Post-Modernism and sustainable architecture referred to earlier, and it is tempting to speculate on the possibility that the intentional architectonic component of the environmental ethic is simply a renewed attempt to get Post-Modernism right, without the pastiche and misdirected inside quotes. Thomas Fisher, in the center of the media fray, has a singular perspective on a significant difference between the two movements and reconfirms the issue of scale, as well, in defining that "in hindsight, Post Modern architecture…was telling us something was wrong. Despite claims of contexturalism, much of the historicist work of the 1980s seemed to get bigger and glitzier as the decade wore on."[2] He goes on to describe the search for an alternative as being driven by economic forces and an awareness that the sheer magnitude of a supply-side bureaucracy was unworkable as a model for the future. This led, he argues, to a counterview of an economy "that is a kind of ecology; which thrives when it is diverse, balanced and well-adapted to the local habitat." He goes on to identify this as the steady-state economy described by Kirkpatrick Sale in his book *Human Scale,* which Sale says "minimizes resource use, sets production on small and self-controlled scales, emphasizes conservation and recycling, limits pollution and waste, and accepts the limits of a single world."[3] Fisher believes green, or sustainable, architecture is a "direct reflection of this economic idea. It conserves energy, uses renewable or recyclable materials, reduces our dependence on fossil fuels, and attempts to create more intimately scaled buildings and communities."[4]

Many people confuse sustainable architecture with singular attempts at energy consciousness in the late 1960s and early 1970s, particularly those that resulted from the oil crisis and the tax credits that followed. Although it encompasses all those sensibilities of energy conservation, solar and photovoltaic technologies, optimum orientation, diurnal zoning, and self-sufficiency, it exceeds them in substance and scope to a significant extent—earlier ecological initiatives typically focused on improving the energy performance of a single object. (Figs. 6.3 and 6.4)

In either an active or passive mode, sustainable architecture tries to make connections to other buildings to take maximum advantage of mass, to local typologies that can be identified as climatically and culturally effective over time, to regional microclimates and materials or to global suppliers if necessary in the implications that some material choices have for nonrenewable resource depletion and for the possibility of technological transfer. This particular aspect of global transfer is especially important, since, rather than having blind faith in biotechnology to solve all the design problems related to the environment (as may have been the case in the past) and waiting for them to be cost-effective enough to implement, there is now more of a willingness to accept what Tom Whiston at Sussex University has referred to as "hybrid technolo-

Sustainable Architecture

Figure 6.3
Passive solar house in
Colorado by Edward
Mazria. A paradigm of
an earlier phase of
ecological consciousness
now surpassed by the
wider concerns of
sustainable architecture.
Photo courtesy of Ed
Mazria.

Figure 6.4
Self-sustaining facility in
northeastern
Pennsylvania by Douglas
Kelbaugh. A similar
approach. Photo
courtesy of Doug
Kelbaugh.

gies which utilize advanced technology and traditional systems."[5]
This new tendency to learn from an existing store of traditional
knowledge worldwide, rather than making costly mistakes by trying to invent new solutions to old problems, he argues, is closer to
the ecological principle of entropy and is far more sensible than
considering techniques from other cultures to be primitive and
beneath consideration. One example would be recent research on
wind towers at the University of Arizona, in which height, width,
and throat dimensions were derived using precedents of Egyptian
malkafs (windcatch), but cellulose filters similar to those used in
cigarettes were used as a substitute for the wet reed mats used in
the original model to keep out dust, with a fine jet spray added for
cooling. This current reification of historical prototypes that have
proved to be environmentally effective over time has reinforced the
study of traditional architecture, increasing appreciation of the
accomplishments of many cultures in responding sensitively to
their surroundings. Rather than trying to adapt environmental tactics or hardware to a functionalistic envelope, vaguely styled to suit
client preferences or current trends, architects using sustainable
principles are increasingly producing work in which this complex

set of imperatives is more integral to the final product, with image a secondary or frequently nonexistent prerogative.

The investigations of Karl Popper into the empirical basis of science that had previously been vehemently denied by its practitioners, who claimed that it was rational, pure, and value free, have helped to propel science even further into the political and social arena. In the ensuing debate about the relationship between facts and values that Popper's work has left in its wake, science is now perceived as less imposing, a social construct that can be adapted to serve human needs. Whereas the political climate in the United States is currently running in the opposite direction, seeking to use funding to force science to serve industry exclusively for national, financial gain, environmental pressures will inevitably force that policy to change. The hybrid or intermediate technologies that have already resulted from this new accessibility hold out the promise for even more ingenious adaptations in the future. These cannot be counted on as panaceas, but should prompt architects to look beyond solar panels and photovoltaic cells to the more interactive elements now being made available to them.

Architects have always been known as generalists, able to assimilate a wide variety of information and convert it into a final design solution. Sustainability challenges that ability, as it encompasses ethics, economics, sociology, ecology, history, and biology for a start. Subsciences in each of these areas are also currently evolving with *environmental* rather than *sustainable* invariably inserted in front of each to make the specialization clear. To remain informed, architects must now digest an exponentially increasing amount of factual data from a wider variety of sources, requiring them to make the effort to search them out and to spend the extra time required to digest them. Recently, obscure critical interpretations may have given the practitioner in the trenches reason for considerable doubt, but sustainability calls upon the skills

Sustainable Architecture

an architect uses best, analysis, cross-comparison, synthesis, and deduction, leading to aesthetic choices that have a basis in fact rather than fashion. Those facts are to be gained primarily from the complex dynamic system that makes up the global ecological network, and knowledge about the level of that complexity has expanded rapidly in the last 30 years. In spite of all the new information that has been gathered, there is still much to know, especially in the area of resource depletion, which will affect future development decisions, particularly once the problems regarding the proper method of economic valuation are solved. Architects can become instrumental in providing the much-needed research that will guide change.

Many of those who are critical of architectural pedagogy today would even go one step further, saying that this description of the opportunities presented to architects in the rapidly evolving field of sustainability simply perpetuates the empiricist-rationalist dichotomy within the profession: by stressing the role of the designer "in the context of practical issues, objective and empirically based knowledge, strong links to research, and a broader view of the scope of architectural practice" over that of the rational image of the architect as abstract aesthete and technician.[6] Some argue for the creation of a third, alternative model of "architect-as-cultivator" (steward), implying both a protector and the person who can inspire an individual or group to a given course of action.[7] That model fits the emerging theoretical stance of reestablishing communication, put forward by Habermaus and Said, even more closely, as well as the architectural alternative that it infers on a global scale. (Figs. 6.5 and 6.6)

Pedagogical critics in recent, concentrated barrages against the standard curriculum now in place in many architectural schools, both in America and Europe, and by extension in the developing world, where Western models are assiduously followed,

Figure 6.5
Wooden mushrabbiya
screen in medieval Cairo
from the sixteenth
century. Photo by James
Steele.

have identified the major barriers to the study of sustainable architecture. Citing the typical dynamics of a studio-driven education,
they have identified a consistently strong emphasis on a hypothetical open-ended creative process developed in relative isolation with
an authority figure evaluating when it is good, without collaborat-
ing with others in the studio, in order to produce a design product that is more often than not an object building, to be reviewed
in abstract terms by a jury.[8] These traits of creative isolation, distrust of collaboration, and focus on a singular design product,
which are amplified in practice, are the main reason that architects
are being increasingly marginalized today and why they are

Sustainable Architecture

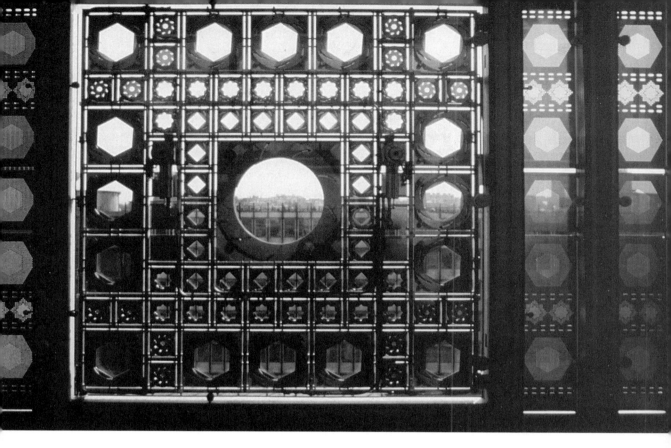

Figure 6.6
Steel computer-activated mushrabbiya screen at the Institute du Monde Arabe in Paris by Jean Nouvel. Photo by Pascal Marechaux, AKAA.

regarded by clients and public authorities as suitable for providing design or drafting services as part of a team of consultants up to a certain point but as untrustworthy in real world or budgetary questions.

In the developing world, where this Western educational model frequently predominates, these characteristics are exacerbated with design studio always emphasized in the credit hour count, as well. Problems, typically not real, are issued in a brief program, and, as one student has described what follows, "design is seen as a geometric puzzle that involves achieving a certain two dimensional arrangement of geometric shapes—mostly rectangles and squares, to meet certain special criteria."[9] In the absence of a real client, or social context, or environmental context, the results are devoid of reality and abstract. In these schools, as in their Western paradigms, the agenda that Thomas Dutton has called "the hidden curriculum," the unstated values, norms, and attitudes conveyed by such exercises, tends to perpetuate the myth of the architect as the aloof form-giver, delivering solutions to the problems of the less-enlightened masses. This image also has a subtext, of nature seen as an enemy that must be conquered, rather than the basis for all life and a milieu to which architecture can and must conform, harmoniously. Both the image and its subtext are completely unsuited to the changes that environmental imperatives are now thrusting upon the profession and must change, or architects will be negated.

By way of contrast, a course of sustainable study would have the following attributes:

- Actual problems, with real clients students can relate to, who may then evaluate their work, with a stress on collective, rather than singular evaluation.
- Collaborative, rather than individual, effort.
- Holistic viewpoints.
- Emphasis on ecological, social, and cultural contexts, with precedents.
- Study of relevant historical typologies.
- Reference and comparison with Third World prototypes, to change the hidden agenda from Western to non-Western values. These prototypes would include collectives, self-help methods, review of appropriate intermediate technologies, and urban models. This comparison will prepare architects not only to deal with the highly complex issues of sustainability but also to work in the rapidly industrializing countries, where the majority of commissions will be found in the future.

- Use of local materials, particularly telluric materials, to best reflect a particular region and save the energy costs of transport.
- Awareness of global politics and the full implications behind material choices as related to resource depletion, cyclical debt service, and balance of trade.
- Awareness of the energy implications of material choices, as indicated in Chap. 5, including the energy costs involved in mining, manufacturing, processing, shipping, and installation, and their pollution potential.
- Instruction on recycling or reuse of materials wherever possible.
- Awareness of new technologies and the literature beyond the usual professional journals, where these are previewed.
- Challenge of institutional regulations that are environmentally damaging. The Grameen Bank is one inspiring example of where such challenges can lead (see Chap. 3). The zoning changes instituted by Duany and Plater-Zyberk are another.
- Reading, or rereading, the classics by the visionaries of the genre, such as Ian McHarg's *Design with Nature,* Hassan Fathy's *Natural Energy and Vernacular Architecture,* as well as the recognized standards of this emerging field.
- An antipositivist viewpoint, of multiple rather than singular realities and meanings, more in tune with a multicultural future.
- Teaching students to think globally, act locally, and live simply, so that others may live.

As an example, the following is the description of a well-known studio which Ralph Knowles has offered at the University of Southern California for over 15 years. It is one of the first to attempt to convey values now identified as sustainable.

ARCH 402: TOPIC STUDIO ON SOLAR DESIGN

Intention

The main purpose of the studio is to test ideas, either about public policy or about design theory. The tests have always been topical, made in a context of current and local interests. As a consequence, they have sometimes met with disagreement and even with active protest from those with conflicting stakes.

Public Policy

An idea that has been tested about public policy is that the solar envelope will not overly constrain either development options or design choices. Two assumptions underlie these tests: first, that Los Angeles has enacted a general zoning policy ensuring sunshine to all properties; and, second, that actual conditions prevail regarding land value, density, building codes, and so on, in order to make the tests as realistic as possible.

The *solar envelope* is defined as the largest hypothetical volume that can be constructed on a lot without overshadowing neighboring properties during critical energy-receiving hours and seasons. The result is a construct of time as well as space. The concept grew out of the energy crisis of the 1970s and today remains viable because of a widening interest in sustainable architecture. Although 15 years of testing have supported this idea, and zoning based on the solar envelope has been instituted in a growing number of communities, protests are still heard from both developers and designers alike.

Developers see the solar envelope as a constraint on size, and yet our tests consistently show little basis for such concern. For example, working under real site constraints near downtown Los Angeles, the solar studio has consistently achieved housing densities of 80 to 100 dwelling units per acre and floor-area ratios (FAR) in excess of 6.0 for office space. In a few urban circum-

Sustainable Architecture

stances, for example, the new subway stops, higher values are planned, but the vast majority of all urban development can easily be accommodated within such limits.

Designers feel threatened by a loss of artistic choice, and yet the solar studio consistently shows enormous diversity of form. The reality of the solar envelope is that its size and shape are not uniform but vary with surrounding conditions. The envelope tends to scale new construction up to meet large, existing buildings and down to meet smaller ones. Its shape tends to be elaborate where the surroundings are complex and simpler where they are plain and orderly. Adding to this inherent variety among parcels is each designer's inclination toward individuality within the constraints of the envelope.

Design Theory

Very recently, an idea that has been tested about design theory is that sunlight adds a dimension of time to our perceptions of architectural space. Two assumptions underlie these tests: first, that space is generated by flux itself, the consequence of daily and seasonal rhythms and corresponding rituals of life in a place; and, second, that the notion of completion is antithetical to all our design activities. Any specific design execution in the studio is, therefore, calculated as a measure of time, the whole process as a consequence of daily and seasonal rhythms of sunlight.

This turns out to be a very difficult notion for students to handle and one often resisted by other faculty in the school. This difficulty seems to result in part from the habit of modern architects of defining space in opposition to chaos and change; they acknowledge that buildings may be transformed or deteriorate over time, but on the whole their artistic idea of space is complete and static. And part of the difficulty students have with a temporal component of space stems from our habit of making decisions in a studio, isolated from nature and the exigencies of change.

The idea that sunlight deepens our understanding of space has been recently tested in the solar studio by using the library as an appropriate building type. Libraries have always implied a sort of gateway in time. For example, medieval libraries served as an opening to the ancient world, preserving and copying existing works with painstaking care. By contrast, modern libraries provide gateways to more than the past. Januslike, they open as well to the future with books on stock market predictions and science fiction. Whether ancient or modern, this linear sense of time has always been modulated by the rhythms of day and season as architects have worked to provide light for reading, copying, preserving, and the like. It is this duality of time, both progressive and cyclic, that the solar studio attempts to connect in an active conception of space.

Procedures

The studio usually depends on selecting an actual site comprised of multiple, adjacent parcels, one for each member of the class. This has twin advantages: First, it allows a better understanding of what happens when solar access is valued as, project by project, a greater landscape evolves. And, second, it places individual designers in a dynamic context where each is continuously modifying the circumstances for the other during the design process.

The studio depends heavily on physical models for use on the sun machine. The models are built at different scales, some quite small and others large, depending on the nature of the assignments as the work progresses.

Studio work progresses in discrete periods. This method allows iteration through a sequence of steps, each advancing understanding of how well the design answers a series of requirements, for example, access to winter sunshine, cross ventilation, pedestrian and vehicular circulation, sun shading in summer. This method of taking smaller, defined steps also puts less emphasis on coming too quickly to a single, comprehensive solution and, instead, allows consideration of alternatives longer into the design process. Students are thus encouraged to see design as a series of discoveries, not as a single act of creation.[10]

A MODEL THAT MUST CHANGE

Ron Herron, of Archigram fame, and the past head of the "Imagination" group in London, addressed a packed hall at the University of Southern California in Los Angeles in late 1993. In a scene that has been reenacted countless times by a burgeoning diaspora of international lecturers that now criss-cross the Atlantic and Pacific to present their work, Herron began by showing his much-published Storr Street conversion, in which a Christolike fabric wrapping has been used to cover a problematic cavern between two existing building blocks near Bedford Square in London. After some derogatory remarks about Prince Charles that quickly and unmistakably established his position in the British debate about traditionalism, Herron showed his conversion of a listed manor house for Lord Rothschild and an underground station in London, among other projects. In each instance his message was clear, an architect must always create an object of identity, in spite of, rather than because of, the context in which that object is to be seen. Place, in short, equals space, and the success of that space is directly proportional to both the "originality" of its conception and technological ingenuity that is used in its fabrication. Storr Street represented this viewpoint most effectively, since the fabric structure used to cover the interior space is held up by custom-made stainless steel trusses and umbrellalike struts that are undeniably elegant as objects in their own right. No matter that the polyvinylchloride material chosen for the cover produces highly noxious black smoke when it burns and is barely insulative, or that the stainless steel supports have been extremely expensive to produce. All attempts by the local council to question such tactics were characterized as intrusive and short-sighted efforts to thwart the creative process. Roark seemed to be rampant once again, and the Modernist emphasis on space and technology virtually unchanged.

Although the venue and name of the speaker may vary, the message remains virtually the same, and it is conveyed in the media and the studio with equal force—be individualistic and iconoclastic at all costs, make a personal statement, in spite of surroundings. Technology stands out as one the most effective ways to make that statement memorable, and publishable.[11] In all this effort to regain the individualistic and elitist aura maintained by the architectural superheroes of the past, in which technology has once again become a symbol of independence from nature and society, several basic facts continue to be overlooked.

By way of contrast, as prophetically pointed out by E. F. Schumacher as early as 1973, is that the United States, as the leader of the "developed nations" of the world, uses an incredibly large portion of its resources in proportion to the population percentage that it represents. He also notes that "An industrial system such as this could be called efficient only if it has obtained strikingly successful results in terms of human happiness, well-being, culture, peace and harmony."[12] Judging from the failure of U.S. architects to act as a catalyst for cultural expression both here and in the developing world, their participation in the use of those resources, in the form of energy-intensive and technologically sophisticated materials, begins to take on an entirely different perspective. According to a recent study by the UN Department of International Economic and Social Affairs, 70 percent of the projected increase in the world's population between now and 2025, which is expected to climb from 5 billion to 8.5 billion in that 34-year period, will occur in 20 of the least developed countries.[13] Considering this fact, the U.S. monopolization of global resources becomes even more reprehensible and moves the question of the promotion of an architecture based on high technology from an aesthetic to a moral plane.

Whereas aesthetic judgments are qualitative, stylistic indulgences of the kind typified by Herron's Storr Street have repercussions that go beyond their obvious disdain for local traditions, inhabitants, or microclimates. Schumacher's test for efficiency may seem superfluous, but he has managed to identify the only possible justification for such indulgence. Human happiness and cultural advancement have not been obvious by-products of such buildings. In our product-oriented society, architecture has become just one more disposable item to be quickly consumed and then discarded in favor of the next model on the line. Architects respond to this by providing that model, and education tends to reflect these ephemeral, object-conscious values. Instead of providing an idyllic life and the increased leisure that was the anticipated by-product of technology in the 1950s, allegiance to the concept of progress in the industrialized world, and the architecture that has resulted from it, have served only to accelerate continuous growth and change at the expense of social stability and global well-being.

Sociologist Marsall Berman's comprehensive definition of the condition of modernity captures the full scope of the kaleidoscopic character of contemporary life, which he traces to many sources. These, as he says, are the

> great discoveries in the physical sciences, changing our images of the universe and our place in it, the industrialization of production, which transforms scientific knowledge into technology, creates new environments and destroys old ones, speeds up the whole tempo of life, generates new forms of corporate power and class struggle, immense demographic upheavals, severing millions of people from their ancestral habitats, hurling them halfway across the

Figure 6.7 Science Museum, Riyadh, Rasem Badran. An earth-berm building.

world into new lives, rapid and often cataclysmic urban growth, systems of mass communication, dynamic in their development, enveloping and binding together the most diverse people and societies.[14] (Fig. 6.7)

There is little consensus as to exactly when the cyclical vision of the world held by traditional societies was replaced by this perception of linear inevitability, but there seems to be little doubt that the transfer from a rural to an industrial way of life, which took place in the majority of the developed world at the beginning of the nineteenth century, and continues to transform the developing world today, seems to mark a growing separation from the cycles of nature itself.

In vivid contrast to the genre of presentation mentioned earlier, in which the preferred self-image of architects and students as autonomous artistic agents is reinforced through the valorization of a succession of technologically sophisticated buildings, Elizabeth Plater-Zyberk and Andreas Duany spoke about the need to break the architecture-as-object syndrome that is so prevalent today. By defining a good designer as someone who extends the parameters of a problem beyond the limits presented by a client program to involve the city or context around that object, Plater-Zyberk also opened up the possibility of expanding them to include consideration of the less developed countries that will dominate the global politics and the architectural choices of the twenty-first century. She spoke with missionary zeal about the need for a wider agenda today, and the attempts by her firm to recapture an America that only exists as a memory for some and an image for others, of small towns and cities that related to people before the automobile took over. Accepting the "neo-Traditionalist" title that has been given to their approach, which involves a return to human scale and personal considerations in urban planning, Plater-Zyberk and Duany have noted that such places actually did exist at the beginning of the Industrial Revolution but have disappeared because of increasingly segregated zoning regulations, which have also served to isolate single buildings in the process. By making a plea to architects to become involved in larger-scale planning, they hope to counteract the myopia now afflicting the profession and to make it politically active and powerful once again. In addition to their concern for the people who live in their projects, and their guerrilla warfare against the car, their approach is also an excellent example of the "technology with a human face" of which Schumacher speaks.[15] Using his own gradation, it is "intermediate" rather than high or low, appropriate to its setting in each case, and not environmentally or energy-intensive. The results that Plater-Zyberk and Duany

Figure 6.8
Environmental
Interpretive Center at
Playa Vista by Angelica
Solis, James Steele
Sustainability Studio,
University of Southern
California School of
Architecture, Los
Angeles.

achieve, without causing a drastic revision of the lifestyles or philosophy of the people who they deal with, are uniformly effective at a humanistic level and have continued to be since they first achieved international recognition for their design of Seaside, Florida, in 1982.

Many practitioners and educators are cognizant of such economic and environmental interrelationships today but continue to follow deeply ingrained patterns because of the creative or financial restrictions that they feel any change in direction would bring, and because of questions about style.

Five entrepreneurs named John Allen, Margaret Augustine, Robert Hahn, Carl Hodges, and Mark Nelson in 1994 completed Biosphere II near Tucson, Arizona, presumptuously named after Biosphere I, which is the earth. They have spared no effort or expense in their search for technological substitutes for the ocean, desert, rainforest, farmland, and savannah ecosystems which are now in danger of extinction in their original form. Six thousand triangular glass windows in a multifaceted aluminum frame shield Biosphere II from an increasingly hostile environment, and its interior is air-conditioned, powered by a 5.2 MW gas burner. The final irony for those who continue to pursue a stylistic direction based on high technology is that the social and economic philosophy to which Biosphere II relates relies entirely upon the depletion of nonrenewable natural resources in order to survive. The environmental repercussions of that depletion, such as the increase of sulfur dioxide and the greenhouse gases carbon monoxide and methane are already irreversible, causing deforestation and desertification, as well as a 2° rise in global temperature by 2025 that has been confirmed by computer modeling.[16] Continued ignorance of the interdependence of all societies today, whether rich or poor, will only hasten these serious problems and at the very least make the questions of style, which seem so important to many today, seem irrelevant. Biosphere II is only one of many signs that those

who want to create and live in a completely technological world may eventually get their wish. A more humane alternative would be to come to terms with the possibilities inherent in altered expectations, as well as the social and material needs of others throughout the world. (Fig. 6.8)

NOTES

Chapter 1

1. Brandt Commission, *Common Crisis,* 1983.
2. Daniel Sitarz (ed.), *Agenda 21: The Earth Summit Strategy to Save Our Planet,* Earth Press Co., Boulder, Col., p. 6.
3. Ibid., 21.
4. Ibid., 32.
5. Ibid., 34
6. Ibid., 40
7. Ibid., 46
8. This was the principle of the Grameen Bank project, which is discussed in Chap. 3.
9. Robert J. Berkebile, Chairman, "NGO Recommendations: Post Rio," *AIA Environmental Resources Guide,* Washington, DC, January 1993, Case R IV-1.

Chapter 2

1. See Gaia: *A New Look at Life on Earth, 1979 and The Ages of Gaia: A Biography of Our Living Earth, 1988,* both Oxford University Press.
2. Michael Jacobs, *The Green Economy,* Pluto Press, London, 1991, p.5. See also William Clarka, "Managing Planet Earth," *Scientific American,* September 1989, vol. 261, no. 2AIA, p.9.

3. Denis Hayer, Committee on the Environment, *Energy, Environment and Architecture* American Institute of Architects (Washington, DC: 1991), p. 9.
4. Ibid, p.10
5. Mark Fienman, "Chaos Grips Somolia as Peacekeepers Leave," *Los Angeles Times,* March 29, 1994, p.1.
6. Hassein Fahim, *The Aswan High Dam,* (N.Y.: United Nations, 1989), p.23.
7. Interview with Hassan Fathy with the Author, June 1988.
8. David Nicholson Lord, *The Independent,* 29 March 1994, London, p. 45.
9. In Chris Abel: "Ecodevelopment, Appropriate Technology and Regionalism," undated, unpublished manuscript, P.S.
10. Op. cit.
11. Ibid., p 217.
12. Ibid., p.222.
13. Melissa Healy, "Group Hopes Greener Cities Will Be Safe," *Los Angeles Times,* 28 June 1994, p. A5.
14. Brian Edwards, "Biodiversity and Building Design," *The Architect's Journal,* 8 June 1994, p. 36.
15. Dousset
16. Peter Calthorpe, "The Pedestrian Pocket: New Strategies for Suburban

Growth," B. Walter, L. Ankin, R. Crenshaw (eds.), in *Sustainable Cities: Concepts and Strategies for Eco-City Development,* EHM, Los Angeles, 1992, p. 26.

17. Shelton H. Davis (ed.), *Indigenous Views of Land and the Environment,* World Bank Discussion Papers, The World Bank, Washington, DC, 1993, p.1.

18. Ibid., p.1.

Chapter 4

1. Robert Goodland, Herman Daly, and Salah El Sorafy (eds.), *Population Technology and Lifestyles: The Transition to Sustainability,* Island Press, Washington, DC, 1992.
2. Ibid.
3. Ibid.
4. Ibid.
5. Ibid.
6. Ibid.
7. See Nishan Manasinghe (ed.), *Environmental Economics and Natural Resource Management in Developing Countries,* World Bank Publications, Washington DC, 1993.
8. Ibid.
9. Goodland, Daly, and Serafy.
10. Ibid.
11. Ibid.
12. Ibid.

Chapter 5

1. Alex Wilson, "Using Concrete Wisely," *Environmental Building News,* March/April 1993, p. 12.

Chapter 6

1. See, for example, Srinivas R. Melkote, *Communication for Development in the Third World,* Sage Publications, New Delhi, 1991, especially Chap. 2.

2. Thomas Fisher, editorial, *Progressive Architecture,* March 1993, vol. 74, p. 9.
3. Ibid, p. 9.
4. Ibid, p. 10.
5. *London Times,* October 8, 1993, p. 18.
6. Linda Grout, "Architects Resistance to Diversity," *Journal of Architectural Education,* September 1993, p. 5.
7. Dana Cuff, *Story of Practice,* MIT Press, Cambridge, Mass., 1991, p. 36.
8. Sanjoy Mazumdar, "Cultural Values in Design Education," *Journal of Architectural Education,* May 1993, p. 233.
9. Ralph Knowles, Course Description for Solar Studio.
10. See Charles Jencks, *The New Moderns,* Academy Editions, London, 1991.
11. E. F. Schumacher, *Small Is Beautiful,* Harper and Row, New York, 1973, p. 110.
12. Cited by Nathan Keyfitz, "The Growing Human Population," *Scientific American,* September 1989, pp. 119–124. The 20 countries are: Bangladesh, Brazil, China, Egypt, Ethiopia, India, Indonesia, Iran, Kenya, Mexico, Nigeria, Pakistan, Philippines, South Africa, Sudan, Tanzania, Turkey, Uganda, Vietnam, and Zaire.
13. Marshall Berman, *All That Is Solid Melts into Air: The Experience of Modernity,* Simon and Simon, New York, 1982, p. 16.
14. Schumacher, *Small Is Beautiful,* p. 158.
16. Bert Bolini, ed., *The Greenhous Effect, Climatic Change and Ecosystems,* John Wiley and Sons, New York, 1986.

BIBLIOGRAPHY

Abel, Chris. "Ecodevelopment, Appropriate Technology, and Regionalism," unpublished.

Adams, Nassau A. *Worlds Apart: The North-South Divide and the International System* (London: Zed Books, 1993).

Adams, William Mark. *Green Development: Environment and Sustainability in the Third World* (London: Routledge, 1990).

Adriaanse, Albert. "Environmental Policy Performance Indicators" (a study on the development of indicators for environmental policy in the Netherlands, 1993).

Agarwal, A., and S. Narain. *Towards Green Villages* (Delhi: Centre for Science and Environment, 1990).

Ahmad, Y., S. El Sarafy, and E. Lutz (eds.). *Environmental Accounting for Sustainable Development* (Washington, DC: The World Bank, 1989), also a UNEP-World Bank Symposium, 1992.

Alexander, Susan, and Brian Greber. *Environmental Ramifications of Various Building Materials Used in Construction and Manufacture in the United States* (U.S.D.A. Forest Service, 1991).

Ambio (Special Issue), *Population, Natural Resources and Development,* February 1992.

American Institute of Architects. *Design and the Environment* (Washington, DC: 1991); *Environmental Resource Guide.* (Washington, DC: 1991).

———. *Energy, Environment, and Architecture* (Washington, DC: 1991).

American Iron and Steel Institute. "Fact Sheet: Steel, Building a History of Recycling Leadership," June 1992.

American Planning Association. "Caring for the Land," *Design and the Environment* (Washington, DC: American Institute of Architects, 1993).

Anderson, Bruce. *Ecologue: The Environmental Catalogue and Consumer's Guide to a Safe Earth* (Englewood Cliffs, NJ: Prentice-Hall Press, 1990).

Anderson, Dennis. "The Economics of Afforestation: A Case Study in Africa," Occasional paper 1 (Baltimore, MD: Johns Hopkins Press, 1987).

Anderson, K. "The Standard Welfare Economics of Policies Affecting Trade and the Environment," in K. Anderson and R. Blackhurst (eds.), *The Greening of Third World Trade Issues* (London: Howester-Wheatsheaf, 1992).

Anderson, Mary, and Peter Woodrow, *Rising from the Ashes* (Boulder, CO: Westview Press, 1989).

Archigui, F., and P. Nijkamp (eds.). *Economy and Ecology: Towards a Sustainable Development* (Dordrecht, The Netherlands: Klower Academic Publishers, 1989).

Arrhenius, Erik, and Thomas W. Waltz, "The Green House Effect: Implications for Economic Development," World Bank discussion paper 78 (Washington, DC: World Bank, 1990).

Arrow, Kenneth J., and Anthony Fisher. "Environmental Preservation: Uncertainty and Irreversibility," *Quarterly Journal of Economics* vol. 88, 1974, pp. 312–319.

Ayres, Robert U., and Allen V. Kreese. "Production, Corruption, and Externality," *American Economic Review* vol. 59, June 1969, pp. 282–298.

Barnett, Harold, and Chandler Morse. *Scarcity and Growth: The Economics of Natural Resource Availability* (Baltimore, MD: Johns Hopkins University Press, 1963).

Barnett, Jonathan. "Sustainable Development: How to Make It Work," *Architectural Record* vol. 181, June 1993, pp. 32–35.

Bartlemus, Peter. *Environment and Development* (Boston, MA: Allen and Unwin, 1986).

Baumol, William J., and Wallace E. Oates. *The Theory of Environmental Policy* (2d ed.) (New York: Cambridge University Press, 1988).

Bello, Walden. "Strategies for Survival in the Global Economy," in *Brave New Third World* (London: Earthscan Publishers, Ltd., 1989).

Bennett Information Group. *The Green Pages: Your Everyday Shopping Guide to Environmentally Safe Products* (New York: Random House, 1990).

Bentley, C. F., and L. A. Leskin. *Sustainability of Farmed Lands: Current Trends and Thinking* (Ottawa: Ministry of Supply and Service, Canadian Environmental Advisory Council, 1985).

Bentrover, Judith D. *Benefits Assessment: The State of the Art* (Dordrecht, Netherlands: D. Reidel Publishing, 1980).

Berman, Marshall. *All That's Solid Melts Into Air: The Experience of Modernity* (New York: Simon & Schuster, 1982).

Berger, John. *Restoring the Earth* (New York: Alfred A. Knopf, 1985).

Berkes, Fikret (ed.). *Common Property Resources: Ecology of Community-Based Sustainable Development* (London: Belhaven, 1989).

Blackwell, Jonathan M., Roger N. Goodwillie, and Richard Webb. *Environment and Development in Africa: Selected Case Studies.* EDI Development Policy Case Series, no. 6 (Washington, DC: The World Bank, 1991).

Blank, Robert. "The Allocation of Scarce Resources: How Much Is the Life of a Baby Doe Worth?" Paper presented to the annual meeting of the American Political Science Association (Washington, DC, 1986).

Blowers, Andrew. "Pollution and Waste—a Sustainable Burden?" *Town and Country Planning* vol. 61, October 1992, pp. 265–268.

———. "Problems, Principles and Prospects," *Town and Country Planning* vol. 61, May 1992, pp. 132–135.

Boadway, Robin, and Neil Bruce. *Welfare Economics* (Oxford: Blackwell, 1984).

Bojo, Jan, Karl-Goran Mäler, and Lena Uremo. *Environment and Development: An Economic Approach* (Boston: Kluwer Academic Publishers, 1990).

Bolin, B., and R. Cook (eds.). *The Major Biogeochemical Cycles and Their Interactions* (New York: John Wiley & Sons, 1983).

Bolini, Bert (ed.) *The Greenhouse Effect, Climate Change, and Ecosystems* (New York: John Wiley and Sons, 1986).

Boserup, Ester. *Population and Technological Change: A Study of Long-Term Trends* (Chicago: University of Chicago Press, 1981).

Boulding, Kenneth. "The Economics of the Coming Spaceship Earth," in Henry Jarett (ed.), *Environmental Quality in a Growing Economy* (Baltimore, MD: Johns Hopkins University Press, 1966).

———. *The Meaning of the Twentieth Century* (New York: Harpers, 1969).

Bower, John. *The Healthy House* (New York: Carol Communications, 1989).

Branch, Mark Alden. "The State of Sustainability," *Progressive Architecture* vol. 74, March 1993, pp. 71–79.

Brandt Commission. *Common Crisis North-South Cooperation for World Recovery* (London: Pan Books, 1983).

Brenton, T. *The Greening of Machiavelli: The Evolution of International Environmental Politics* (London: Royal Institute of International Affairs, Energy and Environmental Programme, Earthscan Publications, 1989).

Bromley, David W., and Michael M. Cerrea. "The Management of Common Property Natural Resources: Some Conceptual and Operational Fallacies," World Bank Discussion 57 (Washington, DC: World Bank, 1989).

Brooks, D. "An Evaluation of 'Our Common Future,'" *Human Economy Newsletter* vol. 12, 1991, p. 4.

Brookshire, David, Larry Eubanks, and Alan Randall. "Estimating Option Prices and Existence Values for Wildlife Resources," *Land Economics* vol. 59, 1983, pp. 1–15.

————, William Schulze, and M. Thayer. *Some Unusual Aspects of Valuing a Unique Natural Resource* (Laramie, WY: University of Wyoming Department of Economics, 1985).

Brown, Harry, Bernard Hamel, Bruce Hedmar, Michael Rolvch, Birar Gajarara, and Philip Troy. *Energy Analysis of 108 Industrial Processes* (U.S. Department of Energy, Contract # E (11-1) 2862, Fairmont Press Edition, 1985).

Brown, K., David Pearce, T. Swanson, and C. Perrings. *Economics and the Conservation of Global Biological Diversity* (Washington, DC: Global Environment Facility, 1993).

Brown, Lester. *Building a Sustainable Society* (New York: Norton, 1981).

————. *State of the World,* 1992 (Washington, DC: Worldwatch Institute, 1992).

————. "State of the World, 1986," a Worldwatch Institute report on progress toward a sustainable society (New York: Norton, annual editions: 1984, 1985, 1986, 1987).

————, Christopher Flavin, and Sandra Postel. *Saving the Planet,* (New York: W.W. Norton, 1991).

Bussel, Abby. "Eco-Evaluators: What Do They Do?" *Progressive Architecture* vol. 74, March 1993, pp. 90–91.

Cairncross, Sandy. "Water Supply and the Urban Poor" in Jorge Hardoy, Sandy Cairncross, and David Satterthwaite (eds.). *The Poor Die Young: Housing and Health in Third World Cities* (London: Earthscan, 1990).

Caldwell, Lynton K. *International Environmental Policy: Emergence and Dimensions* (Durham, NC: Duke University Press, 1984).

Capra, Fritjof. *The Turning Point: Science, Society, and the Rising Culture* (New York: Simon and Schuster, 1982).

————, and Charlene Spretnak. *Green Politics* (New York: Dutton, 1984; updated paperback edition published by Beer & Co., 1986).

Carson, Rachel. *Silent Spring* (Cambridge, MA: Riverside Press, 1962).

Carter, David, Martin Kramper, David Stea, (eds.). *New Directions in Environmental Participation: Ethnoscapes,* vol. 3 (Avebury, Aldershot, U.K.: 1988).

Catton, W.R. *Overshoot: The Ecological Basis of Revolutionary Change* (Chicago: University of Illinois Press, 1982).

Chambers, Robert. *Sustainable Rival Livelihoods: A Strategy for People, Environment, and Development* (Brighton, UK: Institute of Development Studies at the University of Sussex, 1987).

Ciciancy-Wantrup, Siegfried von. *Resource Conservation: Economics and Politics* (Berkeley, CA: University of California Press, 1952).

Clearly, Seamus. *Renewing the Earth: Development for a Sustainable Future* (London: Catholic Fund for Overseas Development, 1989).

Cline, William. *Political Economics of the Greenhouse Effect* (Washington, DC: Institute for International Economics, 1989).

Coe, Gigi. *Present Value: Constructing a Sustainable Future* (San Francisco: Friends of the Earth, 1979).

Cole, Leonard. *Politics and the Restraint of Science* (Totowa, NJ: Rowman and Allanheld, 1983).

Commoner, Barry. *Making Peace with the Planet* (New York, NY: Pantheon Books, 1990).

Commonwealth Group of Experts. *The Debt Crisis and the World Economy* (London: Commonwealth Secretariat, 1984).

Conroy, Czech, and Miles Litrinoff (eds.). *The Greening of Aid: Sustainable Livelihoods in Practice* (London: Earthscan, 1988).

Conservation International. *The Debt for Native Exchange* (Washington, DC, 1989).

Conway, Gordon, and Edward Berbier. *After the Green Revolution: Sustainable Agriculture for Development* (London: Earthscan, 1990).

Coomer, James (ed.). *Quest for a Sustainable Society* (New York: Pergamon Press, 1978).

Cornia, G. A., R. van der Hoeven, and T. Mkardawire. *Africa's Recovery in the 1990s: From Stagnation and Adjustment to Human Development* (New York: St. Martin's Press, 1993).

Costanza, R. (ed.). *Ecological Economics: The Science and Management of Sustainability* (New York: Columbia University Press, 1991).

Court, T. de la. *Beyond Brundtland: Green Development in the 1990s* (London: Zed Books, 1990).

Crosbie, Michael J. "Audubon Society Opens Green Headquarters," *Progressive Architecture* vol. 74, March 1993, pp. 19–20.

Cropper, Maureen. "A Note on the Extinction of Renewable Resources," *Journal of Environmental Economics and Management* vol. 15, 1988, pp. 64–71.

Crowther, Richard. *Ecologic Architecture* (Stoneham, MA: Butterworth Architecture, 1992).

Cruz, H., and R. Repetto, *The Environmental Effects of Stabilization and Structural Adjustment Programmes: The Philippines Case* (Washington, DC: World Resources Institute, 1992).

Cummings, Barbara J. *Dam the Rivers, Damn the People* (London: Earthscan Publications, 1990).

Dahlberg, Kenneth. *Beyond the Green Revolution: The Ecology and Politics of Global Agricultural Development* (Plenum, NY: 1979).

Daly, Herman. "Ecological Economics and Sustainable Development," in C. Rossi and G. Tiezzi (eds.). *Ecological Physical Chemistry* (Amsterdam: Elsener, 1991).

———. "Ecological Economics and Sustainable Development: From Concept to Policy," (Washington, DC: The World Bank Environmental Department Paper, 1991), p. 24.

———. *Economics, Ecology, Ethics: Essays toward a Steady State Economy* (San Francisco: Freeman, 1980).

———. *Steady State Economics: The Economics of Biophysical Equilibrium and Moral Growth* (San Francisco: Freeman, 1977).

———. "Sustainable Development from Conceptual Theory towards Exceptional Principles," unpublished manuscript.

———. "Towards an Environmental Macroeconomics," in R. Costerza, *Ecological Economics* (New York: Columbia University Press, 1991).

———. "Towards a Measure of Sustainable Social Net National Product," in Yusuf J. Ahmad, Salah El Serafy, and Ernst Lutz (eds.), *Environmental Accounting for Sustainable Development, A UNEP-World Bank Symposium* (Washington, DC: The World Bank, 1989).

———. "Toward Some Exceptional Principles of Sustainable Development," *Ecological Economics* vol. 2, 1990, pp. 1–6.

Daly, Herman, and John Cobb, *For the Common Good: Redirecting the Economy towards Community, the Environment, and a Sustainable Future* (Boston: Beacon Press, 1989).

Dasgupta, Partha and Karl Goran Mäller. "The Environment and Emerging Development Issues," *Proceedings of the World Bank Annual Conference on Development Economics, 1990* (Washington, DC: The World Bank, 1991).

———. *An Inquiry into Well-Being and Destitution* (Oxford: Oxford University Press, 1993).

———. "Population and the Local Environment," *Scientific American,* February 1985, pp. 40–45.

———, and Geoffrey Martin Heal. *Economic Theory and Exhaustible Resources* (Cambridge: Cambridge University Press, 1979).

———, and Karl-Göran Mäler. "Poverty, Institutions and the Environmental Resource Base," in Srinivasar et. al. (eds.). *Handbook of Development Economics* vol. 3 (Amsterdam: North Holland Publishing).

Davis, Shelton H. (ed.). *Indigenous Views of Land and the Environment,* World Bank Discussion Paper, 188 (Washington D.C.: The World Bank, 1993).

Dean, Judith M. "Trade and the Environment: A Survey of the Literature," background paper prepared for *World Development Report 1992: Environment* (Washington, DC: World Bank, 1991). Paper processed.

Demas, Ted. *Basic Plywood Processing* (American Plywood Association, December 1992).

Devall, Bill, "The Deep Ecology Movement," *Natural Resources Journal,* vol. 20, 1980, pp. 299–322.

———. George Sessions. *Deep Ecology* (Salt Lake City, UT: Gibbs Smith, 1985).

Devarajan, Shantayanan, and Robert J. Weiner. "Natural Resource Depletion and National Income Accounts" (Cambridge, MA: Harvard University John F. Kennedy School of Government, 1988). Paper Processed.

Dixit, Avinash, and Amy Williamson. "Risk-Adjusted Rates of Return for Project Appraisal," Working Paper 290 (Washington, DC: World Bank Agriculture and Rural Development Department, 1989). Paper processed.

Dixon, John, et. al. *Economic Analysis of the Environmental Impacts of Development Projects* (London: Earthscan Publications in association with the Asian Development Bank, 1988).

———, and Maynard Hufschmidt (eds.). *Economic Valuation Techniques for the Environment: A Case Study Workbook* (Baltimore, MD: Johns Hopkins University Press, 1986).

———, Lee Talbot, and Guy Le Moigne. *Dams and the Environment,* World Bank Technical Paper 110 (Washington, DC: World Bank, 1989).

Domain Biodynamics Research Foundation. *A Global Agenda for Change: Review with Commentary of "Our Common Future"* (Ontario: Breslau, 1987).

Donaldson, Peter. *Economics of the Real World* (2d ed.) (Hermordsworth, UK: Pelican Books, 1973).

Douglass, Gordon (ed.). *Agricultural Sustainability in a Changing World Order* (Boulder, CO: Westview Press, 1984).

Dover, Michael, and Lee Talbot. *To Feed the Earth: Agro-Ecology for Sustainable Development* (Washington, DC: World Resources Institute, 1984).

Dubois, Renee. "So Human an Animal," *Design and the Environment* (Washington, DC: American Institute of Architects, 1993).

Dutton, Thomas A. "Design and Studio Pedagogy," *Journal of Architectural Education,* Fall 1987, pp. 16–25.

Dyson, Freeman. *From Eros to Gaia* (New York: Pantheon, 1992).

Eckholm, Erik. *The Dispossessed of the Earth: Land Reform and Sustainable Development* (Washington, DC: Worldwatch Institute, 1979).

Edmonds, James, and John Reilly. "Global Energy and CO_2 to the Year 2050," *Energy Journal* vol. 4, 1983, pp. 21–47.

Edwards, Steven F. "Option Prices for Groundwater Protection," *Journal of Environmental Economics and Management* vol. 15, 1988, pp. 475–487.

Egan, Timothy. "The Good Rain," *Design and the Environment* (Washington, DC: American Institute of Architects, 1993).

Ehrlich, P., and A. Ehrlich. *The Population Explosion* (New York: Simon and Schuster, 1990).

Elkington, John. "The Green Consumer," *Design and the Environment* (Washington, DC: American Institute of Architects, 1993).

————, and Jonathan Shopley. *The Shrinking Planet: U.S. Information Technology and Sustainable Development* (Washington, DC: Worldwatch Institute, 1988).

El-Sarafy, S. "The Environment or Capital," in R. Costanza (ed.), *Ecological Economics* (New York: Cambridge University Press, 1991).

Fisher, Anthony C. *Resource and Environmental Economics* (Cambridge, MA: Cambridge University Press, 1981).

Fisher, Thomas. "The Paradox of 'Green' Architecture," *Progressive Architecture* vol. 74, March 1993, p. 9.

Flanders, L. *Indigenous Peoples, Environmental Protection and Sustainable Development* (Gland, Switzerland: International Union for Conservation of Native and Natural Resources, 1988).

George, Susan. *A Fate Worse Than Debt* (New York: Penguin Books, 1989).

German Ministry of the Environment. *Advantages of Environmental Protection, Costs of Environmental Pollution* (Bonn: German Ministry of the Environment, 1991).

Girardet, Herbert. "New Directions for Sustainable Urban Living," in *The Gaia Atlas of Cities* (New York: Anchor Books Doubleday).

Goldberg, J., T. Johansson, A. Reddy, and R. Williams. *Energy and a Sustainable World* (Washington, DC: World Resources Institute, 1987).

Golden, David. *Green Cities: Ecologically Sound Approaches to Urban Space* (Montreal: Black Lose Bodis, 1990).

Goldsmith, Edward, and Nicholas Hildyard. *The Earth Report: An Essential Guide to Global Ecological Issues* (New York: Price, Stern, Sloan, 1990).

————, ————, and P. Bunyard. *5000 Ways to Save the Planet* (London: Hamlyn, 1990).

Goodland, R., and H. E. Daly. "Approaching Global Environmental Sustainability," *Journal of Society of International Development.*

————, and ————. "The Missing Tools (for Sustainability)," in C. Mungall and D. J. McLaren (eds.). *Planet under Stress: The Challenge of Global Change* (Toronto: Oxford University Press, 1990).

Goodland, Robert, Herman Daly, and Salah El-Serafy (eds.). "The Transition to Sustainability," in R. Goodland, H. Daly, S. El Serafy, *Population, Technology and Lifestyle: The Transition to Sustainability* (Washington, DC: Island Press, 1992).

———, ———, ———, and Bernd von Droste (eds.). *Environmentally Sustainable Economic Development: Building on Brundtland* (Paris: UNESCO, 1991). Also published as "Paper 36" (Washington, DC: The World Bank, 1991).

Goulet, Dennis. *A New Concept on the Theory of Development* (New York: Atheneum Press, 1971).

Green, Colin H., S. M. Tunstall, A. N'Jai, and A. Rogers. "The Economic Evaluation of Environmental Goods," *Project Appraisal* vol. 5, 1990, pp. 70–82.

Green, Ray. "Sustainable Development of the Built Environment," *Town and Country Planning* vol. 59, May 1990, pp. 142–143.

Greenaway, David, Michael Bleaney, and Ian Stewart (eds.). *Economics in Perspective* (London: Routledge, 1991).

———, and Chris Milner. *Trade and Industrial Policy in Developing Countries: A Manual of Policy Analysis* (New York: Macmillan, 1993).

Gupta, Auijit. *Ecology and Development in the Third World* (London: Routledge, 1988).

Haavelmo, T., and S. Hansen. "On the Strategy of Trying to Reduce Economic Inequality by Expanding the Scope of Human Activity," *Environmentally Sustainable Economic Development: Building on Brundtland* (Washington, DC: The World Bank, 1991).

Hall, Darwin C., and Jane V. Hall. "Concepts and Measures of Natural Resource Scarcity, with a Summary of Recent Trends," *Journal of Environmental Economics and Management* vol. 11, September 1984, pp. 363–379.

Hammond, Allen L. (ed.). *World Resources 1992–93: A Guide to the Global Environment* (Oxford: Oxford University Press, 1992).

Hanley, Nick. "Using Contingent Valuation to Value Environmental Improvements," *Applied Economics,* vol. 20, 1988, pp. 541–551.

Hardin, Garrett J. "The Tragedy of the Commons," *Science* vol. 162, 1968, pp. 1243–1248.

Hardoy, Jorge E., and David Satterthwaite, "Environmental Problems in Third World Cities: A Global Issue Ignored?" *Public Administration and Development* vol. 11, 1991, pp. 341–361.

Hardoy, George E., Sandy Cairncross, and David Satterthwaite (eds.). *Squatter Citizen: Life in the Urban Third World* (London: Earthscan, 1989).

Harrison, Lobert. *Forests: The Shadow of Civilization* (Chicago: University of Chicago Press, 1992).

Harth, Deneke, A. Silva, and S. Silva. "Mutal Help and Progressive Housing Development for What Purpose? (Notes on the Salvadoran Experience)," in Peter Ward (ed.), *Self-Help Housing: A Critique* (London: Mansell, 1982).

Hatfield, Mark. "Old Growth and the Media: A Lawmaker's Perspective," *Evergreen* (Special Issue) (Washington, DC: Island Press, 1991).

Haytar, Teresa. *The Creation of World Poverty* (London: Pluto Press, Ltd. in association with Third World First, 1982).

Hazria, Edward. *The Passive Solar Energy Book* (Emmaus, PA: Rodale Press, 1979).

Henry, C., "Option Values in the Economics of Irreplaceable Resources," *Review of Economic Studies* vol. 41, 1974, pp. 88–93.

Herfindahl, Orris C., and Allen V. Kneese. *Quality of the Environment: An Economic Approach to Some Problems in Using Land, Water, and Air* (Baltimore, MD: Johns Hopkins University Press, 1965).

Hertel, Thomas. *Promoting and Sustaining Development by Increasing the Use of Local Resources* (Washington, DC: World Bank, 1986).

Hibbert, Christopher. *London: A Biography of a City* (London: Penguin Books, 1980).

Hicks, John Richard. *Value and Capital* (2d ed.) (Oxford: Clarendon Press, 1946).

Hileman, B. "Industrial Ecology Route to Slow Global Change Proposal," *Chemical and Engineering News,* August 24, 1992, pp. 21–26.

Hiss, Tony. "The Experience of Place: A New Way of Looking at and Dealing with Our Radically Changing Cities and Countryside," *Design and the Environment* (Washington, DC: American Institute of Architects, 1993).

Holliday, John. "A Sustainable Future for Tomorrow's Communities?" *Town and Country Planning* vol. 60, February 1991, pp. 41–43.

Holmberg, Johan (ed.). *Making Development Sustainable* (Washington, DC: Island Press, 1992).

Hopcraft, D. "Productivity Comparison between Thompson's Gazelle and Cattle, and Their Relationship to the Ecosystem in Kenya," Ph.D. dissertation, Cornell University, 1975.

Hotelling, Harold. "The Economics of Exhaustible Resources?" *Journal of Political Economy* vol. 39, 1931, pp. 137–175.

Hueting, R. "The Brundtland Report: A Matter of Conflicting Goals," *Ecological Economics* vol. 2, 1990, pp. 109–118.

Hughes, Barry, Robert Rycroft, Donald Sylvar, B. Thomas Trout, and James Haif. "Actors Values, Policies, and Futures," *Energy in the Global Arena* (Durham, NC: Duke University Press, 1985).

Hunter, Linda Mason. *The Healthy Home* (Emmaus, PA: Rodale Press, 1989).

Independent Group on British Aid. "Britain and the Third World," *Missed Opportunities* (Oxford: 1986).

Jackson, Wes, Wendell Berry, and Bruce Colman (eds.). *Meeting the Expectations of the Land: Essays in Sustainable Agriculture and Stewardship* (San Francisco: North Point Press, 1984).

Jacobs, Michael. "Environment, Sustainable Development and the Politics of the Future," *The Green Economy* (London: Pluto Press, 1991).

———. "Quality of Life and the Cost of Lollipops," *Town and Country Planning* vol. 59, May 1990, pp. 144–145.

Jacobs, P., and D. Munroe (eds.). "Conservation with Equity: Strategies for Sustainable Development," Proceedings of the Conference on Conservation and Development: Implementing the World Conservation Strategy, Ottawa, Canada, IUCN, Glard, Switzerland, 31 May–5 June, 1986.

Jain, R.K., *Environmental Impact Analysis* (New York: Van Nostrand Reinhold, 1977).

Johan, Holmberg (ed.). "International Institute for Environment and Development," *Making Development Sustainable: Redefining Institutions, Policy and Economics* (Washington, DC: Island Press).

Johansson, Per-Olov. *The Economic Theory and Measurement of Environmental Benefits* (New York: Cambridge University Press, 1987).

Key Fitz, Nathan. "The Growing Human Population," *Scientific American*, Sept. 1989, pp. 119—124.

Kiessling, Kirsten Lindahl, and Hans Landberg. *Population, Economic Development, and the Environment* (Oxford: Oxford University Press, 1994).

Korten, D.C. "Sustainable Development," *World Policy Journal*, Winter 1991–92, pp. 156–190.

Kreimer, Alcira. "Disaster Sustainability and Development: A Look to the 1990s," Paper presented to the World Bank Colloquium on Disasters, Sustainability and Development, Washington, DC, June 9, 1989.

———, Thereza Lobo, Braz Menezes, Mohan Munasinghe, and Ronald Parker.

Towards a Sustainable Urban Environment: The Rio de Janeiro Study, World Bank Discussion Paper, 195 (Washington DC: The World Bank, 1993).

Kreimer, A., and M. Munasinghe (eds.). "Environmental Management and Urban Vulnerability," World Bank Discussion Paper, 168 (Washington, DC: The World Bank, 1992).

Kreps, David M. *A Course in Microeconomic Theory* (London: Harvester-Wheatsheaf, 1990).

Krutilla, John V., and Anthony C. Fisher. *The Economics of Natural Environments* (Baltimore, MD: Johns Hopkins University Press, 1985).

Lamprey, H. *Report on the Desert Encroachment Reconnaissance in Northern Sudan* (Namibia: UNESCO and UNEP, October/November 1975).

Lawry, S. "Tenure Policy towards Common Property Natural Resources" (Madison, WI: Land Tenure Center Paper 134, University of Wisconsin, 1989).

Lee, James. *The Environment, Public Health and Human Ecology* (Baltimore, MD, London: The World Bank and Johns Hopkins University Press, 1985).

Leonard, Jeffrey H. *Environment and the Poor: Development Strategies for a Common Agenda.* U.S. Third World Policy Perspectives 11 (Washington, DC: Overseas Development Council, 1989).

———, D. Morell, "Emergence of Environmental Concern in Developing Countries: A Political Perspective," *Stanford Journal of International Law,* 17.2, pp. 281–313.

Levine, Michael. *The Environmental Address Book* (New York: Putnam Publishing Group, 1991).

Lone, A. *Natural Resource Accounting: The Norwegian Experience* (Paris: OECD, Environment Committee, Group on the State of the Environment, 1988).

Lovelock, James. *Gaia: A New Look at Life on Earth* (Oxford: Oxford University Press, 1979).

———. *The Ages of Gaia: A Biography of Our Living Earth* (Oxford: Oxford University Press, 1988).

MacCleery, Douglas. "Brief Overview of the Condition and Trends of the U.S. Forests" (U.S.D.A. Forest Service, March 15, 1990).

MacNeil, J. "Strategies for Sustainable Development," *Scientific American,* vol. 261, 1989, pp. 154–165.

Magrath, William B. "The Challenge of the Commons: The Allocation of Nonexclusive Resources." Working Paper 14. (Washington, DC: World Bank, Environment Department, 1989). Processed.

Mahar, Denis. *Government Policies and Deforestation in Brazil's Amazon Region* (Washington, DC: The World Bank, 1989).

Mäler, Karl-Goran. *Environmental Economics: A Theoretical Inquiry* (Baltimore, MD: Johns Hopkins University Press, 1974).

———. "Sustainable Development" (Stockholm: Stockholm School of Economics, 1989). Processed.

Marcfa, R. L., and K. K. Lau. "Carbon Dioxide Implications of Building Materials," *Journal of Forest Engineering* vol. 3, January 1992, pp. 11–15.

Marden, Parker, Terry McCoy, Denis Hodgson. "Population in the Global Arena," in James Haif and B. Thomas Trout (eds.), *Actors, Values, Policies, and Futures* (New York: Holt, Rinehart and Winston, 1982).

Markandya, Anil, and David W. Pearce. "Environmental Considerations and the Choice of Discount Rate in Developing Countries," Working Paper 3 (Washington, DC: World Bank Environment Department, 1988). Processed.

———, and ———. "Marginal Opportunity Cost as a Planning Concept in Natural Resource Management," in Gunter Schramm and Jeremy Warford (eds.). *Environmental Management and Economic Development* (Baltimore, MD: Johns Hopkins University Press, 1989).

———, and ———. "Development, Environment, and the Social Rate of Discount," *World Bank Research Observer* vol. 6, 1991, pp. 137–150.

Martel, "Creating Successful Communities, Conservation Foundations," *Design and the Environment* (Washington, DC: American Institute of Architects, 1993).

Maser, Chris. *Forest Primeval: The Natural History of an Ancient Forest* (Sierra Club Books, 1989).

Mazumdar, Savjoy. "Cultural Values in Architectural Education: An Example from India," *Journal of Architectural Education,* May 1993, pp. 230–238.

McGraw-Hill Yearbook of Science and Technology (New York: McGraw-Hill, 1991).

McHarg, Ian. *Design with Nature* (Garden City, NY: Doubleday and Co., Inc., 1971).

McKibben, Bill. *The End of Nature* (New York: Random House, 1989).

McPhee, John. *The Control of Nature* (New York: Noonday Press, 1989).

———. Meadows, D. H. *The Limits to Growth: A Report for the Club of Rome's Project on the Predicament of Mankind* (2d ed.) (London: Earth Island, 1972).

Melkote, Srinivas. *Communication for Development in the Third World: Theory and Practice* (New Delhi: Sage Publications, 1991).

Milbrath, Lester. *Envisioning a Sustainable Society: Learning Our Way Out* (Albany, NY: State University of New York Press, 1988).

Miller, Charles. "From Forest to Grade Stamp," *Fine Homebuilding,* June/July 1988, pp. 38–43.

Miller, Kenton, and Laura Targley. *Trees of Life: Saving Tropical Forests and Their Biological Wealth* (Boston: Beacon Press, 1991).

Mitlow, Diana. "Sustainable Development: Guide to the Literature," *Environment and Urbanization,* vol. 4, April 1992, pp. 34–37.

Mulvihill, Peter Royston. "Caring for the Earth: A Strategy for Sustainable Living; A Review," *Landscape Architecture* vol. 82, February 1992, pp. 120–121.

Munro, R. D., and J. G. Lanners. *Environmental Protection and Sustainable Development: Legal Principles and Recommendations* (London and Boston: M. Nijihoff, 1987).

Myers, Norman. "Economics and Ecology in the International Arena: The Phenomenon of 'Linked Linkages'?," *Ambio,* vol.15, 1986, pp. 296–300.

———, (ed.). *Gaia: An Atlas of Planet Management* (Garden City, NY: Anchor Press, Doubleday, 1984).

Naar, John. *Design for a Livable Planet* (New York: Harper and Row, 1990).

Norway Central Bureau of Statistics. *Natural Resources and the Environment,* 1989 (Oslo: Norway Central Bureau of Statistics. 1990).

O'Riordan, T. "Future Directions in Environmental Policy," *Journal of Environmental Planning,* vol. 17, 1985, pp. 1431–1446.

———. "The Politics of Sustainability," in R. Kerry Turner (ed.), *Sustainable Environmental Management: Principles and Practice* (London: Belhaven Press, 1988).

Oelschlager, M. *Caring for Creation: An Ecumenical Approach to the Environmental Crisis* (New Haven, CT: Yale University Press, 1994).

Office of Technology Assessment. *Energy in Developing Countries* (Washington, DC: U.S. Government Printing Office, 1991).

———. *Energy Efficiency in the U.S. Industrial Sector* (Washington, DC: U.S. Government Printing Office, 1988).

Page, Talbot. *Conservation and Economic Efficiency* (Baltimore, MD: Johns Hopkins University Press, 1977).

Paparek, Victor. "Design for the Real World," *Design and the Environment* (Washington, DC: American Institute of Architects, 1993).

Parker, Ronald. *Sustainability: A Study Undertaken for Foster Parents Plan International* (East Greenich, 1990).

Patterson, Sam H., Horace F. Kurtz, Jane C. Olson, and Cathy Neely. "World Bauxite Resources" (Professional Paper 1076-B), *Geology and Resources of Aluminum* (Washington, DC: U.S. Geological Survey, 1986).

Pearce, David W. "The Social Incidence of Environmental Costs and Benefits," in Timothy O'Riordan and R. Kerry Turner (eds.), *Progress in Resource Management and Environmental Planning,* vol. 2 (Chichester, Wiley, 1980).

———. *Cost-Benefit Analysis* (London: Macmillan, 1986).

———. "Economics of the Environment?" in David Greenaway, Michael Bleaney, and Ian Stewart (eds.). *Economics in Perspective* (London: Routledge, 1991).

———. "Economic Incentives and Renewable Natural Resource Management," in *Renewable Natural Resources: Economic Incentives for Improved Management* (Paris: OCED, 1989).

———, Neil Adger, David Maddison, and Dominic Moran. "Debt and the Environment," *Scientific American,* June 1995, pp. 28–32.

———, Edward Barbier, and Anil Markandya. *Sustainable Development Economics and Environment in the Third World* (Aldershot: Elgar & London: Earthscan, 1990).

———, and Anil Markandya. *The Benefits of Environmental Policy: Monetary Valuation* (Paris: 0rganization for Economic Cooperation and Development, 1989).

———, Anil Markandya, and Edward Barbier. *Blueprint for a Green Economy* (London: Earthscan, 1989).

———, ———, and ———. "Environmental Sustainability and Cost-Benefit Analysis?" *Environment and Planning* vol. 22, 1990, pp. 1259–1266.

———, and D. Moran. *The Economic Value of Biological Diversity* (London: Earthscan Publications, 1994).

———, and R. Kerry Turner. *Economics of Natural Resources and the Environment* (London: Harvester-Wheatsheaf, 1989).

————, and Jeremy J. Waiford. *World Without End: Economics, Environment, and Sustainable Development* (New York and Oxford: Oxford University Press, 1993).

Pearson, David. *The Natural House Book* (New York: Simon and Schuster, 1989).

Perrings, Charles. *Economy and Environment* (New York: Cambridge University Press, 1987).

Peskin, Henry M. "Accounting for Natural Resource Depletion and Degradation in Developing Countries?" Working Paper 13 (Washington, DC: World Bank, Environment Department, 1989). Processed.

Peters, Robert, and Thomas Lovejoy (eds.). *Global Warming and Biological Diversity* (New Haven, CT: Yale University Press, 1992).

Pezzey, John. "Economic Analysis of Sustainable Growth and Sustainable Development?" Working Paper 15 (Washington, DC: World Bank, Environment Department, 1989). Processed.

Phillips, Michael. *The Least-Cost Energy Path for Developing Countries* (Washington, DC: International Institute for Energy Conservation, September, 1989).

Pirages, Dennis (ed.). *The Sustainable Society: Implications for Limited Growth* (New York: Praeger, 1977).

"Planning for Sustainable Development," *Town and Country Planning* vol. 60, January 1992, pp. 16–23.

Plummer, Mark L., and Richard C. Hartman. "Option Value: A General Approach," *Economic Inquiry* vol. 24, 1986, pp. 455–471.

Ponting, Clive. *A Green History of the World: The Environment and the Collapse of Great Civilizations* (New York: St. Martin's Press, 1992).

Postel, Sandra, and John Ryan. *Reforming Forestry: State of the World 1991* (New York: Worldwatch Institute, 1991).

Prince, Raymond. "A Note on Environmental Risk and the Rate of Discount: A Comment?" *Journal of Environmental Economics and Management* vol. 12, 1985, pp. 179–180.

Ramage, Janet. *Energy: A Guide Book* (Oxford: Oxford University Press, 1983).

Randall, Alan. "Total Economic Value as a Basis for Policy," *Transactions of the American Fisheries Society* vol. 116, 1987, pp. 325–335.

Ray, Anandarup. *Cost-Benefit Analysis: Issues and Methodologies* (Baltimore, MD: Johns Hopkins University Press, 1984).

Redclift, Michael. *Sustainable Development: Exploring the Contradiction* (London, Methuen, 1987).

————, and T. Benton (eds.). *Social Theory and the Global Environment* (London: Routlege, 1994).

Reed, D. *Structural Adjustment and the Environment* (Boulder, CO: World Wide Fund for Nature and Westview Press, 1992).

Rees, William. *Planning for Sustainable Development: A Resource Book* (Vancouver: INFO Vancouver and the UBC Center for Human Settlements, 1989).

————. "Sustainable Development as Capitalism with a Green Face: A Review Article," *The Town Planning Review* vol. 61, January 1990, pp. 91–94.

Reinstein, Robert. "Trade and Environment" (Washington, DC: U.S. State Department, 1991). Processed.

Repetto, Robert. "Overview," in Robert Repetto and Malcolm Gillis (eds.). *Public Policies and the Misuse of Forest Resources* (Cambridge: Cambridge University Press, 1988).

————. *World Enough and Time: Successful Strategies for Resource Management* (New Haven, CT: Yale University Press, 1986).

————, *Wasting Assets: Natural Resources in the National Income Accounts* (Washington, DC: World Resources Institute, 1989).

Rifkin, Jeremy. *The Green Lifestyle Handbook* (New York: Henry Holt and Co., 1990).

————, with Ted Howard. *Entropy into the Greenhouse World* (New York: Bantam Books, 1989).

Rousseau, David, and Victoria Schoner. *Global Choices: Environmental Action and the Design Professional* (Denver: American Society of Interior Designers' Convention, 1991).

St. Pierre, G.R. "Iron Metallurgy," *McGraw-Hill Encyclopedia of Science and Technology* (6th ed.), vol. 9 (New York: McGraw-Hill, 1987), pp. 406–409.

Samples, Karl C., Marcia Gowen, and John Dixon. "The Validity of the Contingent Valuation Method for Estimating Non-Use Components of Preservation Values for Unique Natural Resources?" Paper presented to a meeting of the American Agricultural Economics Association, Reno, Nevada. 1986. Processed.

Sathaye, J., A. Kethoff, L. Schipper, and S. Lele. *An End-Use Approach to Developing Long-Term Energy Demand Scenarios for Developing Countries* (Berkeley, CA: Lawrence Berkeley Laboratory, February 1989).

Schmidheiny, Stephen. *Changing Course* (Cambridge, MA: MIT Press, 1992).

Schramm, Gunter, and Jeremy Warford (eds.). *Environmental Management and Economic Development* (Baltimore, MD: Johns Hopkins University Press, 1989).

Schumacher, E. F. *Small Is Beautiful: A Study of Economics as If People Mattered* (London: Abacus, 1974).

Science Council of Canada. "Water 2020: Sustainable Use of Water in the 21st Century," *Report No. 40* (Ottawa: The Council, June 1988).

Sehnke, Errol D., and Patricia A. Plunkert. "Bauxite, Alumina, and Aluminum," *Minerals Yearbook* (Washington, DC: Bureau of Mines, U.S. Department of the Interior, October 1990).

Serageldin, Ismail, and Andrew Steer (eds.). "Making Development Sustainable: From Concept to Action," Environmentally Sustainable Development Occasional Papers, Series 2 (Washington, DC: The World Bank, 1994).

———, and ———. "Valuing The Environment" (Proceedings of the First Award International Conference on Environmentally Sustainable Development) (Washington, DC: The World Bank, 1993).

———, and June Taboroff, (eds.) *Culture and Development in Africa* (Washington, DC: The World Bank, 1993).

Seymour, John, and Herbert Giardet. *Blueprint for a Green Planet* (Englewood Cliffs, NJ: Prentice-Hall, 1990).

Shrybman, Steven. "International Trade and the Environment: An Environmental Assessment of the General Agreement on Tariffs and Trade?" *The Ecologist* 20, vol. 1990, pp. 30–34.

Siebert, Horst. "Spatial Aspects of Environmental Economics," in A. Kneese and J. Sweeney (eds.), *Handbook of Natural Resource and Energy, Economics,* vol. 1. (Amsterdam: North Holland, 1985).

Simmons, Udo Ernest. *Beyond Growth: Elements of Sustainable Development* (Berlin: Sigma Bohn, 1990).

Sitarz, Daniel (ed.). *Agenda: 21 The Earth Summit Strategy To Save Our Planet* (Boulder, CO: The Earth Press, 1993).

Smil, Veclav. *The Bad Earth: Environmental Degradation in China* (New York: M. E. Sharpe, 1989).

Southern California Edison. "The New Adobe," *Sunset,* April 1995, pp. 100–107.

Southgate, Douglas Dewitt. "The Economics of Land Degradation in the Third World," Working Paper 2 (Washington, DC: World Bank, Environment Department, 1988). Processed.

————, and John F. Disinger (eds.). *Sustainable Resource Development in the Third World* (Westview Special Studies in Natural Resources and Energy Management) (Boulder, CO: Westview Press, 1987).

Steeley, Geoffrey. " 'Trend Breach' for Sustainable Transport," *Town and Country Planning* vol. 59, May 1990, pp. 157–158.

Stein, R. G. and Diane Serber. "Energy Required for Building Construction," in D. Watson, *Energy Conservation Through Building Design* (New York: McGraw-Hill, 1979).

Steiner, H. "Markets and Law: The Case of Environmental Conservation," (Manchester, UK: Manchester Polytechnic, 1990).

Stivers, Robert L. *The Sustainable Society: Ethics and Economic Growth* (Philadelphia: Westminster Press, 1976).

Theys, Jacques. "Environmental Accounting in Development Policy: The French Experience," in Yusuf Ahmad, Salah El Serafy, and Ernst Lutz (eds.), *Environmental Accounting for Sustainable Development* (Washington, DC: World Bank, 1989).

Thompson, J. William. "Is It Sustainable? Is It Art?" *Landscape Architecture* vol. 82, May 1992, pp. 56–60.

Tietenberg, Thomas. *Environmental and Natural Resource Economics* (2d ed.) (Glenview, IL: Foresman and Company, 1988).

Tinbergen, J., and R. Heuting. "GNP and Market Prices: Wrong Signals for Sustainable Economic Success That Mock Environmental Destruction," in R. Goodland, H. Daly, and S. El-Sarafy (eds.). *Environmentally Sustainable Economic Development: Building on Brundtland* (Washington, DC: World Bank Environment Department Paper 36, 1991).

Tolba, Mostafa Kanai. *Sustainable Development Constraints and Opportunities* (Boston: Butterworth, 1987).

Turner, John. "Toward Autonomy in Building Environments," *Housing by People* (London: Marion Boyers, 1976).

————. "Uncontrolled Urban Settlements: Problems and Policies" (Report for the UN Seminar on Urbanization, Pittsburgh, PA, 1966).

Turner, R. Kerry (ed.). *Sustainable Environmental Management Principles and Practices* (Boulder, CO: Westview Press, 1988).

United Nations Center for Human Settlements (UNCHS), *Shelter for the Homeless: The Role of Non-Governmental Organizations* (Namibia: United Nations Center for Human Settlements, 1987).

United Nations Development Program (UNDP), *Human Development Report* (New York: 1992).

U.S. Environmental Protection Agency, *Federal Register,* 40 CFR, Parts 260, 261, and 262, *Mining Waste Exclusion,* January 23, 1990 (Washington, DC: U.S. Government Printing Office, 1990).

————. "Environmental Fact Sheet," *Report to Congress on Special Wastes from Mineral Processing* (Washington DC: U.S. Government Printing Office, 1990).

U.S. Joint Economic Committee. *Sustainable Development and Economic Growth in the Third World* (Washington, DC: 1989).

Vale, Brenda, and Robert Vale. "The Future Development of the Built Environment," *Town and Country Planning* vol. 61, November-December 1992, pp. 296–297.

————, and ————. *Green Architecture* (Boston: Little, Brown, 1991).

Van Nostrand Scientific Encyclopedia. "Iron Metals, Alloys and Steel" (New York: Van Nostrand Publishers, 1988).

Vander Ryn, Sim, "Sustainable Communities," *Design and the Environment* (Washington, DC: American Institute of Architects, 1993).

———— and Peter Calthorpe. *Sustainable Communities: A New Design Synthesis for Cities, Suburbs, and Towns* (San Francisco: Sierra Club Books, 1986).

World Commission on Environment and Development (WCED), *Our Common Future* (Brundtland Report) (Oxford: Oxford University Press, 1987).

Warford, Jeremy. "Environments, Growth, and Development, Development," Paper 14 (Washington, DC: World Bank and International Monetary Fund, 1987).

Watson, Donald. "Energy Conservation through Building Design," in *Energy Conservation at the Building Scale: An Innovation Program* (New York: McGraw-Hill, 1979).

Webb, Adrian. "Sustainable Energy—a Question of Restraint and Renewables," *Town and Country Planning* vol. 61, July-August 1992, pp. 198–200.

Whittemore, Claire. *Land for People: Land Tenure and the Very Poor* (Oxford: Oxfam, 1981).

Whittington, Dale. "Estimating the Willingness to Pay for Water Services in Developing Countries: A Case Study of the Use of Contingent Valuation Surveys in Southern Haiti," *Economic Development and Cultural Change* (World Bank Publications, Washington DC: 1990).

Wilson, Edward. *Biophia* (Cambridge, MA: Harvard University Press, 1984).

Woodruff, Tom (ed.). "Alternative Nobel Prize Speeches," in *People and the Planet* (Hertland: Green Books, 1987).

World Bank. *Making Development Sustainable, Fiscal 1994* (Washington, DC: 1994).

———. *Monitoring Environmental Progress: A Report on Work in Progress* (Unpublished, undated manuscript).

———. *World Bank Atlas: 25th Anniversary Edition* (Washington DC: 1992).

———. *World Development Report: 1990* (Oxford: Oxford University Press, 1990).

———. *World Development Report: Poverty* (Washington, DC: World Bank, 1990).

World Commission on Environment and Development. *Energy 2000: A Global Strategy for Sustainable Development* (London: Zed Books, 1987).

———. *Our Common Future* (Oxford: Oxford University Press, 1989).

World Resources Institute with UNEP and UNDP, *World Resources, 1992–93* (New York and Oxford: Oxford University Press, 1992).

INDEX

ABOUT THE AUTHOR

James Steele is an associate professor of architecture at the University of Southern California, where he teaches architectural history and design. He holds Bachelor and Master of Architecture degrees from the University of Pennsylvania, where he studied under Louis Kahn. He is currently pursuing a Ph.D. from the School of Planning and Development at the University of Southern California. Professor Steele is the author of a number of books, including *The Queen Mary, Los Angeles Architecture: The Contemporary Condition, Theatre Builders, Architecture Today, An Architecture for People: The Complete Works of Hassan Fathy, The Faculty Club at the University of California at Berkeley* by Bernard Maybeck, and *Architecture of the Contemporary Mosque,* co-authored by Ismail Serageldin.